JOURNAL FOR THE STUDY OF THE OLD TESTAMENT SUPPLEMENT SERIES
271

Sheffield Academic Press

Until the Spirit Comes

The Spirit of God
in the Book of Isaiah

Wonsuk Ma

Journal for the Study of the Old Testament
Supplement Series 271

Copyright © 1999 Sheffield Academic Press

Published by Sheffield Academic Press Ltd
Mansion House
19 Kingfield Road
Sheffield S11 9AS
England

Printed on acid-free paper in Great Britain
by Bookcraft Ltd
Midsomer Norton, Bath

British Library Cataloguing in Publication Data

A catalogue record for this book is available
from the British Library

ISBN 1-85075-981-2

CONTENTS

PREFACE

As an Asian Pentecostal, and now Old Testament scholar, the years of my study have taught that the Spirit of God works within and for communities, although individuals may experience his presence as well. The present study has proven that, in God's economy, every accomplishment is the result of a cooperative work.

The present work is a revision of my doctoral dissertation, completed in 1996 at Fuller Theological Seminary, Pasadena, California. In the process of revision, only a few new works were added in reference, but the content remains basically identical, except for two major chapters on ancient Near East and early Israel material that are not included in the present work.

The subject of God's spirit in the Old Testament was introduced to me by Revd Robert Houlihan who bought a copy of Lloyd Neve's book, *The Spirit of God in the Old Testament*, published in Tokyo. Throughout the study, the family of the Asia Pacific Theological Seminary in Baguio City, Philippines, was immensely involved. The board and administration were boldly courageous to support the very first Asian missionary faculty member to study at a school in the States, where many theological 'brains' from this part of the world had been 'drained'. Dr William Menzies, President of the seminary during the study, truly believed in me and my future. Students and fellow faculty members were always warm and encouraging. They often told me and my wife, Dr Julie Ma, how often they prayed for us, and we are truly grateful for this spiritual support.

In the process of my study at Fuller Theological Seminary, I was privileged not only to be taught by many fine Old Testament scholars, but also to develop a fond relationship with each one of these esteemed scholars. Dr Leslie C. Allen, my mentor, became a good teacher and wonderful friend. His conscientious attempt to share the struggles and feelings of ancient Israelites makes his scholarship part of his spiritual journey. We are happy that he is going to visit the Philippines soon.

When my wife and I visited his office, the late Dr David Allan Hubbard impressed us greatly as this extremely busy administrator–scholar was interested more in our lives and ministry than my study itself. He went to be with the Lord a day before my graduation, but without failing first to leave a warm word of congratulations. Dr Frederick Bush made many international calls across the Pacific Ocean to prepare my comprehensive exam. Although not directly involved in my study, Dr Colin Brown, the Associate Dean of Fuller's Center for Advanced Theological Studies (CATS), and his wife, Olive, were very supportive of our study and ministry in the Philippines. Another special couple we enjoyed meeting at Fuller were Gordon and Inez Smith. Although Gordon was not able to see the completion of our studies, they adopted us into their warm family circle, and this made our stay in the States a joy.

During my long years of study, many churches and individuals, including those in Asia-Pacific, gave generously to support my study. In the concluding years, Inchon Full Gospel Church in Korea (led by Revd Sung-kyu Choi) was particularly helpful. Numerous times, CATS awarded scholarships to encourage me. The Dilworth Foundation awarded a substantial grant, which helped me to conclude my study. Dr Joseph Ahn of Immanuel Mission Church, Los Angeles, was not only my CATS friend, but also later, through the church he established, helped our family in spite of difficulties in the early years of the church. Many friends contributed to our study and living in California in various ways. We are truly grateful to all of them. My two boys, Woolim and Boram, were a marvel for their uncomplaining support. My father often visited us and entertained them while I, as well as my wife, were hijacked by our studies. They have a great part in this work.

I sent a copy of my dissertation to the editors of the *JSOT* Supplement series, probably out of my ignorant courage. When I received a very kind letter from them, I was truly surprised. I appreciate their special encouragement, which led them eventually to include this work.

In the process of revision, another group of dear friends assisted immensely. Mr Tomoyuki Kisaki read the entire manuscript and improved its readability greatly. Mr Kwang-jin Jang, my administrative assistant, went through all the references and checked them very carefully. Mr Sandy Wilks read the manuscript one more time with his able mind before the final submission. I owe a great deal to them and many others whom I fail to mention.

I would like to dedicate this work to two great women: my mother (Mrs Eunja Ma) and Julie, my wife. The best thing that my mother knows is how to pray. I have seen her pray in my early years and during my Vietnam years. In every part of my schooling, her prayer was the main force that enabled me to continue. Julie has been a special gift of God in my life. She constantly encouraged me while I was uncertain about my study. When I began after much hesitation, she worked to keep our family afloat. When I was finishing, she quickly began her own study at Fuller. While I managed to finish mine after eleven years of dragging, she finished three degrees in four years including two years of PhD study. It was a special treat that we walked across the same stage on the same day. She has been an inspiration to me.

My prayer is that God's people, including my own Pentecostals, will not just talk, read or study about God's Spirit, but earnestly expect to experience him in every aspect of their life and ministry. And if this small work could encourage in any way the reader to draw a step closer to the reality of God's Spirit, this will be my true reward.

Wonsuk Ma
25 March 1998

ABBREVIATIONS

AB	Anchor Bible
AJT	*American Journal of Theology*
AnBib	Analecta Biblica
ANET	James B. Pritchard (ed.), *Ancient Near Eastern Texts Relating to the Old Testament* (Princeton, NJ: Princeton University Press, 1950)
AnOr	Analecta orientalia
AOAT	Alter Orient und Altes Testament
ASTI	*Annual of the Swedish Theological Institute*
BAT	Die Botschaft des Alten Testaments
BDB	Francis Brown, S.R. Driver and Charles A. Briggs, *A Hebrew and English Lexicon of the Old Testament* (Oxford: Clarendon Press, 1907)
BHK	R. Kittel (ed.), *Biblia Hebraica* (Stuttgart: Württembergische Bibelanstalt, 1937)
BHS	*Biblia Hebraica Stuttgartensia*
Bib	*Biblica*
BibOr	Biblica et orientalia
BibRes	*Biblical Research*
BJRL	*Bulletin of the John Rylands University Library of Manchester*
BKAT	Biblischer Kommentar: Altes Testament
BN	*Biblische Notizen*
BSac	*Bibliotheca Sacra*
BZ	*Biblische Zeitschrift*
BZAW	Beihefte zur *ZAW*
CBCOT	Cambridge Bible Commentary on the Old Testament
CBQ	*Catholic Biblical Quarterly*
CBQMS	*Catholic Biblical Quarterly*, Monograph Series
ConBOT	Coniectanea Biblica, Old Testament
CTA	A. Herdner (ed.), *Corpus des tablettes en cunéiformes alphabétiques découvertes à Ras Shamra–Ugarit de 1929 à 1939* (Paris: Imprimerie nationale Geuthner, 1963)
CurTM	*Currents in Theology and Mission*
DSB	Daily Study Bible
ETL	*Ephemerides theologicae lovanienses*
EvT	*Evangelische Theologie*

ExpTim	*Expository Times*
HBT	*Horizons in Biblical Theology*
HKAT	Handkommentar zum Alten Testament
HTR	*Harvard Theological Review*
HUCA	*Hebrew Union College Annual*
IB	*Interpreter's Bible*
ICC	International Critical Commentary
IDB	George Arthur Buttrick (ed.), *The Interpreter's Dictionary of the Bible* (4 vols.; Nashville: Abingdon Press, 1962)
Int	*Interpretation*
ITC	International Theological Commentary
JB	*Jerusalem Bible*
JBL	*Journal of Biblical Literature*
JETS	*Journal of the Evangelical Theological Society*
JPTSup	*Journal of Pentecostal Theology*, Supplement Series
JSOT	*Journal for the Study of the Old Testament*
JSOTSup	*Journal for the Study of the Old Testament*, Supplement Series
JSS	*Journal of Semitic Studies*
JTS	*Journal of Theological Studies*
KAT	Kommentar zum Alten Testament
KHAT	Kurzer Hand-Kommentar zum Alten Testament
NAB	*New American Bible*
NCBC	New Century Bible Commentary
NEB	*New English Bible*
NICOT	New International Commentary on the Old Testament
NIV	New International Version
NRSV	New Revised Standard Version
OTG	Old Testament Guides
OTL	Old Testament Library
OTM	Old Testament Message
OTS	*Oudtestamentische Studiën*
RB	*Revue biblique*
RSPT	*Revue des sciences philosophiques et théologiques*
RSV	Revised Standard Version
RV	Revised Version
SBS	Stuttgarter Bibelstudien
SBT	Studies in Biblical Theology
SJT	*Scottish Journal of Theology*
SOTSMS	Society for Old Testament Study Monograph Series
ST	*Studia theologica*
TC	Theological Commentary
TDNT	Gerhard Kittel and Gerhard Friedrich (eds.), *Theological Dictionary of the New Testament* (trans. Geoffrey W. Bromiley; 10 vols.; Grand Rapids: Eerdmans, 1964–76)

ThWAT	G.J. Botterweck and H. Ringgren (eds.), *Theologisches Wörterbuch zum Alten Testament* (8 vols.; Stuttgart: W. Kohlhammer, 1973–77)
TynBul	*Tyndale Bulletin*
VT	*Vetus Testamentum*
VTSup	*Vetus Testamentum*, Supplements
WBC	Word Biblical Commentary
WBT	Word Biblical Themes
ZAW	*Zeitschrift für die alttestamentliche Wissenschaft*
ZBK	Zürcher Bibelkommentare
ZTK	*Zeitschrift für Theologie und Kirch*

INTRODUCTION

An exilic writer expressed the longing of the new age in Isa. 32.15, 'Until the spirit from above is poured upon us...' This may be an adequate expression of the eschatological expectation of God's restoration. The perspective is from somewhere between two ages: one in the past when the spirit came upon many leaders, and the other in the future when the spirit will again appear, but this time in abundance and upon the entire community. The prophet and God's people were sandwiched between these two blissful realities, but their then-present age had not seen the appearance of the spirit for a long time. The writer of the passage found himself at the dawn of the age of the spirit, still enveloped in darkness, yet witnessing the first light of a fresh revelation of the new age.

The concept of 'spirit', often expressed by רוח (*rûaḥ*), is never a major theological idea in the Old Testament. However, there is enough evidence for us to infer that the idea was more frequently used in the actual 'people's theology' than the formally documented one. This notion achieved a unique development in the Hebrew monotheistic context and later culminated in the person of the Holy Spirit in the New Testament, through various intertestamental evolutions, including the Qumran texts. However, its popular attraction among believers does not end there.

Even today, beside a constant biblical and theological interest, this idea has drawn attention particularly on two fronts: (1) missiology and (2) Pentecostal studies. In the recent emergence of missiology, study of non-Western societies and their religious practices becomes important. Many so-called 'unreached people groups' are animists, and their belief in the spiritual world motivates serious studies of the subject.[1]

---

1. A good example is Lloyd Neve, *The Spirit of God in the Old Testament* (Tokyo: Seibunsha, 1972), whose missionary work in Japan motivated him to study the topic. There are other similar studies by former missionary Old Testament

Similarities in several points between animists and Pentecostal Christians are unmistakable.[2] Even the context in which the idea of the spirit is found in the Old Testament displays many parallels to the contemporary animistic world. The rise of the Pentecostal movement in this century has also brought a renewed interest in the person and work of the Holy Spirit. Among numerous and rather popular works, some studies on the Old Testament 'spirit' tradition have appeared.[3]

In addition to my interest in the Old Testament in general, I reflect also contemporary interests, as a Pentecostal missionary to an animistic people group in the Philippines.

1. *Preliminary Concerns*

1.1 *Study Goals*

References to God's spirit in the Old Testament, especially among the 'classical' prophets, do not appear frequently.[4] However, this scarcity of use of the term in the 'official' religion may not necessarily indicate that the idea is marginal in the mindset of the common people. As they have their own popular theology, or folk-theology, of the 'day of Yahweh' (Amos 5.18-20), there is evidence that the early Hebrews had a rich understanding of the spirit. The prophetic behavior under the

scholars, e.g. H.H. Rowley, *Prophecy and Religion in Ancient China and Israel* (London: Athlone Press, 1956).

2.   E.g. Julie Ma, 'A Comparison of Two Worldviews: Kankana-ey and Pentecostal', in Wonsuk Ma and Robert P. Menzies (eds.), *Pentecostalism in Context: Essays in Honor of William W. Menzies* (JPTSup, 11; Sheffield: Sheffield Academic Press, 1997), pp. 265-90.

3.   For a Pentecostal Old Testament scholar's work, see, e.g., Stanley Horton, *What the Bible Says about the Holy Spirit* (Springfield, MO: Gospel Publishing House, 1976); for a Roman Catholic scholar's, see, e.g., George T. Montague, *The Holy Spirit: Growth of a Biblical Tradition* (New York: Paulist Press, 1976; repr.; Peabody, MA: Hendrickson, 1994).

4.   One can easily recall S. Mowinckel's epoch-making study ('The "Spirit" and the "Word" in the Pre-Exilic Reforming Prophets', *JBL* 53 [1934], pp. 199-227; 56 [1937], pp. 261-65). However, John D.W. Watts, 'Images of Yahweh: God in the Prophets', in Robert L. Hubbard, Jr, Robert K. Johnston and Robert P. Meye (eds.), *Studies in Old Testament Theology: Historical and Contemporary Images of God and God's People* (Dallas: Word Books, 1992), pp. 135-47, esp. pp. 144-46, argues that the prophetic images of God are primarily two: Yahweh as King and Yahweh as the Divine Spirit, although his spiritualized definition of the divine spirit is extremely vague.

spirit's influence is almost an accepted phenomenon during Samuel's time. The term איש הרוח (the man of the spirit; Hos. 9.7) also appears to be a term with a firmly established notion. There is a stereotypical expectation of the spirit's work (e.g. 2 Kgs 18.12). Kapelrud may be correct, after all, that the idea of the divine spirit is so common that it is simply assumed without specific reference.[5]

1.2 *Related Assumptions*

1.2.1. First of all, the term רוח is used in its diverse meanings. And this may point to a possibility that the concept began its life as diverse independent traditions before it was used by the Israelites. This assumption is in direct contrast to most existing works on the subject matter.[6]

1.2.2. Secondly, even in its subsequent developments, the various traditions maintain their distinctiveness and sometimes their own evolution. For this study, the book of Isaiah is selected as a literary example to investigate whether the traditions live their own lives, and if they do so how their evolution continues.

1.2.3. At the same time, as one can detect and trace the diverse and even mutually exclusive threads of traditions, it is equally difficult to conclude that the various ideas are coincidentally expressed by רוח, due, let us say, to the lack of appropriate words. For instance, when the רוח functions as God's agent, the description is not much different from the function of an angel. When a biblical author chooses to refer to it, the concept and word of the angel (מלאך) is readily available. This proves that the term רוח is not used for the various traditions just because of the lack of words. Rather, all the various expressions share one commonality: the רוח expresses God's involvement or even intervention in the situation of individuals, nations or the world. This applies even to the ancient Near Eastern evidence, for whether referring to the 'wind', 'breath' or lower deities such as demons and spirits, it always denotes a divine entity which makes a contact with humans or the world. In the monotheistic Hebrew thought-world, the רוח becomes one of Yahweh's instruments in dealing with humans and the created world. This hypothesis will be in mind throughout this study.

5. Arvid S. Kapelrud, 'The Spirit and the Word in the Prophets', *ASTI* 11 (1977–78), pp. 40-47.
6. For more detail, see below, pp. 26-32.

1.2.4. Denoting an extension of Yahweh's being, the רוח executes God's will, for the רוח, along with God's word and hand, is God's instrument, agent or tool. The רוח contributes to the move of human history toward the definite direction which Yahweh has set. The רוח is often used to bring God's judgment or salvation to Israel and to the nations. As a historical reflection reveals (e.g. Isa. 63.14), the רוח achieves God's definite will in this world. This study will, therefore, examine the eschatological significance of the רוח in the various strata of the book of Isaiah.

1.2.5. In addition to the eschatological significance, the historical evolution of the idea is marked by the increasing spiritual, ethical and democratizational development. The earlier crude and violent effect of the רוח is gradually replaced by a more refined and internalized effect. Through the window of the book of Isaiah, this development will be traced.

1.3 *Study Plan*
1.3.1. *Why the Book of Isaiah?* Isaiah and Ezekiel include the most רוח references among the prophetic books. The book of Isaiah is selected basically for two reasons: (1) its influence on the New Testament which is evidenced by frequent quotations; and (2) the long historical span the book embraces. The book of Isaiah, in all three major historical layers and in its final 'canonical' setting, provides a fertile ground to express the diverse traditions of the רוח idea. The book becomes an excellent window through which the modern reader can see how the concept was used to address a real historical struggle. It is assumed that the רוח of God, with its diverse categories, functions to aid the eschatologization of the book. It takes on a variety of roles: in the blessing on the restored community (e.g. 32.15-20; 44.1-5); in selecting and empowering the future leader (11.1-3a; 28.6; 42.1-4); in the purification of the remnant (4.4); and in the ushering in of the new age.

1.3.2. *Organization.* A study on the background material, especially the ancient Near Eastern and early Israelite, is limited, and therefore the existence of separate רוח traditions and their continued development will be assumed. The main body of this study traces the development of the רוח concept through the Isaianic traditions: pre-exilic, exilic, post-exilic and 'canonical' strata. This study is an attempt to investigate whether the book, as well as the רוח concept, evidences any distinct development. If this is so, I wish to trace the development of the book and further investigate how the הוה concept functions in the development. Throughout the study, attention will also be given to see if the various separate הוה traditions are maintained.

1.4 *Method*
1.4.1 *Textual Unity and Division*.
Recent Old Testament scholarship is characterized by an unsettled state. As the traditional historical-critical method is slowly losing its ground, various new methods are being tried out. Williamson divides the scholarship into two strands: 'those who continue to operate within the established tradition of historical-critical study' and 'those who believe that we should move beyond this to various forms of post-critical literary reading'.[7] Often the book of Isaiah becomes a showcase where much of the battle is fought. There is, however, a 'silent majority'—in Williamson's term—which 'hopes to reconcile these divergent approaches at the rational level'.[8]

This study is a small voice raised by one from the 'silent majority'. In this study, the unity of the book is 'pursued by way of a more intense application of traditional methods rather than an ignoring or bypassing of them'.[9] The validity of the historical-critical approach lies in the fact that a passage is read in its real-life context. The biggest challenge is to discover to what extent one can recover the actual life context and how. However, the uncertainty of recoverable data does not justify the divorce of a text from its historical context. The book will be read as four major chronological collections: pre-exilic, exilic, postexilic and canonical. The divisions do not correspond to the traditional literary blocks of First, Second and Third Isaiah. For instance, Isa. 32.15-20, found in the first literary block or First Isaiah, will be treated with passages belonging to the second, or exilic, block. This deliberately fragmentary and historical reading is designed to recognize the value of the traditional historical-critical approach. A text is a product of a real human life within its own distinct historical, religious and social context.

This approach immediately raises a major concern. The division into the three large chronological blocks leaves almost no room to consider

---

7. H.G.M. Williamson, *The Book Called Isaiah: Deutero-Isaiah's Role in Composition and Redaction* (Oxford: Clarendon Press, 1994), p. vii.
8. Williamson, *The Book Called Isaiah*, p. vii.
9. Williamson, *The Book Called Isaiah*, p. vii.

redactional layers. It is commonly argued that many texts went through
numerous stages of redactional growth. The consideration of the redactional layers would result in more minutely divided blocks. And this
would result in an ideal situation that the given time span is divided
into more time blocks, almost forming a continuum rather than the
abrupt three or four chronological reference points. In spite of the
apparent advantage, I choose to divide the period into four major
reference points. One reason is that redactional layers are often too
ambiguous to assign to a time period with reasonable certainty. The
other is that too many minute divisions may become a hindrance to
achieving clarity. By connecting four major reference points, the development of the רוח idea may be reasonably traced.

To the traditional three time blocks, the 'canonical' layer is added,
for I assume that the 'canonical' formation is still the continuation of
the ongoing hermeneutical process. This stage is still historically rooted,
possibly with a 'universal' and 'normative' intention, and is viewed as
the end stage of the redactional process. For this stage, the texts will be
read in the wider literary and theological context. This four-stage reading not only delineates the historical development of the רוח concept,
but also the four historical layers make a large entirety as the book of
Isaiah. However, the final stage is also the 'canonical reading', that is, a
synchronic reading.[10] This study recognizes both approaches, historical
and synchronic, and attempts to utilize the strengths of both. Thus, the
method can be termed 'a synchronic reading through multiple chronical
readings'. It is my intention to propose a model for a holistic reading.[11]

1.4.2 *Definitions.* Throughout the study, the term 'eschatology' is used
in its broad sense, rather than in the strict definition, which is characterized by the element of finality and the other-worldliness of all the
end-time events.[12] Lindblom's definition represents the broad position:
'All events that refer to the age to come are to be designated as

10. For a more detailed discussion, see Chapter 4, pp. 158-78.

11. One attempt is a rather pre-critical approach by Wilf Hildebrandt, *An Old
Testament Theology of the Spirit of God* (Peabody, MA: Hendrickson, 1995); see
his literature review, p. 24, for detail.

12. For the strict interpretation, see, e.g., J.P.M. van der Plög, 'Eschatology in
the Old Testament', *OTS* 17 (1978), pp. 89-99 (89); Sigmund Mowinckel, *He That
Cometh* (trans. G.W. Anderson; New York: Abingdon Press, 1954), p. 125; and
S.B. Frost, 'Eschatology and Myth', *VT* 2 (1952), pp. 70-80 (70).

eschatological, even when they form part of the historical process.'[13] At the same time, it should be remembered time and again that not all futuristic passages are necessarily eschatological. The working presupposition is, as L. Černy expresses:

> There did not exist any eschatological system at all. This eschatological system was the final result of the work of many generations, and it was developed from originally non-eschatological ideas and materials.[14]

In other words, some messages *became* eschatological.[15]

The ambiguity of the term רוח in Hebrew poses another difficulty. The exact meaning of the term in a given passage may not always be clear. It is primarily due to the wide range of meanings of רוח, that is, from a destructive wind or breath to the highly developed religious idea of 'spirit'. This is in contrast to Arabic, which has two different words for 'wind' and 'spirit'.[16] Every attempt will be made to establish the best possible meaning of רוח in each case, though it is difficult to distinguish between the wind and the spirit in some cases, where the function strongly implies the 'wind' reference, but also has a strong indication that the רוח is specifically used by Yahweh. Among the borderline references, only early texts, such as Exod. 15.8, are considered in this study. The other extreme is the 'spirit of God (or Yahweh)' which is described almost as an independent personality (e.g. 1 Kgs 22.21-22).

1.4.3 *Limitations.* The first parameter to set concerns the word רוח. This study is concerned exclusively with the spirit (רוח) of God: Hence, precluded are human or animal רוח, or the 'wind' as a natural phenomenon. Lys has set commonly used criteria to separate the spirit of

---

13. J. Lindblom, *Prophecy in Ancient Israel* (Philadelphia: Fortress Press, 1962), p. 361. Among others who take a similar position, E. Jenni, 'Eschatology of the OT', *IDB*, II, pp. 126-33 (126); T.C. Vriezen, 'Prophecy and Eschatology', in George W. Anderson (ed.), *Congress Volume: Copenhagen, 1953* (VTSup, 1; Leiden: E.J. Brill, 1953), pp. 199-229 (200); Gerhard von Rad, *Old Testament Theology* (trans. D.M.G. Stalker; 2 vols.; New York: Harper & Row, 1962-65), II, p. 115.

14. L. Černy, *The Day of Yahweh and Some Relevant Problems* (Prague: Filosoficka Fakulta Karlovy University, 1948), p. 100.

15. In this sense, Mowinckel's sharp distinction between eschatology and the national hope of restoration appears too artificial (*He That Cometh*, p. 16).

16. In Arabic, *riḥ* stands for 'wind' and *ruḥ* for 'spirit'. See, e.g., Friedrich Baumgärtel, 'Spirit in the OT', *TDNT*, VI, pp. 359-67 (360).

God from the spirits of others. The presence of the definite article or its equivalence, often appearing in a construct state, is a rule of thumb for judging the spirit of God.

The main objective of this study is to investigate the evolution of the various רוח references in a given literary tradition. Hence, various issues inherent to the book of Isaiah will not receive the attention that they deserve. For instance, intertextuality between the various strata of the book is outside the scope of this study. The book is to function as a window, with good and wide perspectives through which the evolution of the רוח tradition may be observed.

2. *Review of Literature*

When it comes to major works on the spirit of God, there are only seven books written in English, French and German. The authors are Paul Volz,[17] Daniel Lys,[18] Lloyd Neve,[19] Leon J. Wood,[20] Robert T. Koch,[21] Manfred Dreytza[22] and Wilf Hildebrandt.[23] Koch, in addition to his recent work, has an earlier book on a similar topic.[24] For those who are interested in the subject, additional materials covering both the Old and the New Testaments can be found in journals,[25] Festschrifts[26] and

17. *Der Geist Gottes und die Verwandten Erscheinungen im Alten Testament und im Anschliessenden Judentum* (Tübingen: J.C.B. Mohr [Paul Siebeck], 1910).

18. *'Rûach', le souffle dans l'Ancien Testament* (Etudes d'histoire et de philosophie religieuses; Paris: Presses Universitaires de France, 1962).

19. *The Spirit of God.*

20. *The Holy Spirit in the Old Testament* (Contemporary Evangelical Perspectives Series; Grand Rapids: Zondervan, 1976).

21. *Der Geist Gottes im Alten Testament* (Bern: Peter Lang, 1991).

22. *Der theologische Gebrauch von RUAH im Alten Testament: Eine wort- und satzsemantische Studie* (Basel: Brunnen, 1992).

23. *An Old Testament Theology of the Spirit of God.*

24. *Geist und Messias* (Freiburg: Herder, 1950).

25. E.g. Johannes Hehn, 'Zum Problem des Geist im Alten Orient und im Alten Testament', *ZAW* 43 (1925), pp. 210-25; Mowinckel, ' "Spirit" and the "Word" ', pp. 199-227; Claus Westermann, 'Geist im Alten Testament', *EvT* 41 (1981), pp. 223-30; Abraham Pezhumkattil, 'Anthropological Concept of Spirit in the Old Testament', *Bible Bhashyam* 18 (1992), pp. 5-17; *idem*, 'The Spirit as the Power of God in the Old Testament', *Bible Bhashyam* 19 (1993), pp. 283-99.

26. Henri S. Cazelles, 'Prolegomenes à une étude de l'esprit dans la Bible', in W.C. Delsman *et al.* (eds.), *Von Kanaan bis Kerala* (Festschrift J.P.M. van der Plög; AOAT, 211; Neukirchen–Vluyn: Neukirchener Verlag, 1982), pp. 75-90.

books.[27] Also valuable are standard Old Testament theology books[28] and monographs, especially those dealing with Hebrew anthropology,[29] Hebrew worldview and the idea of God,[30] although their treatments are rather brief and general.

In all of these books, except Wood's (whose dealing is not comprehensive), there are divided opinions on various issues including: the possible origin of the Hebrew idea of God's spirit; whether there are different traditions identifiable in the רוח tradition in Hebrew as well as ancient Semitic traditions, or whether there is only one; and if the multiplicity of traditions is viable, how do they merge and fuse together to form a single Old Testament tradition especially projected for the future age?

2.1 *Paul Volz*
The work of Paul Volz is probably one of the first full-size monographs fully dedicated to the subject matter in this century. His historico-grammatical treatment argues strongly that the Hebrew concept of the רוח comes from the Mesopotamian belief in the demonic spirit.

2.2 *Daniel Lys*
Lys's massive work divides the term רוח into three usages: wind as an element of nature, human רוח and divine רוח. These three uses of the

27. E.g. Hans Heinrich Schmid, 'Ekstatische und charismatische Geistwirkungen im Alten Testament', in C. Heitmann and H. Mühlen (eds.), *Erfahrung und Theologie des Heiligen Geistes* (Hamburg: Agentur des Rauhen; Munich: Kösel, 1974), pp. 83-100; Norman H. Snaith, 'The Spirit of God in Jewish Thought', in *The Doctrine of the Holy Spirit: Four Lectures* (London: Epworth Press, 1937), pp. 11-37.

28. Paul van Imschoot, *Theology of the Old Testament* (trans. Kathryn Sullivan and Fidelis Buck; Paris: Desclée de Brouwer, 1965); Walther Eichrodt, *Theology of the Old Testament* (OTL; trans. J.A. Baker; 2 vols.; Philadelphia: Westminster Press, 1967), especially II, pp. 46-68.

29. E.g. Hans Walter Wolff, *Anthropology of the Old Testament* (trans. Margaret Kohl; Philadelphia: Fortress Press, 1974).

30. E.g. Luis I.J. Stadelmann, *The Hebrew Conception of the World* (AnBib, 39; Rome: Biblical Institute Press, 1970); Aubrey R. Johnson, *The One and the Many in the Israelite Conception of God* (Cardiff: University of Wales Press, 1961); *idem, The Vitality of the Individual in the Thought of Ancient Israel* (Cardiff: University of Wales Press, 1964). For a more comprehensive bibliography, see S. Tengström, 'רוח *rûaḥ*', *ThWAT*, VII, cols. 385-418 (386-88).

concept are investigated in material divided by historical and literary
divisions: pre-exilic, exilic and postexilic periods, and poetic and
wisdom literature. In this sense, his work is exhaustive. The title of the
book suggests that Lys defines the word רוח narrowly as the breath
(*souffle*), and in doing so, he further implies that the possible origin is
found in its anthropological use. In truth, the overwhelming discussion
of the *nepeš* appears overly to influence the anthropological aspect of
the idea to Lys's interpretation.

2.3 *Lloyd Neve*
Neve developed his interest in the subject during his missionary work
in Japan. In many ways, he closely follows Daniel Lys, except for
Neve's narrowly defined scope. Neve divides the material and assigns
passages to various respective periods utilizing Lys's method, as he
follows Lys's dating and his separation of the 'רוח of God' texts from
the other passages. For the origin of the idea of רוח, he suggests two
possibilities: anthropomorphic derivation, and the divine wind; and he
places more weight on the latter. He detects an Egyptian influence in
early material, especially in Exod. 15.8.[31] His approach is historico-
grammatical, but with less discussion of dates or textual uncertainties
about several passages. Since he is tracing the development of the
concept, sufficient attention should have been given to the matter. He
also failed to consult with important works that are available in his
time, such as those by Baumgärtel,[32] Koch,[33] Lys and Volz.

2.4 *Leon J. Wood*
The title of his book, *The Holy Spirit in the Old Testament*, indicates
his assumption: the book is written with the New Testament and even
contemporary interests in the Holy Spirit in mind. His treatment is
more popular, lacking critical exegetical treatment or any reference to
critical works, especially the one by Lloyd Neve. Nor is his work comprehensive, in spite of an impression one can have from the title. Thus,
his work is characterized by selectivity: this is the strength as well as
the weakness of the book. Selected topics imply that he has a contemporary interest in making the work usable and relevant in today's

31. Neve, *The Spirit of God*, p. 7.
32. F. Baumgärtel, *Spirit of God* (London: A. & C. Black, 1960); *idem*, 'Spirit
in the OT', pp. 359-67.
33. Koch, *Geist und Messias*.

church world. Because of his interest in contemporary issues, his work does not discuss the origin of the רוח tradition in Israel or its historical development.

2.5 *Robert T. Koch*

Koch, a German scholar, has long shown an interest in the subject, particularly in connection with the future age, that is, the spirit of God in the messianic age.[34] He places רוח along with 'word' (דבר) as a main element of God's revelation. It is an agent of the 'supernatural and superhistorical God' who deals with humans in covenant and in history.[35] Thus, רוח is 'the personal potency of the acting God' (*die personeigene Potenz des handelnden Gottes*).[36] Because of his interest in the role of רוח in the messianic, his treatment of some passages is in detail: the messianic figure (e.g. Isa. 11.1-9; 28.5-6; 42.1-4; 61.1-3); and people (e.g. Isa. 4.2-6; 32.15-20; 44.1-5; 59.21; Ezek. 36.25-29; cf. Jer. 31.31-34; Ezek. 37.1-4; Joel 3.1-5). Koch's treatment is a tightly organized work around the concept of 'messiah' and the eschatological role of the רוח.

2.6 *Manfred Dreytza*

In his revised Basel dissertation (1989), Manfred Dreytza takes a lexical and semantic approach. His search through Ugaritic, Eblite, Aramaic, Akkadian and Phoenician–Punic material does not yield any promising result. With a survey of literature which is rarely replicated by other scholars, he identifies his approach: a diachronic semantic investigation from the perspective of salvation history and history of religion. He seems to locate the original usage of the term רוח in the meteorological use denoting the functions of 'move', 'transport' and other effects of the wind. In this important work, Dreytza investigates a long-neglected area of a linguistic and semantic study. The lexical and semantic study is basically paradigmatic and syntagmatic analysis for him, and the patterns are studied to determine the theological meaning

34. His earlier work includes *Geist und Messias*. This work is not a revision of the earlier monograph. His usage of terms like messianic age, eschatological time or *Endzeit* is interchangeable, and they are used broadly. There is no definition of the terms. Koch tends, therefore, to regard any futuristic passage as referring to the messianic age.

35. Koch, *Der Geist Gottes*, p. 13.

36. Koch, *Der Geist Gottes*, p. 32.

of the רוח. In comparison with Koch's microscopic study, Dreytza's work is wider in scope encompassing meteorological and anthropological meanings of the רוח.

2.7 *Wilf Hildebrandt*
Hildebrandt, teaching in Africa, adds a welcome volume to the scarce רוח study in the English-speaking world. Well acquainted with Pentecostals, if not one himself, he divides passages not according to historical periods, but into four conceptual networks: creation, God's people, Israel's leaders, and prophecy. The rest of the book investigates passages in the four set categories. However, his canonical approach fails to overcome the problem of reading passages from different periods and contexts as if they were from one hand. Juxtaposing chs. 14 and 15 of Exodus, for instance, results in an indifferent treatment of two distinct literary genres and their different historical origins. He concludes his book with a discussion of the significance of his findings for New Testament pneumatology. This valuable and extensive research, by a non-Westerner probably for the first time, is weakened by a methodological shortfall: his synchronic 'canonical' reading puts the passages on a mono-dimensional plane, almost indifferent to their literary genre or various dates and historical contexts. A synchronic reading, without recognizing the rich depth of the engaging growth of a passage, may not be much different from the pre-critical reading.

2.8 *Reflection*
German scholarship has shown constant interest in the subject of the spirit, as evidenced by Koch and Dreytzer.[37] Neve's work will probably remain the standard work on the topic available in English, in spite of its limited availability (the book was produced by a foreign press and has been out of print). His balanced and serious scholarly work is analogous to Irving Wood's work at the turn of the century.[38] Generally speaking, however, English-speaking scholarship is geared more toward popular readership as shown in the several books dealing with the spirit in the Old Testament and the Holy Spirit in the New Testament

---

37. Two additional articles by German scholars should also be mentioned: Tengström, 'רוח'; Baumgärtel, 'Spirit in the OT'.

38. Irving F. Wood, *The Spirit of God in Biblical Literature* (London: Hodder & Stoughton, 1904).

together. Among them, Montague displays a balanced scholarship with easy readability.

French literature on this present topic is represented by Lys's magisterial work, as well as by numerous articles produced by Imschoot (1934–54). It is unfortunate that the latter's six works are scattered in four journals,[39] and his Old Testament theology book did not incorporate all his findings.

3. *The* רוח *of God before Isaiah*

From the study of conceptual parallels in ancient Near Eastern material and early Israelite Hebrew literature, the possible meaning and origin of the רוח may be argued as follows.

3.1 *Preliminary Observations*

Depending on which רוח tradition a text reflects, the meaning and emphasis varies. For example, in a judgment context, the רוח often reflects the violent and destructive movement of the wind, but in a salvation setting, the idea of a life-giving force appears. In this context, the רוח takes a crucial role in creation, and the imagery of life-sustaining water is associated with it. When it is specifically granted to a human being, it results in a superhuman ability in the form of physical or military prowess and in prophetic inspiration in words and behavior. The following are preliminary observations.

3.1.1. The majority of the רוח usage displays a tension between two concepts: it is closely attached to God, and it produces unique effects. The רוח in most cases can be called the 'extension of Yahweh's personality'[40] or of his being. It does not display any personal feature, and remains as an impersonal force, though the distance between רוח and

---

39. Paul van Imschoot, 'L'action de l'esprit de Jahvé dans l'Ancien Testament', *RSPT* 23 (1934), pp. 553-87; *idem*, 'L'esprit de Jahvé et l'alliance nouvelle dans l'Ancien Testament', *ETL* 13 (1936), pp. 201-20; *idem*, 'L'esprit de Jahvé, principe de vie morale dans l'Ancien Testament', *ETL* 16 (1939), pp. 457-67; *idem*, 'L'esprit de Jahvé, source de la piété dans l'Ancien Testament', *Bible et Vie Chretienne* 6 (1954), pp. 17-30; *idem*, 'L'esprit de Jahvé, source de vie dans l'Ancien Testament', *RB* 44 (1935), pp. 481-501; *idem*, 'Sagesse et esprit dans l'Ancien Testament', *RB* 47 (1938), pp. 23-49.

40. Johnson, *The One and the Many*, pp. 6-7, 19-22, 36-37.

Yahweh varies. The Old Testament is not ready to declare that the spirit is Yahweh or vice versa; rather, its affinity to God is often expressed in a parallel construct with other anthropomorphic expressions such as mouth (Isa. 34.16) or hand (Exod. 15.6).[41] This expresses part of God himself with a distinct function. At the same time, there are usages more detached from God such as the spirit of judgment and burning (Isa. 4.4) which almost sounds like '*a spirit of...*' (cf. 1 Kgs 22.22-23). Also a water imagery is often employed as if רוח is a substance which God pours out (Isa. 32.15; 44.3). Although this usage also refers to God himself, the רוח almost takes its own personality (Isa. 63.14). However, once it assumes a definite personality, that tradition (1 Kgs 22.17-23) eventually develops its own separate category—angel (מלאך). In the later tradition, these two are clearly distinguished (Isa. 63.9, 10-14).

3.1.2. When it comes to function, the רוח, as מלאך, executes Yahweh's will and purpose in the human world. Once the רוח is moved beyond the human realm, the details may differ significantly. In contrast to the purely messenger role of the angel, the רוח is used often in the context of God's power (e.g. Isa. 11.1),[42] whether equipping an individual to produce a secondary effect (e.g. Isa. 11.1-3a) or directly affecting the people (e.g. Isa. 32.15). It is God's personal influence, in reference to his power, either directly or indirectly, as an empowering agent.

3.2 *Toward the Origin of the* רוח
For the possible origin of the spirit ideas there is no scholarly consensus, although the majority argues from the 'wind'/breath phenomenon.[43] As Dreytza observes, philological investigations of the ancient Near Eastern languages have not produced fruitful results.[44] The conceptual inquiry so far has proved that the various uses of the

---

41. For the correlation between רוח and יד, see Dreytza, *Der theologische Gebrauch von RUAH*, pp. 146-58.

42. For this contrast, the Gideon narrative is illuminating, as first the angel appears as God's messenger with its distinct human-like personality (Judg. 6.11-21), and later Gideon encounters the spirit of God with totally impersonal features (Judg. 6.34).

43. See, e.g., Lys, '*Rûach*', p. 1, for his etymological study of the 'air family' words; Eichrodt, *Theology*, II, pp. 46-47; Tengström, 'רוח', col. 389. For another argument of a single demonic origin, see Volz, *Der Geist Gottes*, pp. 2-6. For a more recent view see Hildebrandt, *Old Testament Theology of the Spirit*, pp. 3-5.

44. Dreytza, *Der Theologische Gebrauch von RUAH*, chs. 1 and 2.

concept in 'wind', 'atmosphere', divine elements in prophets, kings and ordinary human beings have their unique meanings. One can even go further to say that their uses and meanings are almost mutually exclusive.

One can assume the ancient Near Eastern influence in the formation of the Hebrew רוח concept, for the reason that the Hebrew writers already presume that the existence of the idea indicates the influence. The ancient Near Eastern evidence demonstrates that the notion of the wind is significant in creation and in divinity. But the notion of the wind is not present in kingship, prophecy and 'soul'. Therefore, it is obvious that at least three ancient Near Eastern ideas to which Hebrew רוח is related cannot be combined with the idea of the wind. A single origin of the tradition cannot account for this. The only common element is the presence of the divine element, but this is not specific enough to be regarded as the origin.

In the monotheistic ideal of Hebrew, various ancient Near Eastern deities or their influences come under one Hebrew expression of רוח. However, this does not bring the diverse traditions into one category: it is only one aspect of these diverse traditions combined under the idea of רוח. Among the pre-exilic uses, there are extremes; for instance, while Isa. 31.3 implies that God is spirit, 1 Kgs 22.19-23 implies that the רוח maintains the Mesopotamian demonic tradition. The plurality of the רוח tradition in Israel is also apparent.

The question is, how is the רוח concept used to encompass all these diverse ideas? It is possible that the 'wind' as a powerful divine weapon comes to signify God's instrument. As is commonly argued, the ancient mind could have viewed the breath in general as a divine life-giving wind. However, this does not adequately explain the spirit of God as seen upon the leaders and the prophets. The process of appropriation has already begun prior to the 'biblical era'. The only seeming fusion of more than one spirit tradition is found in the story of Saul and the 70 elders where the 'leadership' and 'prophetic' spirit temporarily merge. Otherwise, the multiplicity of the spirit traditions is evident throughout the Old Testament.

3.3 *Toward the Basic Meaning of* רוח

Questions regarding the meaning of the spirit of God have not been difficult to answer for many scholars. Arguing from the word רוח, they highlight the power element of God's activity *'as he relates himself* to his world, his creation, his people'.[45] Eichrodt's definition is typical of most scholars. Drawing heavily from the 'wind' notion of רוח, the spirit of God refers to 'the mysterious nearness and activity of the divine'.[46] Most definitions emphasize the elements of power and mystery of the רוח.

As seen in Mesopotamian and Ugaritic texts, the 'wind' highlights the power element either as a divine weapon or as a powerful storm to bring rain. Yet, the power element is not always prominent, or even present. Egyptians relate the 'wind' concept more to life than to power. It is evident in early Israelite traditions that Gen. 6.3 does not refer to the activity of God, although the exact notion of the רוח is much debated. (It may refer to the breath of God in Gen. 2.7.) At any rate, the רוח refers to the presence of the God-given quality in the 'sons of God'. In this sense, the Egyptian ideas of *ba* (soul) and *ka* (double) are close to the spirit of God.[47] Eichrodt's idea of nearness is appealing, although he still singles out the role of the spirit as related to God's 'activity'.

Ugaritic texts also shed light on this. Out of nine occurrences of *rwḥ*, or *rḥ*,[48] only three refer to what Hebrew רוח does. First, *rḥ* is easily rendered as 'wind' or 'breath' in its parallelism with *npš* (*CTA* 18 iv 24, 25, 36). Secondly, in a parallelism between *rḥ* and *brlt* (17 i 37-38; 19.88, 93; 18.25, 37); *brlt* is rendered either 'soul' by Gordon[49] or 'spittle' by Gibson.[50] Thirdly, *CTA* 7 v 6-11 describes the armory of Baal which is the wind (*rḥk*) and its associated elements. Certainly the deified natural forces are at the disposal of Baal. At the same time, the term is also in parallel with the life principle in human beings.

45. Neve, *The Spirit of God*, p. 2 (my emphasis).

46. Eichrodt, *Theology*, II, p. 46. The spirit of God is viewed as one of three cosmic powers of God.

47. For *ka*, see James H. Breasted, *Development of Religion and Thought in Ancient Egypt* (New York: Harper & Brothers, 1959), p. 64. For *ba*, the best illustration is found in Hans Goedicke, *The Report about the Dispute of a Man with his Ba: Papyrus Berlin 3024* (Baltimore: The Johns Hopkins University Press, 1970) (p. 20 for its origin).

48. G. Douglas Young, *Concordance of Ugaritic* (AnOr, 36; Rome: Pontificio Istituto Biblico, 1956), pp. 62-63 (Glossary, items 1745-51).

49. Cyrus H. Gordon, *Ugaritic Textbook: Grammar, Texts in Transliteration, Cuneiform Selections, Glossary, Indices* (AnOr, 38; Rome: Pontifical Biblical Institute, 1965), p. 375 (Glossary, item 520).

50. J.C.L. Gibson, *Canaanite Myths and Legends* (ed. G.R. Driver; Edinburgh: T. & T. Clark, 1956), pp. 112-13.

A.R. Johnson proposes an attractive expression to describe the spirit of God: the 'extension of God's personality'.[51] This definition is more desirable than the one proposed above, because the expression includes not only God's activity, but also the representative function of God's being. The only disadvantage of this definition is an impression from 'personality' that spirit also assumes the personhood of God.

The spirit of God is an element or aspect of the divine being, or an instrument at the divine disposal, manifested as God relates himself to human beings, nature, and later the nation. This divine element is present among humans, as in Gen. 6.3, or carries out God's will, as in Exod. 15.8, or 'invades' human agents, as among the 70 elders, the judges, the kings, Joseph and the prophets.

3.3 *Spirit Traditions*

One can divide the use of the notion of divine spirit into two broad categories: charismatic and non-charismatic. The former has the primary function of enabling. The spirit of God is given to equip, enable or empower a selected individual to perform a divinely commissioned task. In a strict sense, therefore, there are two layers of recipients: one that receives the spirit as God's agent; and one that will experience consequences of the spirit-empowerment. Into the first category fall spirit-empowered leaders and, to a lesser degree, spirit-empowered prophets. The latter category has a single layer of the recipients, that is, only those who experience the spirit as sole recipients. The purpose of the spirit's presence is to empower the immediate recipient without an intended consequence for a secondary group of people. The rest of the spirit tradition belongs to the latter category. Not all the spirit traditions, however, may neatly fall into one of these two categories. The following are various spirit traditions found in the Old Testament.

3.3.1 *Leadership Spirit.* This tradition is found in the judges, kings (present and future) and the 70 elders. The main feature of this category is the dual role of the presence of the spirit, to authenticate and to equip the recipient.

As a regular feature of charismatic leadership before the monarchical period, a leader is chosen by God. Due to the lack of any established system whereby a leader emerges and he or she is accepted by the

---

51. Johnson, *The One and the Many*, pp. 6-7, 19-20, 36-37.

ancient Israelite society, the authentication of the divinely elected leader is essential. Sometimes the leader is chosen through a human initiative, as are the 70 elders, and later God authenticates the selection. But in most cases, it is God who makes the selection. The judges (e.g. Judg. 2.16), Saul (1 Sam. 10.1) and David (1 Sam. 16.1) are such cases. That the latter is a norm is substantiated by how the future king or leader is elected (Isa. 11.1-2; 28.6; 42.1, etc.). Regardless of who initiates the process, the authentication is essential for the leader to be accepted by the people. The presence of the spirit of God is probably the most common means of authentication (Num. 11.25; 1 Sam. 10.10-11). The element of equipping or enabling appears in a varying degree, although this element is often assumed. For instance, the judges are almost always associated with military expeditions after the spirit comes upon them. The successful organization of an inter-tribal army and a successful military campaign are proof of the spirit's presence. In the case of Saul, especially in 1 Samuel 11, the action of the spirit exactly follows the pattern of the judges. However, in the case of the 70 elders (Num. 11.25, E) and David (1 Sam. 16.13), there is no explicit or implicit reference to the equipping role of the spirit. However, for the future leader figures, the equipping feature returns (e.g. Isa. 11.1; 42.1-2).

3.3.2 *Prophetic Spirit.* Another early charismatic tradition is related to prophetic phenomena. There are at least two categories for the prophetic spirit: (1) the presence of the prophetic phenomenon as the spirit comes upon non-prophetic figures; and (2) the coming of the spirit upon the prophets. In both cases, a prophetic behavior is commonly perceived as an important sign for the presence of the divine spirit.

Saul leads the first category. After he is anointed by Samuel (1 Sam. 10.1), he experiences three signs to affirm his anointing. The last of them is the coming of the spirit upon Saul as he is to encounter a band of prophets in Gibeath-elohim (1 Sam. 10.5). As a result of his encounter with the 'sons of the prophet' he begins to prophesy (1 Sam. 10.10-11). The prophetic experience is to authenticate the presence of the spirit, which in turn authenticates God's selection. A similar story is found in the 70 elders: as the proof of the presence of God's spirit, the 70 elders prophesy (Num. 11.25).

For the second category, an example is the presence of God's spirit upon the 'sons of the prophet' (1 Sam. 10.10; 16.13). In both cases, the coming of the spirit upon them is just assumed rather than argued. This indicates that the connection between the prophetic movement and the spirit of God is an ancient phenomenon, and, by the tribal period, it is already expected to take place. Possibly the idea of ecstasy arises from the presence of the spirit which in turn causes an abnormal behavior, as evidenced in Saul's experience (1 Sam. 19.24).

3.3.3 *Creation Spirit.* This usage is often regarded as a late development. The association of the divine spirit in Gen. 1.2 (P) is a good example. Metaphorically, the restoration of the nation, agricultural prosperity, peaceful life (Isa. 32.15-20) and spiritual restoration (Isa. 44.3-5) are of this same category where the divine spirit is portrayed as a creation force. Due to the nature of this usage, the spirit is given not only to individuals, the entire community (Isa. 32.15) or the nation, but also to the land (Isa. 32.15b-16), and to people to increase (Isa. 44.4).

3.3.4 *The Spirit as God's Independent Agent.* This may be another old usage found throughout the ancient Near Eastern environment as well as in the Old Testament. The spirit's association with God is rather loose, as it functions as an independent entity. There are two kinds of spirit in this category: the spirit with personality and the one without. 1 Kings 22.19-23 uses a heavenly court scene; a courtier is called 'spirit'. One of them is permitted to become a 'lying spirit' in the mouth of Ahab's prophets. This usage is increasingly frequent in Ezekiel. The later reference of wisdom to the spirit (Prov. 1.23) may belong to this usage. The non-personality usage abounds. For instance, in Exod. 15.8, the 'blast [רוח] of your [God's] nostril' is the impersonal agent, in this case the east wind, which carried out God's will. Zechariah's often quoted declaration may fall into the same category, ' "Not by might, nor by power, but by my spirit", says Yahweh of hosts' (Zech. 4.6). The former usage may have developed into, or been included in, the idea of angels as God's agents in the later times.

3.3.5 *The Spirit as Part of God's Person of Sign of God's Presence.* Often anthropomorphic usage is an indication of this category. For instance, Isa. 31.3 compares Yahweh with Egyptian horses by declaring, 'their horses are flesh, and not spirit' (NRSV). Another example is Isa. 34.16b where a parallelism is evident: 'For the mouth of Yahweh has commanded, and his spirit has gathered them [animals]'. Both the

mouth and the spirit are God's agent, but the usage is clearly different
from the 'spirit' in the divine court in 1 Kgs 22.19-23. Isaiah 40.13
identifies God's spirit as a faculty of his wisdom. Another reference is
found in the enigmatic Gen. 6.3, 'Then Yahweh said, "My spirit shall
not abide in mortals forever..."'. The exact identity of the spirit is
hotly debated, as the exact interpretation of the 'sons of God' or the
'daughters of men' is equally difficult. Nevertheless, it is not difficult to
identify the 'spirit' as something closely associated with God himself,
graciously granted to the 'sons of God'. A.R. Johnson, in fact, identifies
the spirit throughout the Old Testament as the 'extension of God's
personality'.[52]

3.3.6 *The Spirit Practically a Substitute for God.* This could be a later
feature, along with the development of the transcendental emphasis on
God over the human realm. For instance, Isa. 63.7-19 is a historical
prayer recounting God's mighty work and human failure throughout
Israel's history. Verse 10 reads, 'But they rebelled and grieved his holy
spirit; therefore he became their enemy...' The first line can simply
mean, 'they grieved him [God]'. In v. 14, it reads, 'the spirit of Yahweh
gave them [Israelites] rest'. The next line continues, 'Thus you [God]
led your people...' The 'spirit of Yahweh' is virtually synonymous
with 'you' (God). This may be compared with the Deuteronomic development of 'name theology' to avoid a direct reference to God himself.

52. Johnson, *The One and the Many*, pp. 6-7, 19-20, 36-37; *idem*, *Vitality of the Individual*, pp. 2-3.

Chapter 1

PRE-EXILIC ISAIANIC SPIRIT TRADITION

S. Mowinckel points out that at this time the prophets hardly referred to the רוּחַ of Yahweh in connection with the prophetic inspiration of their own and of other prophets.[1] This study will focus on early Isaianic references to God's רוּחַ. Some passages will be read in their unique pre-exilic eschatology.

1. *Passages*

11.1-2[2]
1   And a shoot shall go out from the stump of Jesse
    A branch from his roots shall bear fruit.

---

1.   Mowinckel, '"Spirit" and the "Word"', pp. 199-227.
2.   For vv. 11.1-9 as a unit, Brevard S. Childs, *Myth and Reality in the Old Testament* (SBT, 27; Naperville: Allenson, 1960), p. 65; Margaret B. Crook, 'A Suggested Occasion for Isa 9.2-7 and 11.1-9', *JBL* 68 (1949), pp. 213-24 (216); Georg Fohrer, *Das Buch Jesaja* (Zürcher Bibelkommentar; 3 vols.; Zürich: Zwingli-Verlag, 1960–64), I, pp. 165-66; Norman K. Gottwald, *All the Kingdoms of the Earth: Israelite Prophecy and International Relations in the Ancient Near East* (New York: Harper & Row, 1964), p. 197; W. Harrelson, 'Nonroyal Motifs in the Royal Eschatology', in Bernhard W. Anderson and Walter Harrelson (eds.), *Israel's Prophetic Heritage: Essays in Honor of James Muilenburg* (New York: Harper & Row, 1962), pp. 147-65 (154); Mowinckel, '"Spirit" and the "Word"', p. 202; *idem, He That Cometh*, p. 17; Neve, *The Spirit of God in the Old Testament*, p. 55; John N. Oswalt, *The Book of Isaiah Chapters 1–39* (NICOT; Grand Rapids: Eerdmans, 1968), pp. 276-77; R.B.Y. Scott, 'The Book of Isaiah Chapters 1–39', *IB*, V, pp. 149-381 (247); J. Skinner, *The Book of the Prophet Isaiah, Chapters I–XXXIX* (Cambridge Bible for Schools and Colleges; Cambridge: Cambridge University Press, 1958), pp. 103-105. But for vv. 1-10 as a unit, see, e.g., John D.W. Watts, *Isaiah 1–33* (WBC, 24; Waco, TX: Word Books, 1985), pp. 167-77. A number of commentators see the beginning of the unit in 10.33, presumably due to the repetition of the tree imagery in 10.34 and 11.1.

> 2   And the spirit of Yahweh shall rest on him:
>   a spirit of wisdom and understanding,
>   a spirit of counsel and might,
>   a spirit of knowledge, and the fear of Yahweh.

The affinity to the royal psalms (particularly, to Ps. 72) leads Wildberger to conclude that vv. 1-5 is an oracle of a future king.[3] The
uncertainty of the oracular setting prompts Watts to see it as a 'poem
that deals with royal ideology'.[4] A cultic use of the passage seems
feasible. Attached to this royal poem is a description of a mythological
paradisiacal world (vv. 6-9).

A logical structure is visible: the description of the coming ruler (1-
3a) and equipment for his office (3b-5). The strict parallelism is evident
throughout the passage, and the parallelism of the three pairs after a
general statement in v. 2 ('the spirit of Yahweh...') is noteworthy.

Arguments both for Isaianic authorship and for a later redactional
origin are posited by an equally impressive number of scholars. The
matter boils down to two factors; the interpretation of גזע, 'stump', and
the positive nature of the oracle.

Mowinckel contends that, as far as the 'stock of Jesse' is concerned,
there is no sidestepping of it. For him it is natural to assume that the
Davidic family tree has toppled after the fall of Judah.[5] Further, in
another connection, Mowinckel asserts that גזע here, and in Job 14.8
means 'the stump of a tree which has been felled', although he does not
rule out the possibility that the term in other places may refer also to
the living stem of a plant.[6] R.E. Clements argues that a postexilic hand
had a definite intention to balance out the preceding negative message
(10.26-32) with a positive one.[7] He also draws attention to a close
similarity to Mic. 5.2-4 as a clue for the later origin.[8] This view is
shared by a number of scholars.[9]

---

3.   Hans Wildberger, *Isaiah 1–12: A Commentary* (trans. Thomas H. Trapp;
Minneapolis: Fortress Press, 1991), p. 463.

4.   Watts, *Isaiah 1–33*, p. 169.

5.   Mowinckel, '"Spirit" and the "Word"', p. 202. Also Ronald F. Youngblood, *The Book of Isaiah: An Introductory Commentary* (Grand Rapids: Baker
Book House, 2nd edn, 1993), p. 55.

6.   Mowinckel, *He That Cometh*, p. 17.

7.   Ronald E. Clements, *Isaiah 1–39* (NCBC; London: Marshall, Morgan &
Scott, 1980), p. 122.

8.   Clements, *Isaiah 1–39*, p. 121.

9.   Among them are Otto Eissfeldt, *The Old Testament: An Introduction* (trans.

Those who argue for the Isaianic origin acknowledge that גזע is most commonly applied to a fallen tree.[10] However, they assert that 'the realization of the judgment announced [earlier] by Isaiah is a sufficient reason for the use of such an expression'.[11] Stacey contends that 'every time the king dies, a tree from the root falls; but a shoot from the same stock, a new son of David, takes his place';[12] while Hayes and Irvine argue this to refer to the territorial reduction in Isaiah's early career.[13] It is also true that messages of salvation are not uncommon in Isaiah 1–39, although they are less frequent than in Second and Third Isaiah.[14]

It is not an easy task to weigh between these two convincing presentations. Yet at least two additional factors should be taken into consideration. As Gottwald observes, one is that, in Isaiah, there are two types of expectations of God's rule, namely, with a human agency, which is mostly a kingly figure (9.2-7; 11.1-9), and without any human instrumentality (12.4-6; 14.25; 17.12-14; 29.5-8).[15] This is in contrast to the expectation of Second and Third Isaiah, which does not describe a definite royal figure of this kind. The description is more vague and less royal as seen, for instance, in the Servant Songs. This difference is

Peter R. Ackroyd; New York: Harper & Row, 1965), p. 319; Fohrer, *Das Buch Jesaja*, I, p. 160; O. Kaiser, *Isaiah 1–12* (OTL; trans. John Bowden; Philadelphia: Westminster Press, 1983), pp. 253-54; Lindblom, *Prophecy in Ancient Israel*, p. 281 n. 100; William R. Schoemaker, 'The Use of "Ruach" in the Old Testament and of "Pneuma" in the New Testament', *JBL* 23 (1904), pp. 13-67 (31).

10. John H. Hayes and Stuart A. Irvine, *Isaiah, the Eighth-Century Prophet: His Time and his Preaching* (Nashville: Abingdon Press, 1987), p. 212, point out that in Isa. 40.24, the term refers to 'the stalk of a recently planted tree before branches have sprouted', thus meaning simply the Davidic house.

11. Helmer Ringgren, *The Messiah in the Old Testament* (SBT, 18; London: SCM Press, 1956), p. 31. Also Josh Pedersen, *Israel, its Life and Culture* (4 vols. in 2; London: Milford, 1926–40), III–IV, p. 678, gives examples to show that the term can refer to the living stem of a plant as seen in Isa. 40.24.

12. David Stacey, *Isaiah 1–39* (Epworth Commentaries; London: Epworth Press, 1993), p. 87.

13. Hayes and Irvine, *Isaiah*, p. 212.

14. Bernhard Duhm, *Das Buch Jesaja: Übersetzt und erklärt* (HKAT, 3; Göttingen: Vandenhoeck & Ruprecht, 1902), p. 77; Hugo Gressmann, *Der Messias* (Göttingen: Vandenhoeck & Ruprecht, 1929), p. 247; Walther Eichrodt, *Der Heilige in Israel: Jesaja 1–12* (BAT, 17.1; Stuttgart: Calwer Verlag, 1960), p. 137; Wildberger, *Isaiah 1–12*, pp. 465-67. See also Oswalt, *Isaiah Chapters 1–39*, pp. 276-77 and Watts, *Isaiah 1–33*, p. 176.

15. Gottwald, *All the Kingdoms*, p. 197.

further argued because of Isaiah's interest in the continuity of the
Davidic monarchy. Hence, the postexilic date of the Micah passage on
which Clements asserts the postexilic origin of the present passage
should be re-examined.[16] The other factor to be considered is the *Sitz
im Leben* of the passage. The literary features betray a definite connection with 9.2-7 which appears not to be a prediction but an announcement in a royal ceremony. Isaiah 11.1-5 may possibly be another royal
oracle,[17] although Crook's detailed argument for a ninth-century origin
of the tradition is yet to be established.[18] The absence of a typical
expression for a distant future, like 'in the end of days' or 'in that day',
supports the cultic function of the passage.[19] In addition, the appearance
of the typical paired words of Isaiah, 'justice' and 'righteousness' gives

16. E.g. Leslie C. Allen assumes the eighth-century origin of the passage, *The
Books of Joel, Obadiah, Jonah and Micah* (NICOT; Grand Rapids: Eerdmans,
1976), p. 342. James L. Mays, *Micah: A Commentary* (OTL; Philadelphia: Westminster Press, 1976), p. 112, attributes the messianic promise to Micah at the end of
the eighth century. Delbert R. Hillers, *Micah* (Hermeneia; Philadelphia: Fortress
Press, 1984), p. 65, suspects an exilic reworking of the original pre-exilic oracle;
similarly Hans W. Wolff, *Micah: A Commentary* (trans. Gary Stansell; Minneapolis: Augsburg, 1990), pp. 135-36.

17. Gottwald, *All the Kingdoms*, p. 276, regards the passage as an enthronement
song, whereas Crook, 'A Suggested Occasion', p. 213, explains the passage as a
coronation liturgy and 9.2-7 as an enthronement liturgy. William L. Holladay,
Jeremiah. I. A Commentary on the Book of the Prophet Jeremiah Chapters 1–25
(Hermeneia; Philadelphia: Fortress Press, 1986), p. 617, identifies the oracle, along
with Jer. 23.5-6, as an 'announcement of a royal savior'. He bases his argument on
Akkadian prophecies and the Egyptian 'Prophecy of Neferti'. Also, see John M.
Wiebe, 'The Form of the "Announcement of a Royal Savior" and the Interpretation
of Jeremiah 23.5-6', *Studia Biblica et Theologica* 15 (1987), pp. 1-22 (6-7). The
royal figure is often identified with Hezekiah, e.g. Richard J. Sklba, *Pre-Exilic
Prophecy: Words of Warning, Dreams of Hopes, Spirituality of Pre-Exilic Prophets*
(Collegeville, MN: Liturgical Press, 1990), p. 86; and archaeological evidence is
claimed for this identity, see D.P. Cole, 'Archaeology and the Messiah Oracles of
Isaiah 9 and 11', in M.D. Coogan *et al.* (eds.), *Scripture and Other Artifacts:
Essays on the Bible and Archaeology in Honor of Philip J. King* (Louisville, KY:
Westminster/John Knox Press, 1994), pp. 53-69.

18. The narrative of 2 Kgs 11 where a royal child was saved leads Crook, 'A
Suggested Occasion', p. 216, to conclude the specific origin of the tradition.

19. In that sense, like the majority of modern scholars, Joachim Becker, *Messianic Expectation in the Old Testament* (trans. David E. Green; Philadelphia:
Fortress Press, 1980), p. 38, argues that the expectation of a future royal savior is
within the immediate historical context.

a slight affirmative nod in favor of the early date of the passage.[20]

The endowment of the spirit of Yahweh to the coming ruler recalls an old tradition in which רוח is closely associated with Yahweh's chosen charismatic leaders, the judges (Judg. 3.10; 6.34; 11.29; 13.25; 14.16, 19; 15.13, 14; 19.9, 20, 23) and the first two kings (1 Sam. 10.6, 10; 11.6; 16.13, 14; 19.9). This idea might have survived in the northern kingdom,[21] while in Judah the dynastic succession has replaced God's direct intervention in the selection and equipping of national leaders.[22] After a long silence of Yahweh's רוח in the monarchy, the tradition of charismatic leadership and the Davidic succession are combined here for the future king.

This divine equipment with the רוח of Yahweh is distinguished from the ancient Near Eastern understanding of kingship, in which the divine equipment of the king is attributed to a supernatural conception or birth, or to nursing at the breast of a goddess.[23] Here the charismatic endowment of the future king is the source of all his royal virtues.[24] H. Ringgren notices an allusion to 1 Sam. 16.13, where David is anointed and as a consequence the spirit 'will rest' upon him.[25] The permanency and gentle nature of the endowment are noted against the temporary effect of the spirit upon the earlier leaders such as the judges.

20. Some scholars leave the question undecided as the passage is 'under investigation', e.g. Williamson, *The Book Called Isaiah*, p. 233.

21. As in Albrecht Alt, 'Das Königtum in den Reichen Israel und Juda', *VT* 1 (1951), pp. 2-22 (4-6, 12-13).

22. Neve, *The Spirit of God*, p. 55, suspects that the charismatic succession from Moses to the elders, to the judges, to Saul and David himself has been terminated with David, although in Solomon, the endowment of wisdom seems to be a substitute for the gift of the spirit.

23. P. Robert Koch, 'Der Gottesgeist und der Messias', *Bib* 27 (1946), pp. 241-68, 376-403 (248-49).

24. J.J.M. Roberts, 'The Divine King and the Human Community in Isaiah's Vision of the Future', in H.B. Huffmon, F.A. Spina and A.R.W. Green (eds.), *The Quest for the Kingdom of God: Studies in Honor of George E. Mendenhall* (Winona Lake, IN: Eisenbrauns, 1983), pp. 127-36 (132), notes a close parallel with the royal psalms, particularly Ps. 72. The evidence is obvious in the enabling of the spirit of Yahweh and the administration of judicial justice and righteousness (Isa. 11.4a; Ps. 72.2) and the vindication of the poor as well as the slaying of the wicked (Isa. 11.4b; Ps. 72.4).

25. Ringgren, *The Messiah*, pp. 31-32.

However, this ideal king is never pictured as independent from Yahweh, not only because of the ultimate divine source of his virtues, but also because of his constant subjection to God in the fear of Yahweh. This appears to be reminiscent of the pre-monarchic leadership which was characterized by Yahweh's direct rule with earthly leaders as his instrument of salvation. It is not the king who uses the רוח of Yahweh, but vice versa, just as the spirit of Yahweh 'clothes' itself with Gideon (Judg. 6.34). Yahweh is the true ruler over Israel, and not a king or even with all the idealized qualifications. Yet the significance of the endowment of the spirit does not totally rest in the idealized virtues of the king. According to Mowinckel, the exclusive endowment with the spirit separates the king from ordinary human beings.[26] Although his understanding of Yahweh's רוח here goes beyond a justifiable limit,[27] the association of the רוח of Yahweh certainly gives the king 'the quality of "holiness"', closer to the idea of sacral kingship. It implies a direct association of the king with divinity, although in the case of Saul there are two distinct effects of the presence of the spirit (1 Sam. 19.23-24 and 10.5-6, 10; 11.6-7).

The three pairs of attributes of the ruler are all virtues that belong to the old ideal of a king.[28] A close connection between wisdom and kingship is common in the ancient Near Eastern world. That Israelites share this common idea is made clear here in the explicit expression of 'wisdom' and in Isa. 9.6 in the name of 'wonder of a counselor'.[29]

---

26. Harrelson, 'Nonroyal Motifs', pp. 154-55, argues that the writer portrays the coming ruler as non-royal. There is no mention of a specific king and the uses of uncommon terms such as חטר, גזע and נצר are the clues to the non-royal nature. However, the effect of his rulership, which is peace and righteousness, can only be attributed to a royal figure.

27. Mowinckel, *He That Cometh*, p. 65, contends that the spirit of Yahweh is exclusive to the ideal king, just as ancient manas (power which is present in an object) and taboos were exclusive to the sacral king in Egypt and the Near Eastern region. He also argues that the spirit here represents the life-giving, wonder-working, power-filled 'wind' or 'breath' of the deity. However, the life-giving role is not applied in this passage. Even the description of the paradisiacal era has no notion of a life-giving spirit.

28. Youngblood, *The Book of Isaiah*, p. 55, calls the three pairs intellectual, practical and spiritual qualities and thus explains in three words, 'wisdom, strength and fear of God'.

29. J.W. Whedbee, *Isaiah and Wisdom* (Nashville: Abingdon Press, 1971), p. 142, contends that this set of charismatic gifts is 'centered fundamentally in

Wisdom is the 'ability to act according to what the circumstances demand'[30] in his capacity as a judge in its premonarchical sense. In the Israelite tradition, as in the ancient Near Eastern world, the royal wisdom is mainly for judicial and political purposes as the paired word 'understanding' further clarifies (for David and Solomon, 2 Sam. 14.20; 1 Kgs 4.29-34 and particularly the paired words in 1 Kgs 3.12, 'a wise and understanding heart'). Moreover, Isa. 11.4 makes it clear that the protection of the underprivileged is the foremost task of the king.[31] This definitely reflects the keen interest of Isaiah in social unrighteousness and injustice (e.g. the frequent reference to 'righteousness' in Isa. 1.21, 26, 27; 5.7, 16, 23; 9.6[7]; 10.22; 28.17 and 'justice' in 1.17, 21, 27; 5.7, 16; 9.6[7]; 10.2; 16.5; 28.6, 17). The practice of the crediting of wisdom to a divine source is not widely shared, as seen in the claim of the king of Tyre who boasts himself as the source of wisdom (Ezek. 28.2-7, 12, 17).[32] In Isaiah, however, the reliance of the future ruler upon Yahweh is absolute. He is called 'prince' (שׂר), an official commissioned by a higher authority, who receives advice from the universal king (2 Sam. 16.23).[33]

The influence of wisdom tradition in Isa. 11.1-5 is further attested by the employment of עצה in the second pair.[34] This often used pair,

wisdom...' See also Leo G. Perdue, *Wisdom and Creation: The Theology of Wisdom Literature* (Nashville: Abingdon Press, 1994), p. 222.

30. J. Lindblom, 'Wisdom in the Old Testament Prophets', in M. Noth and D. Winton Thomas (eds.), *Wisdom in Israel and in the Ancient Near East: Essays Presented to H.H. Rowley* (VTSup, 3; Leiden: E.J. Brill, 1955), pp. 192-204 (198).

31. Tryggve N.D. Mettinger, *King and Messiah: The Civil and Sacral Legitimation of the Israelite Kings* (ConBOT, 8; Lund: C.W.K. Gleerup, 1976), p. 249 takes 'the spirit of counsel and wisdom' in a martial sense. Moshe Weinfeld, ' "Justice and Righteousness"—משפט וצדקה—The Expression and its Meaning', in Henning Graf Reventlow and Yair Hoffman (eds.) *Justice and Righteousness: Biblical Themes and their Influence* (JSOTSup, 137; Sheffield: JSOT Press, 1992), pp. 228-46, argues that the pairing of צדקה and משפט primarily refers to the establishment of social justice.

32. N.W. Porteous, 'Royal Wisdom', in M. Noth and D. Winton Thomas (eds.), *Wisdom in Israel and in the Ancient Near East: Essays Presented to H.H. Rowley* (VTSup, 3; Leiden: E.J. Brill, 1955), pp. 247-61 (255).

33. Von Rad, *Old Testament Theology*, II, pp. 171-72.

34. Whedbee, *Isaiah and Wisdom*, p. 142. Also see below (pp. 45-50) for the discussion of עצה in a wisdom context. William M. Schniedewind, *The Word of God in Transition: From Prophet to Exegete in the Second Temple Period* (JSOTSup, 197; Sheffield: Sheffield Academic Press, 1995), p. 69 n. 99, argues that

'counsel and might' (for a human being, 2 Kgs 18.20; Isa. 36.5; and for God, Job 12.13), however, has a political interest with its paired word 'might'.[35] It refers to an 'ability to weigh the facts and come to the right conclusions' and 'a courage and strength to carry out' decisions the ruler makes that apparently are God's will.[36] The fact that the ruler does not need counselors is aligned to the thought of 40.13-14. With little martial reference, the description of the ruler seems to reflect more of the administrative 'judging' function than the 'savior' role of the judges.[37] The spirit of Yahweh is the source of executing his עצה which is also established by the same source. Here, two main elements of kingship ideology, עצה from wisdom tradition and 'might' stemming from the role of the judges, are ideally combined for the future ruler.

The last group appears slightly different from the first two.[38] The 'spirit of knowledge and fear of Yahweh' is an effect of the endowment rather than the quality of the ruler.[39] This line certainly distinguishes

the passage characterizes the military function of the king.

35. Mettinger, *King and Messiah*, p. 249, sees an echo of Jer. 9.5 in this pair.

36. Franz Delitzsch, *Bible Commentaries on the Prophecies of Isaiah* (trans. James Martin; 2 vols.; Grand Rapids: Eerdmans, 1954), I, p. 282.

37. Mettinger, *King and Messiah*, p. 249, argues for a strong reference to the charisma of a hero. He finds a strong support in 'understanding and wisdom' of 2 Kgs 18.20 (cf. גבורה in a martial sense in 1 Kgs 15.23; 16.5, 27, and שׂר שׁלום in 9.5). On the contrary, Wildberger, *Isaiah 1–12*, p. 472, rules out any martial implication. It is evident that there is no physical reference as in the judges, or military power as in Saul and David. Rather the effect of his rule is the destruction of the evil and wicked with 'his mouth' and the 'breath of his lips' (v. 3) which results in the administration of justice and universal peace.

38. Watts, *Isaiah 1–33*, p. 168, renders 'a spirit of knowledge, and fear, of Yahweh' to maintain the parallelism as well as to imply 'the knowledge of Yahweh'. Wildberger, *Isaiah 1–12*, p. 460, also maintains the parallelism, 'Spirit [sic] of knowledge and of fear of Yahweh'. 'A spirit of' is understood before 'the fear of Yahweh' as much as 'a spirit of' is presumed before 'might' or 'understanding'. However, idiomatic expression of 'the fear of Yahweh' itself serves as a royal virtue. This does not disturb the meter.

39. See J.A. Alexander, *The Prophecies of Isaiah* (Grand Rapids: Zondervan, 1953), p. 163. The three pairs may not form a perfect parallel. There are expressions like the 'spirit of righteousness' or the 'spirit of justice' to indicate an equipment of people by Yahweh (e.g. 28.5-6; 4.4) that can be put in a same category as the first two pairs of the passage. In this sense, an old description of the passage is proved too artistic: the spirit of Yahweh is like the central shaft of a sevenfold candlestick of a lampstand, the first pair intellectual, the second practical, and the

itself from the first two.[40] In Hebrew thought, knowing or knowledge is more than intellectual processes or achievement. It is 'practical acknowledgment of God which is implemented in thought and action'.[41] This naturally leads to the fear of Yahweh which is not just 'numinous awe, but moral conduct' (Prov. 1.7, 29; 9.10).[42] The secret of the earthly king's success lies in the intimate knowledge of the divine king and in his total subjection to Yahweh. There is no doubt that this pair, too, shows a strong wisdom influence with the 'knowledge of Yahweh' and the famous Wisdom motif, the 'fear of Yahweh'.[43]

The effect of his rule is described in two ways: the administration of righteousness and justice, which inevitably involves the judgment of the evil and wicked (v. 3),[44] and the paradisiacal peace in the human and animal world,[45] probably attached later. If the historical context of the passage is, as von Rad argues, the Assyrian attack and its defeat,[46] the oracle may well reflect the unjust society and the king's failure to match the Israelite's lofty kingship ideology. Historically speaking, the expectation of a messiah is not in the distant future, but in the immediate future, as is the case in other great 'messianic' passages (7.23b–9.6[7]).[47] At the same time, Isaianic eschatology has the expectation of a radical fulfilment with a new David who is 'the root of Jesse', the one

third his attitude to God; see, e.g., Delitzsch, *Prophecies of Isaiah*, I, pp. 282-83.

40. In spite of the general rule that 'not more than one construct can stand before the same genitive' (A.B. Davidson, *Hebrew Syntax* [Edinburgh: T. & T. Clark, 3rd edn, 1901], no. 27[b]), many favor this translation, e.g. Skinner, *Isaiah, Chapters I–XXXIX*, p. 105.

41. Kaiser, *Isaiah 1–12*, p. 256.

42. Kaiser, *Isaiah 1–12*, p. 256.

43. This rejects the sharp distinction between the technical wisdom of the wisdom schools and the 'prophetic wisdom' which is found among the prophets, e.g. Lindblom, *Prophecy in Ancient Israel*, p. 199. The prophetic wisdom shares with the conventional wisdom, the same root which is the 'fear of Yahweh'.

44. A discussion on 11.3b-4a is found in Daniel N. Freeman, 'Is Justice Blind? (Isaiah 11.3f)', *Bib* 52 (1971), p. 536.

45. For the treatment of mythological material in vv. 6-9, see Childs, *Myth and Reality in the Old Testament*, pp. 65-68.

46. Von Rad, *Old Testament Theology*, II, p. 171. Verse 5 may imply a royal ritual as the real life situation of the passage.

47. E.g. von Rad, *Old Testament Theology*, II, p. 171; Joseph Klausner, *The Messianic Idea in Israel: From its Beginning to the Completion of the Mishnah* (trans. W.F. Stinespring; New York: Macmillan, 1955), p. 56.

whom Micah expects from Bethlehem, not from Jerusalem. Naturally,
the רוח of Yahweh too becomes an eschatological element in the
'messianic' expectation. The passage is looking forward, while at the
same time looking back to the spirit of God as a distinct mark of a
chosen vessel of God.

28.5-6[48]

[5]In that day Yahweh of hosts will be a beautiful crown and a glorious
diadem to the remnant of his people; [6]and a spirit of justice to him who
sits in judgment, and strength [to] those who turn back the battle [at the]
gate.

The majority of scholars agree that vv. 5-6 are to be treated sepa-
rately from vv. 1-4 and vv. 7-10. The change from poetry (vv. 1-4) to
prose (vv. 5-6),[49] and to poetry again (vv. 7-10), and the change from
Unheil (judgment) to *Heil* (salvation) are the main arguments.[50] These
drastic changes lead some to believe that a later hand is responsible for
vv. 5-6.[51]

At the same time, the passage shows continuity, by using the imagery
of the drunken leaders of Ephraim and their fallen crown (as vv. 1-4).[52]
The writer describes the eschatological days.[53] 'In that day' (ביום ההוא)

48. A few scholars dispute the pre-exilic origin of the passage: David L.
Petersen, 'Isaiah 28, A Redaction Critical Study', in Paul J. Achtemeier (ed.), *SBL
1979 Seminar Papers* (2 vols.; Missoula, MT: Scholars Press, 1979), II, pp. 101-22
(107); Marvin A. Sweeney, *Isaiah 1–4 and the Post-Exilic Understanding of the
Isaianic Tradition* (BZAW, 171; Berlin: W. de Gruyter, 1988), p. 180 n. 222, notes
a strong link between this passage and 4.2-6 whose late date is firmly set.

49. Kaiser, *Isaiah 13–36*, p. 241, calls this a 'rhythmical prose'.

50. E.g. Simon John DeVries, *Yesterday, Today and Tomorrow: Time and
History in the Old Testament* (Grand Rapids: Eerdmans, 1975), p. 309 n. 84.

51. E.g. Scott, 'Isaiah Chapters 1–39', pp. 149-381 (314); Fohrer, *Das Buch
Jesaja*, II, pp. 48-49; Stacey, *Isaiah 1–39*, p. 170 and Clements, *Isaiah 1–39*, pp.
225-26, although the majority of scholars contend for a pre-exilic date, e.g. Hans
Wildberger, *Jesaja 28–39* (BKAT, 10.3; Neukirchen–Vluyn: Neukirchener Verlag,
1982), pp. 1041-42; Hayes and Irvine, *Isaiah*, p. 324; Gerhard F. Hasel, *The
Remnant: The History and Theology of the Remnant Idea from Genesis to Isaiah*
(Berrien Springs, MI: Andrews University Press, 3rd edn, 1980), pp. 301-309;
Skinner, *Isaiah, Chapters I–XXXIX*, p. 221; Lindblom, *Prophecy in Ancient Israel*,
p. 467.

52. This leads Hayes and Irvine, *Isaiah*, pp. 123-24, to conclude that vv. 5-6
continue vv. 1-4.

53. Kaiser, *Isaiah 13–36*, p. 241, calls the passage 'proto-apocalyptic' and
hence assigns a much later date.

may refer to a more general future rather than a specific eschatological moment.[54] The presence of a remnant which presumes a near-total destruction of a nation[55] also reinforces the eschatological emphasis.[56] 'That day' is the period of salvation in spite of the need for military defense, which is another characteristic of realistic eschatology of the pre-exilic period.

The subject, Yahweh of hosts,[57] is described as 'becoming' (היה ל־)[58] four different things: a beautiful crown and a glorious diadem to the remnant of his people; a spirit of justice to the one sitting in judgment; and strength to warriors. It is not that 'the spirit of the Lord' will do this, but rather 'the Lord...will be...a spirit...'[59] This equation does not immediately result in the conclusion that 'Yahweh is the spirit'.

54. Kaiser, *Isaiah 13–36*, p. 241, renders 'then'; S.H. Widyapranawa, *The Lord Is Savior: Faith in National Crisis: A Commentary on the Book of Isaiah 1–39* (ITC; Grand Rapids: Eerdmans, 1990), p. 168, renders 'an eschatological moment'. However, Wildberger, *Jesaja 28–39*, p. 1050, renders 'the day when *Unheil* turns into *Heil*', referring to an unspecified eschatological future. I.W. Slotki, *Isaiah: Hebrew Text and English Translation with an Introduction and Commentary* (rev. A.J. Rosenberg; London: Soncino, rev. edn, 1983), p. 127, is closer to the historically grounded meaning: 'after the fall of Samaria and the survival of a faithful remnant'.

55. F.W. Dobbs-Allsopp, *Weep, O Daughter of Zion: A Study of the City-Lament Genre in the Hebrew Bible* (BibOr, 44; Rome: Pontificio Istituto Biblico, 1993), p. 151.

56. The redactional literary arrangement makes the remnant include the northern survivors, and this leads Clements, *Isaiah 1–39*, p. 226, to date the passage to the postexilic time. But this can refer only to the northern survivors in its historical context. Similarly J. Cheryl Exum, '"Whom Will He Teach Knowledge?" A Literary Approach to Isaiah 28', in David J.A. Clines, David M. Gunn and Alan J. Hauser (eds.), *Art and Meaning: Rhetoric in Biblical Literature* (JSOTSup, 19; Sheffield: JSOT Press, 1982), pp. 108-39 (109-10), argues that a reference to Jerusalemites appears only in v. 14. However, Francis Landy, 'Tracing the Voice of the Other: Isaiah 28 and the Covenant with Death', in J. Cheryl Exum and David J.A. Clines (eds.), *The New Literary Criticism and the Hebrew Bible* (JSOTSup, 143; Sheffield: JSOT Press, 1993), pp. 140-62 (149 n. 25), contends that vv. 5-6 refer to Judahites.

57. Wildberger, *Jesaja 28–39*, p. 461; Kaiser, *Isaiah 13–36*, p. 252; *BHK* adopts an emendation of versions: LXX, ἀναβήσεται; Tg, יחרב׳; Syr, *nafraʿ*; Vg, *ascendet*, reflecting the emendation of יפרה, 'will bear fruit', to יפרח, 'will sprout forth'. *BHS* retains the MT reading.

58. *BHS* adds ל־.

59. Montague, *The Holy Spirit*, p. 39.

The loosely attached predicative noun is a common Semitic phenomenon. In the restored kingdom, the administration of justice is
ensured by the very presence of Yahweh. The parallel position between
the 'spirit of justice' and the 'strength' shows the effect of Yahweh's
presence rather than indicating the quality of Yahweh himself.

What, then, is the 'spirit of justice'? The use of the qualifying construct state recalls similar expressions such as an 'evil spirit' (1 Sam.
16.14) and a 'lying spirit' (1 Kgs 22.22) from God. The narratives
reveal that the qualifying elements refer not to the nature of the spirit,
but to the consequences of its activities. At any rate, in these two cases,
the רוח is a personified force or reality readily available to carry on
Yahweh's will. However, in the present passage, there is no indication
that the 'spirit of justice' assumes personality. The verbal construction
('Yahweh...will be') further rules out the possibility.

However, similar construct states are found in Isa. 11.1-3. As the
future king is given God's spirit, it will become the 'spirit of wisdom'
and other spirits in the king. They are specific manifestations of the
spirit, that is, consequential qualities or attributes within the person of
the king. They may be viewed as forces, or elements, but not personified realities. Hence, the spirit of justice indicates the effect of
Yahweh's presence. In the restored kingdom, the administration of
justice is ensured by the very presence of Yahweh.

Who, then, is the one who sits in judgment? The singular expression,
in contrast to 'the warriors', may refer to everyone who sits in judgment (cf. 32.1b). On the contrary, it can also refer to the eschatological
ideal ruler who will administer justice and righteousness (11.2-3).[60] The
pre-exilic understanding of the leadership spirit is confined to one
single chosen leader of God as evidenced in the judges and the first two
kings. The only exception is the group of 70 elders. But they were 'sub-
leaders' under the supreme leadership of Moses. The use of the singular
appears to be deliberate, denoting the future king.

The parallel position between the 'spirit of justice' and 'strength'
cause some to consider the latter as a short form of 'a spirit of
strength'.[61] Hebrew would not normally have a double-duty construct

60. Clements, *Isaiah 1–39*, p. 226, and Stacey, *Isaiah 1–39*, p. 170. In contrast,
Hayes and Irvine, *Isaiah*, p. 324, identify it with a group of people that adheres to
the treaty instituted between Hoshea and Shalmaneser. However, it is difficult to
see the treaty as the principle of justice.

61. Kaiser, *Isaiah 13–36*, p. 242. Cf. Widyapranawa, *The Lord Is Savior*,

state. Here, the king is described as the administrator of justice, especially to protect the unprotected such as orphans and widows (Isa. 11.4).[62] In this way, God will guarantee the internal security of the remnant community.[63] The external security will be provided as God becomes 'strength to its warriors', who will be able to turn back the battle at the gate (cf. Zech. 12.7-9).[64]

The pre-exilic eschatology retains the social and political parameters set by its social structure. This realistic eschatology pictures the new Israel to dwell in the same real world with the presence of the king and warriors.

30.1-2[65]

1　Woe, rebellious people,
　　　the oracle of Yahweh,
　Making a plan, but not from me,
　　　pouring out libations, but not by my spirit
　　　in order to add the sin upon the sin.
2　Those who go down to Egypt,
　　　without asking my advice;
　To take refuge in the stronghold of Pharaoh,
　　　and to take refuge in the shadow of Egypt.

The proclamation of woe is followed by a series of qualifying words such as infinitives and a participle which explain the reasons for the following judgment (1-2). In close parallel with an oracle of judgment, the participles function as an accusation. The announcement of judgment is introduced in the form of a prophetic reversal with 'but' (v. 3).

p. 169, who wrongly subordinates the 'strength' to the 'spirit of justice'.

62. Widyapranawa, *The Lord Is Savior*, p. 169, defines 'justice' as the 'dynamic meaning of fighting against all kinds of injustice or attacks by one's enemies', hence closely connected with a 'strength' which appears to be overly generalized.

63. Kaiser, *Isaiah 13–36*, p. 241.

64. Again, Hayes and Irvine, *Isaiah*, p. 324, consistent with their assumption of the unity of vv. 5-6 with vv. 1-4, reject the 'warrior' reference, but identify them with those who were against rebellion in the deliberation of rebellion which normally took place at the gate. Syr. and Θ read 'from the gate'. But the reading has to account for the ה-directive in שַׁעַר and the insertion of מִן, notion.

65. See Wildberger, *Jesaja 28–39*, p. 1147, and Kaiser, *Isaiah 13–36*, p. 282, for this division. For a much longer unit, see Watts, *Isaiah 1–33*, pp. 390-92, which is characteristic of his 'vision' approach (vv. 1-18). For verses 1-7 as a unit, see T.K. Cheyne, *The Prophecies of Isaiah: A New Translation with Commentary and Appendices* (2 vols.; New York: Thomas Whittaker, 5th edn, 1892), I, p. 175.

The announcement reuses the same language found in v. 2, but in an opposite sense. Verse 5 further offers an explanation as to why the announced judgment is inevitable.

The authenticity of the passage has not been seriously questioned.[66] Typical Isaianic style and terminology like עצה give evidence of the hand of the eighth-century prophet. The single issue at hand is to pinpoint the exact historical setting. Many favor the 705–701 Assyrian crisis,[67] although the range stretches from the Ashdodite rebellion in 713–711,[68] Josiah's reign (640–609)[69] to the period following the death of the Seleucid king, Antiochus III (187 BCE).[70]

This woe oracle has two main parts as an oracle of judgment: the accusation, or description, of evildoers (vv. 1-2), and the announcement of judgment (vv. 3-5).[71] The powerful rhetorical device, 'woe', not only attracts the attention of hearers, but also adds a sense of tragedy commonly associated with the funeral lament.[72] The target audience is called 'rebellious children' (v. 1) which assumes a parent–child relationship, where unquestioned obedience to the parent is expected.[73]

66. Kaiser, *Isaiah 13–39*, p. 282, however, sees v. 3 as a case of explanatory exegesis added by a later hand.

67. Herbert Donner, *Israel unter den Völkern: Die Stellung der klassischen Propheten des 8. Jahrhunderts v. Chr. aur Aussenpolitik der Könige von Israel und Juda* (VTSup, 2; Leiden: E.J. Brill, 1964), p. 132; Clements, *Isaiah 1–39*, p. 234; Oswalt, *Isaiah Chapters 1–39*, p. 544; Edward J. Young, *The Book of Isaiah* (NICOT; 3 vols.; Grand Rapids: Eerdmans, 1965–69), II, p. 336; John Day, 'The Problem of "So, King of Egypt" in 2 Kings XVII 4', *VT* 42 (1992), pp. 289-301 (296).

68. E.g. Wildberger, *Jesaja 28–39*, p. 1150; Skinner, *Isaiah, Chapters I–XXXIX*, p. 240.

69. Watts, *Isaiah 1–33*, p. 396.

70. For the discussion, see Kaiser, *Isaiah 13–39*, p. 238.

71. Waldemar Janzen, *Mourning Cry and Woe Oracle* (BZAW, 125; Berlin: W. de Gruyter, 1972), p. 56, writes, '[the passage] presents itself as a *Gerichtsrede* as completely as any *hoy*-pericope in Isaiah'. However, it lacks some elements, e.g. a hinge-word 'therefore', typical of an oracle of judgment.

72. R.J. Clifford, 'The Use of *Hoy* in the Prophets', *CBQ* 28 (1966), pp. 458-64 (458-59), defines three different functions of הוי; (1) actual funeral lament as its original usage; (2) attention gathering; and (3) prophetic הוי. Yet he rightly cautions that the prophetic הוי should not be sharply separated from the funeral הוי.

73. Literally 'rebellious sons'. F. Charles Fensham, 'Father and Son as Terminology for Treaty and Covenant', in Hans Goedicke (ed.), *Near Eastern Studies in Honor of William Foxwell Albright* (Baltimore: The Johns Hopkins Univer-

This may refer to the strong covenant relationship between Israel and Yahweh.[74] However, the actual target is the political leadership of Judah, which ignored Yahweh's claim over political decisions, rather than Israel as a whole.[75] The tone of judgment is strengthened by the direct divine speech indicated in the oracle formula, which may be a variation of a messenger formula, 'the oracle of Yahweh'.[76]

Their offense against Yahweh is depicted in the parallel construction of vv. 1b and 2. It is the carrying out of an עצה ('plan, advice or counsel')[77] which does not originate from Yahweh. The Old Testament

sity Press, 1971), pp. 121-35 (134), argues that this expression refers to treaty-based covenant partners, such as the relationship between Ahaz and Tiglath-pileser of Assyria (2 Kgs 16). However, the expression, 'I am your servant and your son', is different from this text, since the personal pronouns 'your' or 'my' have a much stronger nuance of personal intimacy. Hence, Fensham's suggestion is far-fetched.

74. Claus Westermann, *Basic Forms of Prophetic Speech* (trans. Hugh C. White; London: Lutterworth, 1967), pp. 191-94, contends that the series of covenant curses (e.g. Deut. 27) is the origin of the woe-saying as seen here and in ch. 31. The original covenant relation is abandoned by Israel. However, Edhard Gerstenberger, 'The Woe-oracles of the Prophets', *JBL* 81 (1962), pp. 249-63 (250-52), argues that the origin is found in popular sayings, in lists of acceptable and unacceptable conduct such as those in Eccl. 10.16-17 and Isa. 3.10.

75. As Westermann, *Basic Forms*, pp. 191-94, points out, this woe oracle is a variation of an oracle of judgment against an individual or individuals rather than the nation.

76. נאם is either the singular of a noun meaning 'utterance' or the masculine passive participle of the verb. The 'utterance of Yahweh', or 'oracle of Yahweh', can be taken either as an introductory call, or as a phrase leading into the actual matter of prophecy; see, e.g., Norman H. Snaith, *Notes on the Hebrew Text of Isaiah Chapters XXVIII–XXXII* (London: Epworth Press, 1945), p. 41. For Mitchel Dahood, 'Accusative *ʿēṣāh*, "Wood", in Isaiah 30,1b', *Bib* 50 (1969), pp. 57-58, it is 'wooden idols'. This oracle is not a typical woe oracle in a strict sense, for the messenger formula is unusually present here. This phenomenon can not be sufficiently explained, as in Westermann, *Basic Forms*, pp. 191, 193, by the specific historical occasion of the oracle.

77. According to William McKane, *Prophets and Wise Men* (SBT, 44; London: SCM Press, 1965), p. 65, עצה is a typical wisdom term. Henri S. Cazelles, 'Les milieux de Deutéronome', in Heather A. McKay and David J.A. Clines (eds.), *Of Prophets' Visions and the Wisdom of Sages: Essays in Honour of R. Norman Whybray on the Occasion of his Seventieth Birthday* (JSOTSup, 162; Sheffield: JSOT Press, 1993), pp. 288-306 (294), points out that the political counselors were called חכמים by Isaiah (29.14; cf. 5.21), Jeremiah (9.11; cf. 8.9) and Ezekiel (28.3-4). However, Dahood, 'Accusative *ʿēṣāh*', p. 57, repoints עצה as ע ץ, 'wood[en

provides ample evidence that on the occasion of any act by a ruler an oracle was required and sought from Yahweh through a prophet (cf. 1 Kgs 22.5-6; Jer. 37.17; 38.14-23).[78] This is commonly practiced throughout the ancient Near East.[79] 'And did not ask for my counsel' (v. 2) further elaborates that the king failed to seek prophetic advice. There is a conflict between the prophet who brings the עצה of Yahweh and the court politicians who bring their עצה to the king.[80] McKane goes further by saying that the controversy is between Yahwism represented by the prophet and the wisdom tradition to which the political leaders belonged.[81] It is evident that in the more professionalized court of Hezekiah (Prov. 25.1), court politicians had full influence, while the role of the prophet, or of Yahweh, was often neglected. However, the folly of those who 'hid their plan from Yahweh' is severely condemned in 29.15-16.

The spirit of Yahweh is mentioned in the second member of the parallelism. 'Pouring out libation' is a hypothetical translation as other renderings are possible.[82] Duhm points out that an ancient practice is referred to in which the name of a deity would be invoked as the libation was being poured out.[83] The argument is that, although the representative of Judah invokes the name of Yahweh, Yahweh does not give the plan his assent since that עצה did not originate from him. In

idol]' with the accusative ending ה־—as in Isa. 37.19; 44.19; 45.20, etc., and especially Jer. 6.6. See also William H. Irwin, *Isaiah 28–33: Translation with Philological Notes* (Rome: Pontifical Biblical Institute, 1973), p. 69.

78. Verse 2 literally reads 'my mouth', although LXX renders 'me' and Tg 'the words of the prophets'.

79. In a recent Mari prophecy (A. 1968), Zimri-Lim is told, 'When you participate in a campaign, by no means set out without consulting an oracle' (A. Malamat, 'A New Prophetic Message from Aleppo and its Biblical Counterparts', in A. Graeme Auld [ed.], *Understanding Poets and Prophets: Essays in Honour of George Wishart Anderson* [JSOTSup, 152; Sheffield: JSOT Press, 1993], pp. 136-241 [238]).

80. Whedbee, *Isaiah and Wisdom*, p. 132, claims that 'this passage contains in the sharpest form the conflict between Judah's counsel and Yahweh's'. Also Youngblood, *The Book of Isaiah*, p. 90, links v. 1 with v. 10.

81. McKane, *Prophets and Wise Men*, p. 71. It seems dubious whether one can make as sharp a distinction as McKane between the two traditions.

82. Literally 'to pour out libations' as the conclusion of an agreement as in LXX. But Vg, Aq, etc., have 'weaving of a web'.

83. Duhm, *Das Buch Jesaja*, p. 185.

addition to this, the ceremonial act would involve the recognition, if not worship, of an Egyptian deity.

If מנּי corresponds to and rephrases רוּחִי, as it appears to do, here רוּח certainly refers to Yahweh himself. Montague also interprets '[by] my spirit' simply as '[by] me' and so does NAB.[84] Neve claims that this is a rare instance where רוּח refers to the center of volition in Yahweh himself, that is, his mind.[85] A.R. Johnson defines רוּח as all that is involved 'in the grasping of a totality and the exercises of self-control that the forceful and indeed purposeful individual is revealed'.[86]

Another interpretation is that of prophetic רוּח as Duhm elaborates. For him, 'not [with] my spirit' may mean 'not on the עצה of my prophet', making it more synonymous with the first member of the parallelism.[87] This view is based on the assumption that מנּי in v. 1 is explained by 'without asking my advice' of v. 2. Therefore, it implies that the רוּח of Yahweh is the source of prophetic counsel. The argument of the entire passage, that is the conflict between the prophet and the court politicians, favors this. The only flaw in this interpretation is that nowhere else does Isaiah claim the spirit of Yahweh as the source of his prophetic message. Mowinckel aptly discusses the phenomenon with the conclusion that the pre-exilic reforming prophets deliberately avoided the use of the term.[88] It is true that the usage is significantly rare among the pre-exilic prophets, but it is premature to claim non-existence. A strong line of evidence, besides here, is Mic. 3.8, the later origin of which has not been successfully established.[89] As Kapelrud has suggested, the spirit of Yahweh as the inspirer of prophetic messages might be an idea so established that it is not necessary to mention

---

84. Montague, *The Holy Spirit*, p. 41.

85. Neve, *The Spirit of God*, pp. 52-54. According to him, the term is used in the place of לב as a part of the divine being, cf. 40.13. Also Fohrer, *Das Buch Jesaja*, II, pp. 86-87.

86. Johnson, *Vitality of the Individual*, p. 35.

87. Duhm, *Das Buch Jesaja*, p. 185; Oswalt, *Isaiah Chapters 1–39*, p. 545; Skinner, *Isaiah, Chapters I–XXXIX*, p. 239.

88. Mowinckel, '"Spirit" and the "Word"', pp. 199-227. A different approach to the same phenomenon is taken by Kapelrud, 'Spirit and the Word in the Prophets', pp. 40-47.

89. Against Mowinckel's contention of a later date ('"Spirit" and the "Word"', p. 201), numerous commentators assume the authenticity of the passage; e.g. Allen, *Joel, Obadiah, Jonah and Micah*, p. 313; Hillers, *Micah*, p. 46.

it.[90] If this is feasible, then Mowinckel's thesis requires re-examination.

The judgment is announced in an ironic reversal of the intention of the עצה of the leaders. Instead of the protection they seek, shame will be the result. The message of the prophet is clear that the security of Judah does not reside in foreign alliances which are brought about by the עצה of human wisdom, but in acknowledging Yahweh's sovereignty over his people. The spirit of Yahweh stands, together with the prophet, in direct opposition to the human plan which deliberately ignores the plan of God.[91]

31.1-3[92]

1   Woe, Those going down to Egypt for help,
        who rely on horses.
    They trust in chariots so numerous,
        and upon horses so very strong.
    They do not look to the Holy One of Israel,
        nor of Yahweh do they seek.
2   And indeed he is the Wise One.
        He will bring evil;
        and does not retract his words.
    He will rise up against the house of the wicked,
        and against those who help evil-doers.
3   Egypt is human and not God!
        Their horses [are] flesh and not spirit!
    When Yahweh stretches out his hand,
        the helper will stumble, the one helped will fall.
    They will all be finished off together.

Again, as is typical of the woe oracle, the description of sin (or 'accusation' in the oracle of judgment) begins with a 'woe', followed by a series of plural participles. Each participle depicts the detail of the crime. The sudden appearance of a descriptive statement in 2b breaks the ordinary flow of a woe oracle. The announcement of judgment

---

90. Kapelrud, 'Spirit and the Word', p. 46.

91. P.A.H. de Boer, 'The Counselor', in M. Noth and D. Winton Thomas (eds.), *Wisdom in Israel and in the Ancient Near East: Essays Presented to H.H. Rowley* (VTSup, 3; Leiden: E.J. Brill, 1955), pp. 42-71 (47).

92. For this division, see Cheyne, *Introduction to the Book of Isaiah*, p. 183; Duhm, *Das Buch Jesaja*, p. 199; Fohrer, *Das Buch Jesaja*, II, pp. 110-11; Kaiser, *Isaiah 13–36*, p. 311; Oswalt, *Isaiah Chapters 1–39*, p. 569; Skinner, *Isaiah, Chapters I–XXXIX*, p. 251; Wildberger, *Jesaja 28–39*, p. 1226. But for vv. 1-9, see Watts, *Isaiah 1–33*, p. 406. For Irwin, *Isaiah 28–33*, p. 107, vv. 1-2 make a unit.

appears in 2b, and 2a is seen as a logical support of 2b. 'And indeed' may be the substitute for a transitory conjunction like 'therefore' or 'but' before the announcement of judgment. Verse 3 amplifies the coming judgment.

The striking prophetic reversal between vv. 1 and 3 is unmistakable. The might of Egypt and its horses (v. 1) is contrasted with the almost nothingness of them (v. 3). Parallelism is frequently employed to reinforce the message.

As in 30.1-5, this passage shows strong evidences of Isaianic tradition: language like 'the holy One of Israel'; the prophet's opposition against Judah's reliance upon Egypt; the polemic between the prophet and political leader; a similar, if not an identical, historical situation to that of 30.1-5, the 'head-on collision' between the Yahwism of the prophet and political professionalism;[93] and the 'woe' element like that of 30.1-5.

At the same time, minor differences need to be noted. For example, Whedbee observes that there is no appearance of עצה, which is a strong wisdom term, and yet a direct reference to Yahweh's wisdom is actually present.[94] Form-critically speaking, Janzen argues that there is 'no specific mark of *Gerichtsrede*' (trial speech) nor claim of divine speech.[95] In that sense, this is closer to a typical woe oracle than the previous passage.

The only 'muddying of the waters' in this passage occurs in v. 2. The strange statement and rough transition between the accusation (v. 1) and the announcement of judgment (v. 3) have prompted discussions.[96] Childs believes the verse to be secondary,[97] while Wildberger[98] and Barth,[99] among others, reject the argument of a later interpolation. The

---

93. The clash is between the Yahweh religion and court professionalism rather than prophetism and wisdom tradition (the latter as McKane, *Prophets and Wise Men*, p. 65, supposes).

94. Whedbee, *Isaiah and Wisdom*, p. 133.

95. Janzen, *Mourning Cry*, p. 56.

96. For more discussion, see below (p. 52).

97. Brevard S. Childs, *Isaiah and the Assyrian Crisis* (SBT, Second Series, 3; Naperville: Allenson, 1965), pp. 34-35.

98. Wildberger, *Jesaja 28–39*, p. 1227.

99. Hermann Barth, *Die Jesaja-Worte in der Josiazeit* (Neukirchen–Vluyn: Neukirchener Verlag, 1977), pp. 79-80.

main point of difference concerns the significance of the 'historical and existential situation' of the message.[100]

As is typical of woe oracles, the woe is followed by a plural participle which specifies to whom the warning is directed. At the same time the phrase articulates the reason for the following announcement of judgment.[101] Their evil is relying on Egyptian military power[102] without inquiring or seeking of Yahweh.[103] The issue is, as seen in v. 2, the court politicians' doubt of Yahweh's wisdom and power. Not only their influential presence in the court (Isa. 5.19; 28.23-29; 29.15), but also their claim of being wise in their own eyes (30.21), are evident throughout the pre-exilic references.

The problematic expression, 'he too is wise to bring disaster', is a biting irony against those 'wise men'.[104] Yahweh, the prophet argues, is not only wise to bring about judgment[105] and to direct the course of history, but is the possessor of ultimate wisdom which Yahweh shares with the future ruler (11.2). This description of Yahweh introduces the announcement of judgment in general terms: Yahweh rises against the evildoers. In more specific terms (v. 3b) the destruction of both the helper and helped is announced.

100. Whedbee, *Prophets and Wise Men*, p. 134.

101. Janzen, *Mourning Cry*, p. 56.

102. This reading is supported by Snaith, *Notes*, p. 62. The niphal imperfect of שׁעע means 'they support themselves', while many read ישׁעו which follows LXX's rendering, πεποιθότες, 'who rely on', e.g. Watts, *Isaiah 1–33*, pp. 407-408. A disadvantage of this translation, however, is that the same verb is used in a different sense ('seek, inquire') in a later part of the same verse.

103. דרשׁ, reflecting an old tradition, is to consult deity for advice, either directly (e.g. Gen. 25.22; 2 Kgs 1.2, 3, 6, 16; Isa. 8.19) or, more often, through a mediator such as a prophet (e.g. 1 Kgs 14.5; 22.5; 2 Kgs 3.11; 8.8). This term is more traditional than שׁאל in 30.2.

104. R.B.Y. Scott, 'Solomon and the Beginning of Wisdom', in M. Noth and D. Winton Thomas (eds.), *Wisdom in Israel and in the Ancient Near East: Essays Presented to H.H. Rowley* (VTSup, 3; Leiden: E.J. Brill, 1955), pp. 262-79 (277); Whedbee, *Prophets and Wise Men*, p. 135. Also Snaith, *Isaiah Chapters XXVIII–XXXII*, p. 63, reads an 'emphatic ironical expression'; contra Irwin, *Isaiah 28–33*, p. 110.

105. 'Bring evil' in v. 2 as in MT, רע. See also Cheyne, *Introduction to the Book of Isaiah*, p. 183; Kaiser, *Isaiah 13–36*, p. 311; Fohrer, *Das Buch Jesaja*, II, p. 111; Wildberger, *Jesaja 28–39*, p. 1226. But Watts, *Isaiah 1–33*, p. 407, repoints to רע, 'purpose', thus rendering, 'He achieves [his] purpose'. Irwin, *Isaiah 28–33*, p. 108, also prefers this reading because 'disaster is not to be expected with חכם'.

An uncompromising distance is clearly drawn not only between his wisdom and the 'wise men', but also between his power and Egyptian military strength. So רוח is used here to sharpen the distinction further, as A.R. Johnson describes:

> [The] distinction is here made explicit, for the parallelism, coupled with the foregoing illustrations, will surely warrant our saying that Yahweh, like the heavenly forces under his control, differs from mankind as being of a more rarefied substance 'like fire'—in short, רוח or spirit.[106]

The contrast between flesh and spirit is particularly pronounced when the difference between God and his created world is being stressed.[107] The characteristic of God in his power is said to be רוח[108] as that of humans and animals, even if they are many and strong,[109] is בשׂר (flesh) in their weakness and frailties.[110] This opposition may have an allusion to Gen. 6.3. Yet רוח is not a general word for power, but 'it is power only because it partakes of and stems from the source for all power, God himself'.[111] רוח apart from God becomes void as wind, for the spirit is neither a substance nor an entity standing apart from Yahweh. It becomes evident in the following judgment which will be brought about by God or Yahweh himself. However, the prophet is not ready to say, 'God is spirit'. In a sense, on the one hand, this shows a connection to an old tradition as found in the book of Judges in which the רוח of Yahweh is described as the source of extraordinary physical strength for national heroes. But on the other hand, the passage differs from the Judges traditions. Here, Yahweh is directly involved in the conflict between Pharaoh's horses with horsemen and the רוח which characterizes God.

Since the otherliness of Yahweh is at stake, 'God' here is not used as a generic term. No other deity is known in this polemic. Naturally

106. Johnson, *The One and the Many*, p. 14.

107. Donald E. Gowan, *Eschatology in the Old Testament* (Philadelphia: Fortress Press, 1986), p. 74.

108. The strong adherence to the 'power' issue leaves no room for other implication of God's רוח. Cf. Charles A. Briggs, 'The Use of *Ruach* in the Old Testament', *JBL* 19 (1900), pp. 132-45 (143), and Wildberger, *Jesaja 28–39*, p. 1234, who argue for the reference to the life-giving and transforming energy.

109. כי in v. 1 is an emphatic use (Irwin, *Isaiah 28–33*, p. 109); although a simple causal clause, 'for they are many, or strong', is grammatically possible.

110. Wolff, *Anthropology of the Old Testament*, p. 30.

111. Neve, *The Spirit of God*, p. 46.

foreign gods are ignored.[112] Wildberger rightly observes that אל rather than אלהים or יהוה is used in Isaiah (e.g. 7.14; 9.5) to denote the quality of divine being, that is being *göttlich* (of God).[113] Pharaoh, in spite of his claim of divinity and of being the 'sweet breath of life' to the people, is only בשר.[114] Here בשר is 'not "material" nor "physical" but that which comprises the entire being of humans'.[115] It is possible that the prophet further denounces the deification of the Egyptian army, along with the Egyptian king.

2. *God's* רוח *in the Pre-Exilic Isaianic Theology*

The task of this discussion is to investigate possible contributions of the concept of God's רוח to the theology and eschatology of pre-exilic Isaianic tradition. The small number of relevant passages warrants no over-generalization.

2.1 *Yahweh*

Yahweh as King of Judah is a predominant motif in pre-exilic Isaianic tradition. His absoluteness is focused in two realms: his power and his wisdom. יהוה צבאות well expresses God as the one who controls all the powers of heaven and earth (1.9, 24; 2.12; 3.1, 15; 5.7, 9, 16, 24; 6.3, 5; 8.13, 18; 9.6 [12], 18; 10.16, [23, 24, 26], 33; 14.24, 27; 17.3; 18.7; 19.12; 22.5, [14]; 28.5, 22, 29; 29.6; 31.4, 5; [37.32]). He is also ישראל אביר, 'the Mighty One of Israel' (1.24), and this expression is found in only two other places (Gen. 49.24; Ps. 132.2, 5). This uncompromisable distance between Yahweh and his creature is expressed by the use of רוח for God and בשר of human and animal (31.3).

Yahweh's wisdom is often depicted in the context of divine counsel (verb יעץ in 14.24, 26, 27; 19.12; or noun עצה in 5.19; 14.26; 28.29; 30.1). The counsel is not to determine a future, but to carry out Yahweh's decree. Thus, Isa. 30.1 is a typical declaration that the prophetic

112. Duhm, *Das Buch Jesaja*, p. 205.
113. Wildberger, *Jesaja 28–39*, p. 1233. The contrast of 'man...God' (אדם and אל) has its Ugaritic parallel of *'il* and *'ab 'adm* (Krt 135-36; 150-51, etc.). For אל, Tg has רב, 'noble, prince'.
114. Wildberger, *Jesaja 28–39*, p. 1233.
115. Wildberger, *Jesaja 28–39*, p. 1234. For a similar and more detailed discussion, see Daniel Lys, *La chair dans l'Ancien Testament 'Basar'* (Paris: Editions Universitaires, 1967), pp. 49-50, 52-53, 56-57, 64-66.

counsel represents the wisdom of the divine counsel. Among the qualities of the coming ruler, wisdom plays a definite role (11.2). As seen
above, wisdom is implicitly, if not explicitly, present in all the three
pairs of attributes. Wisdom is accompanied by strength in the pair
(11.2). Even the declaration of Yahweh's supreme strength because of
the divine quality of רוח is closely linked with his wisdom (31.2).

During the ministry of Isaiah there were two major political events
which threatened the continuity of the kingdom. They were the Syro-
Ephraimite War (735–734 BCE) in the time of Ahaz, and the Assyrian
invasion (701 BCE) in Hezekiah's reign. In both instances, the prophet
calls for total trust in Yahweh for the nation's security (7.1-2; 30.1-5;
31.1-3). Recognition of God's lordship is demanded in every facet of
life, including national and international matters.

In this connection, the frequent occurrence of יעץ/עצה (5.12, 18-19,
25-30; 7.7; 8.9-10; 9.7-20; 11.2; 14.24-27; 19.17; 22.11; 25.1; 30.1, 3)
is noted. This originally secular concept is frequently applied to the
idea of Yahweh's divine counsel.[116] As the Lord of Israel, Yahweh
formulates his definite plans, and he puts them into effect in history.
His supreme lordship is to be realized in his firm plan and its implementation in history (e.g. 14.24-27). It demands that any plans contrary
to that of God will inevitably come to grief (7.7; 8.10; 30.1, 3) along
with those who formulate and carry out plans. Human problems arise
because God's plans are often strange, alien, and yet conversely, they
are wonderful (28.29). Blenkinsopp observes two reasons for this
complexity. First, plans are 'for', as well as 'against', Judah; and secondly, often the plans defy conventional wisdom.[117] Isaiah, therefore,
does not believe in *Realpolitik*, and often Isaiah insists that Yahweh's
plan is against political feasibility.[118] The human dilemma exists
because God requires a human role as partner in the process. Old Testament history is God's work through his plan in his encounter with
humans, Israel and the nations.[119]

---

116. Von Rad, *Old Testament Theology*, II, p. 162.

117. Joseph Blenkinsopp, *A History of Prophecy in Israel* (Philadelphia:
Westminster Press, 1983), p. 118.

118. Joseph Jensen, 'Yahweh's Plan in Isaiah and in the Rest of the OT', *CBQ*
48 (1986), pp. 443-55 (445).

119. Gottwald, *All the Kingdoms*, p. 349. Also H. Wolff, 'The Understanding of
History in the O.T. Prophets', in Claus Westermann (ed.), *Essays on Old Testament*

The supremacy of Yahweh's plan is attributed to his incomparable
wisdom in his planning and his strength in implementing his עצה. In
the Syro-Ephraimite war (7.1-9) Yahweh assures the king, through the
prophet, that he has a definite עצה for Judah which surpasses human
wisdom. The prophetic call to trust in God's plan is intensified with the
offer of a sign to the king. The explicit reference to the רוח of Yahweh
appears in the context of the Assyrian crisis. In 30.1 the prophet
condemns those who carry on human plans which are not by Yahweh's
רוח. The רוח can mean the very thought and mind of God.[120] To ignore
his counsel is to deny the lordship of Yahweh in Judah's affairs. The
strong reference to עצה seems to suggest a reference to Yahweh's
wisdom. At the same time, רוח can refer to the prophetic spirit through
which Yahweh's mind, or thought, is revealed. The following verse
supports the prophetic reference. The prophet may have both meanings
in his mind. In 31.1-3, a similar condemnation is pronounced on those
who rely on human military power rather than Yahweh for the protection of Zion. Throughout the prophetic argument, wisdom and strength
are two realms within which context the quality of Yahweh is identified
to be רוח whereas that of horses is בשר (31.3). It is Yahweh's plan that
will eventually prevail in human history. It is not only because of his
wisdom which formulates it, and his רוח through which Yahweh's will
is proclaimed, but also the רוח, the quality of Almighty God which will
bring about his plan.

2.2 Israel
In the preaching of Isaiah the cycle of guilt–judgment–demand for faith
is a set pattern. The primary guilt of Judah is, as Vriezen rightly
points out, purely religious, although its effect is multidimensional.[121]

Hermeneutics (trans. James L. Mays; Richmond, VA: John Knox Press, 1963),
pp. 336-55 (339).
　120. E.g. Neve, *The Spirit of God*, pp. 52-53, 'Yahweh's mind'.
　121. T.C. Vriezen, 'Essentials of the Theology of Isaiah', in Bernhard W.
Anderson and W. Harrelson (eds.), *Israel's Prophetic Heritage: Essays in Honor of
James Muilenburg* (New York: Harper & Brothers, 1962), pp. 128-46 (134),
describes Israel's sin as revolt against Yahweh (1.2, 4); contempt for Yahweh (3.8-
9; 5.4-5, 24; 8.6; 28.12; 29.15-16; 30.9-13, 15); derision of Yahweh (5.18-19);
neglecting God (17.10; 22.11); pride (2.7; 3.16-26; 9.8-10; 10.5; 22.15; 28.1-4, 14-
15); not having faith in God (7.9; 22.11; 31.1); not being willing to be obedient
(28.12; 30.9, 15; [1.19]); being a godless people (9.16; 10.6); being wise in its own
eyes (5.21; 28.14-15).

'Rebellious' (סר, 1.5; 31.6) or 'rebellion' (סרר, 1.23; 30.1) summarizes the attitude of the people toward their God. For Isaiah, as for Amos and Micah, Israel is the 'people of God'. The intimate covenant term 'my people' (1.3; 3.12, 15; 55.13; 10.2[24]; 22.4; 32.13, 18) has its frequent counterpart 'this people' throughout the book (6.10; 8.6, 11, 12; 9.15; 28.11, 14; 29.13, 14). There is no doubt that Yahweh deliberately distances himself from Israel. The prophet always sides in this case with Yahweh. It is, in fact, Judah that has distanced itself from its God against God's intention of intimate fellowship.

Judah's sin is a failure to know and understand its God (1.3; cf. Hos. 4.6). The prophet calls Jerusalem 'Sodom and Gomorrah' (1.10; 3.9) not only in a moral, but also in a religious sense. The powerful accusation against the people in the beginning of the book (1.2-3) puts them below the animal level. God demands the knowing of him instead of religious ritual (1.11-17, cf. Hos. 6.6), and the cleanness of heart instead of myriad sacrifices. For the prophet, other problems like idolatry (2.20-21) and social injustice stem out of this unacceptable attitude toward God. Political and religious leaders of the people are severely attacked (1.23; 3.1). Judah and its leaders fail to recognize Yahweh's lordship and his wisdom and strength. This human failure is contrasted with the future ruler's total dependence upon Yahweh's will by the gift of רוח of Yahweh (11.2-3). A prophetic reversal is obvious in the depiction of the future age. Leaders of the future kingdom are faithful servants of Yahweh through the endowment of the spirit of God (e.g. 11.2-4; 28.5-6).

Israel's sin is also found in dealings with fellow citizens. The claim of ethical living is not based on any legalistic obligation,[122] but on a living relationship between Yahweh and Israel.[123] That there is no mention of the covenant relationship between Yahweh and Israel as a whole supports the stress of the organic relation. Another basis on which Yahweh demands ethical life is the divine law. The striking emphasis on the Torah forms the central element in Isaiah's preaching. It is widely understood that the prophet's concept of Torah is not the code, but its 'instruction'.[124] The recurrent appearance of two key

122. On the legalistic understanding of 'righteousness' and 'justice', see von Rad, *Old Testament Theology*, II, p. 149.
123. Henry S. Gehman, 'The Ruler of the Universe: The Theology of First Isaiah', *Int* 11 (1957), pp. 269-81 (280).
124. For a fine discussion, see Joseph Jensen, *The Use of tôrâ by Isaiah: His*

words, 'righteousness' (1.21, 26, 27; 5.7, 16, 23; 9.6[7]; 10.22; 28.17)
and 'justice' (1.17, 21, 27; 5.7, 16; 9.6[7]; 10.2; 16.5; 28.6, 17) further
illustrates the inseparable relationship between the religious and social
dimensions of Israel. The administration of Torah is a mirror that
reflects the attitude of humanity to God. The apparent failure of Israel,
particularly among its leaders, is manifested in a lack of civic interest.
The underprivileged, particularly the fatherless and widows, easily fell
prey to a strong party. Therefore, the protection of the rights of the
underprivileged functions as a common criterion for a just society
throughout the ancient Near East. Those who take advantage of them,
rather than protecting them, are the leaders of the people, the 'princes'
(1.23), 'mighty men', soldiers, judges, and even prophets (3.1-2). The
corruption has already permeated every level of the society.

The collapse of the existing order of society (3.1-26) is well illustrated by the description of women who are sophisticated, selfish and
thoughtless (3.16-23; cf. Amos 4.1-3). Degradation by strong drink
(5.11-12, 22-23; cf. Ephraim's drunkenness, 28.1, 3, 7, 8) is compared
with the liberal women who cause their husbands to do unacceptable
things to attain their end. J. Love aptly argues that the trouble is
'inward weakness and the slow process of moral rot' (1.30-31).[125]

As a consequence, the future shows a drastic reversal of the present
situation, and the full administration of justice and righteousness is
often described as a direct influence of the spirit of Yahweh (11.1-2;
28.5). This eschatological expectation is undoubtedly in contrast to the
present failing leadership.

2.3 *Jerusalem and the Davidic Monarchy*
In the midst of a strange silence about such past deliverances as the
exodus tradition, Zion and Davidic motifs are freely used.[126] These
traditions, probably first used by court circles as the basis of their own
legitimation, are often applied with a completely new concept.

Zion occupies the center of pre-exilic Isaianic theology. At least 11
times, the prophet mentions the holy place with strong references such
as 'Yahweh founded' (14.32), 'dwells' (8.18; 31.9) and 'reveals him-

Debate with the Wisdom Tradition (CBQMS, 3; Washington: Catholic Biblical
Association, 1973).

125. J.P. Love, 'The Call of Isaiah: An Exposition of Isaiah 6', *Int* 11 (1957),
pp. 282-96 (286).

126. Von Rad, *Old Testament Theology*, II, p. 174.

self' (2.3; cf. 6.1). Zion, therefore, is closely linked with the kingship of Yahweh. It is where God's rule is realized, either his direct rule or rule through the earthly representative.[127] God's special plan for Zion (10.5-19; 14.24-27) explains the centrality of Zion theology in the prophet's thought. This is commonly expressed by the popular belief in the inviolability of Zion as found in Pss. 46, 48 and 76. This focus upon Zion might be shared, not only by the Judeans in general, but also by the prophet himself, as the mysterious defeat of enemies in the Assyrian crisis suggests. For the common belief, the presence of the temple in Zion is the basis of false security (1.11-17). It is also possible that the Davidic promise plays a strengthening role to it. For the prophet, however, it is the real presence of God that protects and strengthens the people (6.1). This also explains why there is no reference to past history. Zion remains purely a religious place, with no political role at all.[128]

Therefore, Yahweh's protection of Zion is not a blanket promise, as often he is against his abiding place (29.4), although it is subsequently followed by a deliverance (30.27-33). This calls for a total trust in Yahweh for the security of the nation (31.1-8). Such security is present only when the people look to Yahweh, not based on past history but on the intimate relationship that the prophet assumes between Yahweh and Judah.

The lack of trust in God is shown in two ways: self-reliance and reliance on external power. In the two eighth-century crises, Judah, or more specifically its leaders, choose to rely on external powers, at first Assyria and later Egypt. It is precisely in this context that the absolute claim of Yahweh is linked with the Zion tradition. רוח, the supreme quality of Yahweh, is that on which Judah can base her trust (31.5) over the false trust in בשׂר, the human power. Therefore, it is the faith and confidence on the human part (36.5-7; 37.10) and subsequently Yahweh's zeal (37.32) that will result in a positive outcome.[129] The descriptive expression of this trust is viewed as consulting and obeying Yahweh's prophet whose message of עצה is from Yahweh's רוח

127. For this reason, William J. Dumbrell, *The Search for Order: Biblical Eschatology in Focus* (Grand Rapids: Baker Book House, 1994), p. 154 n. 83, describes the city where 'divine and earthly spheres intersect'.

128. Vriezen, 'Essentials', p. 130.

129. In this case, a remnant will emerge. This seems to be a reflection of a later time as von Rad, *Old Testament Theology*, II, p. 168, contends.

(30.1-2). The total submission of the future leader to God's will is also attributed to the spirit of Yahweh endowed upon him (11.2-3).

As seen already, kingship in Judah is closely related to Zion theology. The prophet's interest in the continuation of the monarchy is evident in his call for the king to trust in Yahweh in the time of crisis. For instance, in the Syro-Ephraimite war, the prophet assures his audience that the Davidic monarchy has a firm foundation, whereas that of Rezin and Pekah's rule is extremely shaky (Isa. 7.4). Therefore, the central issue of national continuity revolves around trust in Yahweh (7.4, 9). This similar situation occurs in the Assyrian invasion, and the prophet utters the same urge to trust in God for protection rather than the intention of foreign powers (e.g. 30.1-5; 31.1-3). Isaiah, although attacking Ahaz for his unwillingness to trust in Yahweh, never denounces the monarchy itself.

The welfare of the king is closely interwoven with the Zion theology. The prophetic faith in Davidic kingship leads to the promise of an ideal ruler from the Davidic lineage.[130] In chs. 33–35, the prophet's assurance that God will not abandon his promises to the king and to Zion is reinforced by later oracles which are placed side by side. The editor of chs. 36–39 has moved a step further by providing historical evidence (chs. 36–37) that Yahweh delivers the king of Judah. At the same time, the prophet, as did Micah his contemporary, dismisses the present monarch (11.1) and envisages the coming ruler in the immediate future. The description of the ideal qualities of the ruler certainly reveals the failure of the present monarch.

2.4 *Prophets*

The prophet's self-identity is heavily influenced by the call experience (ch. 6). The tradition has been well established that a prophet takes part in the counsel of King Yahweh.[131] In this sense, the role of the prophet

130. 'Dynastic messianism' is the expression used to refer to a belief that all Davidic descendants will match David himself in administrating righteousness and justice; see Daniel Schibler, 'Messianism and Messianic Prophecy in Isaiah 1–12 and 28–33', in Philip E. Satterthwaite, Richard S. Hess and Gordon J. Wenham (eds.), *The Lord's Anointed: Interpretation of Old Testament Messianic Texts* (Carlisle: Paternoster Press; Grand Rapids: Baker Book House, 1995), pp. 87-104 (97); S. Talmon, *King, Cult and Calendar in Ancient Israel* (Jerusalem: Magnes Press, 1986), ch. 1; P.D. Wegner, *An Examination of Kingship and Messianic Expectation in Isaiah 1–35* (Lewiston, NY: Edwin Mellen Press, 1992), pp. 307-308.

131. De Boer, 'Counselor', p. 55.

parallels that of a 'spirit' in the council of Yahweh (1 Kgs 22.19-23). He is an earthly representative of the council, and many times he is in direct conflict with the earthly wise in their wisdom (28.13-16). The רוח of Yahweh is the prophetic inspiration with strong reference to divine wisdom (30.1-2). Micah 3.8 also claims the spirit of God as the source of his prophetic vocation and inspiration (cf. Hos. 9.7). The call narrative of Isaiah well represents both elements: Yahweh as king, and the prophet as a messenger of the counsel of Yahweh (6.1-8).

2.5 Eschatology

2.5.1 The Remnant. This primarily secular concept is not peculiar to the preaching of the prophets nor is it an invention of the prophets.[132] It was by the prophets, however, that this military and civil concept came to bridge the 'abyss between the eschatology of doom and weal', in Gressmann's terms,[133] that is between judgment and salvation. To the prophets, the attitude toward the remnant is primarily negative (e.g. Amos 3.12; 9.1-4, 9; cf. 2 Kgs 21.10-15). Often it is depicted with its feebleness, smallness, barely escaping and ruthlessly hunted down by the wrath of God (Isa. 16.14). Hence, the concept is closely linked with the message of the judgment of God in the prophets (e.g. Amos 5.15; Mic. 5.6). Yet the message of a few faithful survivors is never abandoned (Isa. 1.25-26; 28.5-6; cf. Zeph. 3.13; Mic. 5.8; 1 Kgs 19.18) and here is given a new interpretation. The presence of the remnant serves a dual purpose: to be a nucleus for the future people of God, and to be a witness to God's judgment and his saving act. Both motifs affirm that the survival of the remnant is only by 'constraint of the justifying grace and love of God'.[134] This can be an expression of God's חסד, 'the love which goes an extra mile and grants another chance for a fresh start, which he [God] does not have to do'.[135]

In Isaiah, a vivid presentation of belief in a remnant is found in 7.1-17. In the midst of the Syro-Ephraimite war Yahweh instructs Isaiah to

---

132. Von Rad, *Old Testament Theology*, II, pp. 19-20; Hugo Gressmann, *Der Ursprung der israelitisch-judischen Eschatologie* (Göttingen: Vandenhoeck & Ruprecht, 1905), pp. 229-30.

133. Gressmann, *Der Ursprung der israelitisch-judischen Eschatologie*, p. 237.

134. J.C. Campbell, 'God's People and the Remnant', *SJT* 3 (1950), pp. 78-85 (82).

135. This definition of חסד is by Leslie C. Allen (Fuller Theological Seminary, Winter, 1987).

confront Ahaz (7.3b). On this occasion, a son of the prophet with the
name of שְׁאָר יָשׁוּב (a remnant will return) was present. His name is a
message of hope as well as threat.[136] In the confrontation between
religion and politics, the prophet demands the king and Judah to have
faith in Yahweh only (9b). Here, Isaiah eliminates much of the secular
meaning of the term, making it a radical religious entity. In the same
historical orbit, however, the promise of Immanuel after the refusal of
the king to trust Yahweh is another promise of a remnant (7.10-17). In
the negative and distancing context (e.g. the shift of personal pronoun),
Yahweh is no longer the God of the king ('your God') but becomes the
God of those who put their trust in him ('my God'). The sign, the birth
of Immanuel, is a sign of doom, destruction and judgment. But the
same sign is, on the other hand, a promise of his presence in the midst
of those who choose to put their total trust in him. A similar message is
repeated in the Assyrian crisis. The prophet urges Hezekiah (30.15-17)
to return to Yahweh with the promise of security and protection (e.g.
28.7-13, 14-22; 29.9-12, 13-14). Preservation of a remnant is an act of
grace, even after his people rejected his protection.

The historical reality of a remnant is described in 1.7-9 (cf. 2 Kgs
18.13-16). To the historical remnant, the remaining 'daughter of Zion',
Isaiah announces another chance to return to Yahweh in faith. The
prophet's understanding of a historical remnant is not identical with a
religious or spiritual entity. It does not just return, but is converted. It is
characterized by total obedience and giving up of every possible
security other than God's.[137] The same distinction is found in 37.30-32,
where the 'survivors' (v. 32) serve as the historical entity out of which
the future remnant will emerge. Even though these two are not identical, the existence of the historical remnant is crucial to the emergence
of the eschatological remnant. A remnant motif in an eschatological
context is found in 11.10-16.[138]

---

136. The ambiguity of the name has been noted by a number of commentators.
For a summary, see Michael E.W. Thompson, *Situation and Theology: Old Testament Interpretations of the Syro-Ephraimite War* (Sheffield: Almond Press, 1982),
pp. 23-26.

137. J. Fichtner, 'Jahves Plan in der Botschaft des Jesaja', *ZAW* 63 (1951), pp.
16-33. See also Hans Wildberger, 'Jesajas Verständnis der Geschichte', in *Congress Volume: Bonn, 1962* (VTSup, 9; Leiden: E.J. Brill, 1963), pp. 83-117 (110).

138. The question of authenticity is coupled with the universal scope of the

As to who is the remnant in Isaiah's understanding, Isa. 8.16 is often referred to. In fact, Skinner identifies the 'band of his disciples' formed after the refusal of Ahaz with the nucleus of the future people of God.[139] This view, however, is correctly objected to in that 'it envisages the people of God as being reconstituted on the basis of an idea or programme or body of doctrine propagated by the remnant'.[140] Rather, they are signs and wonders in Israel, or 'prophetic representatives of the eschatological remnant'.[141]

In spite of the demand for trust, the remnant is not described as if it merits a better fate. It is to bear the burden of the judgment in humility and hope. The primarily negative portrayal of the remnant is met by the promises of future glory by later hands. The remnant is not only saved in the Day of Yahweh (4.2-3; 6.13; 10.21-22; 17.4-6), but also material and spiritual blessings are promised to it.

Furthermore, in Isa. 28.5-6, a leader is promised for the remnant, to whom is given a spirit of justice. With this leader and warriors to whom God will grant might, the remnant community will enjoy the eschatological promise of restoration which includes the return of the exiles.

2.5.2 *God's Reign in Zion*. The manifestation of Yahweh's kingship over the nations as well as over Israel is a post-judgment sequel. The initial judgment upon the nations that are identified as Israel's enemies functions as an implicit message of salvation and vindication for Israel (e.g. judgment upon Edom in 34.5-17). Yet, the nations in the future reign of Yahweh are not only seen in a context of judgment (e.g. Assyria in 10.7, cf. 13-14), but also in the celebration of the universal rulership of Yahweh (e.g. 2.2-4).

At that time, Zion will be the city of righteousness (1.26, also 28.6), the redeemed city, with righteous people (1.27) in it. Zion will be the dwelling place of Yahweh in its full sense. Its leadership will be restored (1.26) and justice will prevail everywhere (28.1-6), for the Lord will be 'a crown of glory, and a diadem of beauty unto the remnant of his people' (28.5). Fruitfulness and fertility of the land (7.22,

message. Hasel, *The Remnant*, p. 315, attributes it to the 'undogmatic flexibility' of the prophet as far as the idea is concerned.

139. Skinner, *Isaiah, Chapters I–XXXIX*, p. lxiv.

140. Campbell, 'God's People', p. 80.

141. Hasel, *The Remnant*, p. 286.

30.23, 24, cf. 4.2), bliss on animals and nature (30.23), and the ingathering of exiles (11.11) often allude to another exodus (11.15-16). This feature is fully developed in the exilic Isaianic tradition (43.14-21; 48.20-21; 51.10-11; 52.11-12; 55.12).

There is no direct reference to the רוח of Yahweh in the pre-exilic Isaianic tradition, except an implicit description of the redemptive future as seen above. A more explicit expression of the role of רוח in God's kingship is found in the role of the coming Davidic ruler.

2.5.3 *The Coming Ruler.* As far as the future reign of God is concerned, the scriptural evidence is not consistent. On the one hand, the coming age is viewed with God's direct rule over his people and the nations. But on the other hand, his rule is mediated by human agents even in the future. It ranges from judges (28.6) and soldiers (28.6) even to a ruler that is equivalent to a king (11.1) from which the 'messianic' idea emerges. How to reconcile these two contradicting evidences is beyond the scope of this study.

Like other elements of eschatology, this expectation was originally a historical prediction of an ideal ruler in a specific historical context. It is argued that the prophet believe the fulfillment of the coming king to be the near future. Only after the realization that the prediction was not fulfilled historically is it moved to the distant future and 'becomes messianic' in its proper sense.

In the pre-exilic material, the so-called 'messianic' prophecy is found in chs. 7–11 which consist of three major passages. The Immanuel oracle (7.10-16) is clearly given in the context of the Syro-Ephraimite war. In spite of the obscure identity of the promised child, the cultic origin of the oracle is supported in two ways. First, a Ras Shamra text attests that 'the young woman shall bear a son' is a cultic announcement of the birth of a divine, or a royal child.[142] Secondly, some royal psalms seem to indicate that Immanuel, 'God with us', is a cultic exclamation (e.g. Ps. 46, 'The Lord of hosts is with us ...'). These evidences appear to favor testimony to a royal birth on the historical level.[143] Ringgren describes the prophet's intended messages as follows,

142. Gordon, *Ugaritic Literature*, p. 64 (Glossary, *Nkl* I, 8).
143. The similarity between this text and the Egyptian oracle concerning the birth of Queen Hatshepsut is also noted by Widengren (*Religion och Bible* 7 [1949], pp. 28-29) as quoted by Ringgren, *The Messiah*, p. 27.

> Take your cultic confession seriously. You say that God is with you; why do you not trust in him? You take the ancient words of the birth of the royal child into your mouths, but you dare not trust the expectations that are bound up with the traditional formula.[144]

The main emphasis in this passage is the destruction of the two threatening powers. The birth of Immanuel serves as a sign which God himself offers after the rejection of the king to trust in Yahweh.

The second 'messianic' passage is found in 9.2-7 where the birth of a royal child is expected. Without any hint of its historical context, this announcement of salvation is placed right after the depressing description of the present situation. Anguish, trouble and darkness may describe the Assyrian conquest of the northern kingdom (v. 2).[145] To chaos and disorder, the light of salvation breaks through (v. 2). Yahweh is to act as a warrior who saves his people with his might (9.4-5). However, v. 6 suddenly presents an implied message that this bright salvation is brought about by a newborn child, the son of a king. Israelite kingship ideology is well reflected in the throne names.[146] Similar expressions are scattered throughout the Old Testament. Among them are 'son of God' (Ps. 2.7, cf. 89.26), 'everlasting ruler' (Mic. 5.2), 'righteous judge' (Isa. 11.4), 'prophet' (Ps. 2.7), 'perpetual priest' (Ps. 110.4) and so on. These terms, as well as those in Isaiah 9, however, refer to the office rather than to the man, or to the man in his ideal role.[147] This ideal Davidic child will be a ruler in a special relation to God, as royal psalms claim (Ps. 2.7; 45.16).[148] Against its Egyptian counterpart,[149] the Israelite notion of kingship maintains that a king is not divine. Yet, a king is not an ordinary human as seen in a suzerain–vassal relationship. The king certainly is a superhuman whose unique

144. Ringgren, *The Messiah*, p. 27.

145. Ringgren, *The Messiah*, p. 28.

146. E.g. Gowan, *Eschatology*, p. 35, 'a prophetic affirmation of traditional kingship ideology'. Also Kaiser, *Isaiah 1–12*, pp. 125-30; Wildberger, *Isaiah 1–12*, pp. 378-87; Mowinckel, *He That Cometh*, pp. 102-10.

147. R.B.Y. Scott, 'Biblical Research and the Work of the Pastor: Recent Study in Isaiah 1–39', *Int* 11 (1957), pp. 259-68 (266).

148. Gehman, 'Ruler of the Universe', p. 275, asserts that the theophanic name of the child cannot be used to prove that he is divine (contra Ringgren, *The Messiah*, p. 31).

149. For the kingship ideology of Egypt and Mesopotamia, see Henri Frankfort, *Kingship and the Gods: A Study of Ancient Near Eastern Religion as the Integration of Society and Nature* (Chicago: University of Chicago Press, 1948).

relation to deity is well attested by some throne names such as 'Mighty God' and 'Everlasting Father' in Isa. 1.6.[150] Strength and wisdom, which are two main qualities of an ideal king, are well represented in the names. The effect of his rule is described with two key words of Isaiah, 'righteousness' and 'justice' which, in turn, is summarized as 'peace'. Even though the prophet is silent as to who the child is,[151] the certainty of his coming is evident. Yet, historically, no king appeared to fulfill the qualification of the child and this oracle of salvation becomes 'messianic' in that it is to be realized in the coming age.

The third passage is 11.1-9 which is discussed above in some detail. Three pairs are used and correspond to the throne names in 9.6 to a certain extent. Attributes found in both passages are to be summed up in the two concepts of 'wisdom' and 'strength' resulting in 'righteousness' and 'justice' under his rule. His intimate dependence on Yahweh is increasingly emphasized here. Whoever is responsible for the final arrangement, the unfulfilled expectation of an ideal ruler[152] is neatly rounded off with the expectation of universal peace and the return of a perfect era. The use of mythological language in the description of universal peace[153] distinguishes the biblical tradition from the surrounding religious milieu.

It is in this last passage that the רוח of Yahweh is explicitly associated with the quality of the ideal king. Two traditions are present in the making of the ideal ruler. First is the charismatic tradition of kingship. The charismatic leadership of Moses, attributed to the spirit of God (Num. 11.17), is succeeded by the judges (Judg. 3.10; 6.34; 11.29; 13.25; 14.6, 19; 15.14) before the monarchy. The religious role of the prophetic spirit is not clearly distinguished from its secular role as the leadership itself is inclusive (e.g. Moses, Num. 11.16-17 and also Samuel as prophet, 1 Sam. 3.20; 9.9; as priest, 2.11, 18; 3.1; and as

150. Gehman, 'Ruler of the Universe', p. 275. Cf. Christopher R. North, 'The Religious Aspects of Hebrew Kingship', *ZAW* 50 (1932), pp. 8-38 (10), who is blamed for minimizing this super-human element by Mowinckel, *He That Cometh*, p. 456.

151. He could be a newly crowned king. Some suggest Hezekiah, e.g. de Boer, 'Counselor', p. 45; Cole, 'Archaeology and the Messiah Oracles', pp. 53-69.

152. Klausner, *The Messianic Idea in Israel*, p. 56 suggests that it was after Hezekiah's failure to fulfill the expectation that this became an everlasting ideal.

153. Childs, *Myth and Reality*, pp. 63-67. Also Mowinckel, *He That Cometh*, p. 186.

judge, 7.3-14).[154] The secular role of Yahweh's רוח upon leaders develops radically as the first two kings (1 Sam. 10.5-6, 10; 11.6-8; 16.13),
and also Solomon (1 Kgs 3.4-15) (to a certain extent) are equipped by
the spirit of God. Through the mouth of David, the Deuteronomistic
writer confirms רוח as the way by which Yahweh intends rulers of
Israel to be equipped (1 Sam. 23.2). This should be seen as a reaction to
the typical *Anfangserscheinung* (early phenomenon), subject to gradual
Veralltäglichung (routinization).[155] It is argued that the tradition survived in the northern kingdom as an inroad to legitimate kingship, and
it later infiltrated to the south.[156]

Another tradition evident here is the covenant theology expressed in
2 Samuel 7 and Psalm 89 which seems to support the Jerusalem monarchy. The unconditional and eternal nature of the covenant 'did not permit so radical a judgment of repudiation as that expressed in the Mosaic
or amphictyonic covenant'.[157] The expectation of the coming ruler is
that he will be from the Davidic lineage (Isa. 11.1 and Mic. 5.2). The
two old traditions are integrated together once again to interpret what
lay ahead for the people of God. They function well as a 'kind of pro-
totype for the shaping of their eschatology, even the royal eschatology'.[158]

3. Concluding Observations

3.1 *The* רוח *in the Traditions*
Where does the pre-exilic usage stand in the various רוח traditions? At
least four out of the six identifiable traditions are present in the pre-
exilic Isaianic traditions. First of all, for the first time, רוח is used to
refer to the incomparable quality of God (31.3). The distinctive element
of Yahweh is described as רוח, in contrast with Egyptian military power
which is בשר (31.3). The absoluteness of Yahweh is the underlying
basis for the pre-exilic Isaianic tradition. And רוח, in reference to God's
wisdom and power, contributes to this understanding of Yahweh.

---

154. In the case of Samuel, there is no reference to רוח associated with him.
155. Mettinger, *King and Messiah*, p. 246.
156. Alt, 'Das Königtum in den Reichen Israel und Juda', p. 12; M. Noth, 'Gott,
König, Volk im Alten Testament', *ZTK* 47 (1950), pp. 159-91 (187-88).
157. Robert J. Marshall, 'The Structure of Isaiah 1–12', *BibRes* 7 (1962), pp.
19-32 (25).
158. Harrelson, 'Nonroyal Motifs', p. 164.

However, a specific link between רוח and the idea of God's holiness is
not yet established (e.g. 'holy spirit' in Isa. 63.10-11, cf. Ps. 51.11).[159]
The emphasis is heavy on the issue of power. Probably this is a significant development from the common notion, 'God's spirit'. רוח is a
distinct quality exclusively found in the deity.

Secondly, רוח is a superhuman element granted to God's chosen ves-
sels, and this is the dominant tradition in the pre-exilic Isaianic thinking
(11.1-3; 28.5-6). They have a divine quality extended to them, due to
their special position. It may be worthwhile to compare the role of
Yahweh's רוח in the Israelite kingship ideology and *ka* in the Egyptian
idea, both being divine elements granted to divinely appointed rulers.[160]
As seen in the selected leaders, the presence of the spirit of God is a
sign for a legitimate leader. In addition, the granting of God's רוח has a
practical function, that is, to equip for the administration of justice
and righteousness. On the one hand, this continues the pre- and early
monarchical kingship ideology. On the other hand, the lack of any
violent feature of the spirit of God as previously seen in the judges
(Judg. 13.25; 14.6, 19) and Saul (1 Sam. 11.6-7) indicates either the
refinement of kingship ideology, the spiritualization of רוח tradition, or
both. In both passages (11.1-5 and 28.5-6), the leader is an eschatological figure.

For these two traditions, the idea of 'extended personality', in Johnson's term is aptly applied. Isaiah 31.3 articulates, for the first time, that
רוח is God's essential element. The distinguishing element of God from
his creature is רוח. This distinctively divine quality is extended or
granted to the leader. In the ancient Near East, early kings are gods,
while in Israel, the king has God's spirit.

Thirdly, the most obvious impression is that the spirit of God seems
to function just as one of various divine agents. The context is well set
in an old tradition where a member of the divine counsel becomes a
'lying spirit' to achieve a divine plan. To certain activities of רוח of
Yahweh are attached a distinctive functional description, as the 'evil
spirit' (1 Sam. 16.14), the 'spirit of fire' (Isa. 4.4), as well as the 'lying
spirit' from the divine counsel (1 Kgs 22.20-22). Isaiah 11.2-3 can be
viewed in this way, but in a positive way for the first time. The divine

159. The specific reference to the 'holy spirit' of Yahweh is found in Isa. 63 as
well as in Ps. 51.

160. A good beginning point can be Hehn, 'Zum Problem des Geist', pp. 210-
25.

representative of Yahweh is upon the coming ruler too. Its influence is described as if the spirit of God is realized as the spirit of wisdom and understanding. In Isa. 28.6, Yahweh will be 'the spirit of justice' in the coming age. The usage is not much different. However, this positively described instrument of God exhibits almost no sign of personality. This is in clear contrast to the negative usages referred to above. The 'lying spirit' in particular displays a specific and explicit personality in the council of God.

The fourth tradition is that of the prophetic spirit. In a vague reference in Isa. 30.1, the prophetic counsel is expressed as seeking a plan revealed by God's spirit to the prophet. Its strong link with wisdom is unavoidable. Its ambiguity and the single reference make the conclusion tentative.

Only one רוח is not present in the pre-exilic Isaianic traditions: the רוח of creation. Within just four passages, a wide variety of traditions is represented.

3.2 Characteristics

In comparison with the understanding of the רוח of God in the earlier period, there are at least four apparent characteristics of רוח at this stage.

3.2.1 *Refinement/Spiritualization*. The relative scarcity of the spirit of Yahweh in the pre-exilic Isaianic tradition as observed by Mowinckel and Kapelrud, may be a reaction to the claim of the violent possession of the prophetic spirit (e.g. Hos. 9.7). Nonetheless, as argued above, at least two passages have a reference to the prophetic רוח of Yahweh, but with careful elimination of any violent feature. Also the royal figure in 11.1-5 and the leader 'judge' in 28.6 show less martial references. This can be seen as part of a long process toward the 'spiritualization' of the רוח. In the case of the king, this phenomenon is not unrelated to the 'spiritualization' of the royal functions.[161] This phenomenon is also seen in the internalization of the effect of רוח approaching and during the exilic period (Ezek. 36.26-27). On the other hand, the old super-human tradition still survives in the direct association with strength upon the coming ruler (11.2). The power reference is also found in Yahweh against human plans (e.g. 30.1-5; 31.1-3).

161. Wildberger, *Isaiah 1–12*, p. 477.

3.2.2 *The Wisdom Connection.* The association of רוח and wisdom is a new development. Rylaarsdam observes correctly,

> Thus we see now that the integration of the Hebrew concept of deity, wisdom and spirit, two elements in it that begin at opposite poles, are gradually drawn together and begin to operate in the same orbit.[162]

There are explicit (11.2), as well as implicit, references relating the spirit of God to wisdom (30.1-5; 31.1-3). Yet wisdom has been a part of the charisma which Yahweh bestows, through his spirit, to his chosen servants. Moreover, wisdom has been closely connected with the traditional royal ideology. Similarly, for the first time, piety, that is knowing and fearing God, is attributed to the spirit of God (11.2).[163]

3.2.3 *Exclusiveness.* In spite of the significant development of the concept, the pre-exilic period still perceives Yahweh as bestowing his רוח only upon selected leaders (in this discussion, the future ruler). It is within the orbit of an old tradition where the spirit of God is exclusively given to legitimate leaders. Yahweh's רוח is the very element that turns an ordinary person into an extraordinary one suitable for the work of God. Moreover, the continual endowment of the spirit is limited to the coming ruler as to David. It is only during the exilic period that the concept becomes fully democratized (32.15). This change can be attributed either to the developed concept of רוח, or to the different understanding resulting from the exilic nature of the community.

3.2.4 *The Eschatological Connection.* The most distinguishing development of the concept is its association with the Israelite eschatology. Isaiah 11.1-9 is a clear example that the prophet's expectation of the idealized coming ruler is closely associated with the spirit of Yahweh. Historically, up to this point, the רוח of Yahweh has its immediate function always in the present situation (e.g. the judges, the first two kings, the prophets). With 11.1-9 as the starting point, however, the idea of the רוח of God experiences a significant development, particularly in connection with the coming age.

---

162. John Coert Rylaarsdam, *Revelation in Jewish Wisdom Literature* (Chicago: University of Chicago Press, 1946), p. 103.
    163. Neve, *The Spirit of God*, p. 56.

Chapter 2

Exilic Isaianic Spirit Traditions

As observed in the previous chapter, among the pre-exilic prophets there is an avoidance of the use of the phrase (רוח יהוה or רוח אלהים), particularly in relation to the prophetic inspiration.[1] During and after the exile, however, the concept appears to have gained a new significance with the noticeably increasing frequency of its occurrences in this period.[2]

This chapter is concerned with the exilic understanding of the divine רוח concept evidenced in the exilic Isaianic literature.[3] As evidenced in the pre-exilic traditions, it is assumed that the eschatological implications of God's רוח continue to persist to this period, and that the eschatological significance is further developed.

1.   See Chapter 1 for more discussion, e.g. pp. 60-61.
2.   The almost loose, certainly prolific, use of the word רוח during the exilic period is aptly illustrated in the book of Ezekiel. See Daniel I. Block, 'The Prophet of the Spirit: The Use of *rwḥ* in the Book of Ezekiel', *JETS* 32 (1989), pp. 27-50.
3.   Recently the traditional notion of the origin of Second Isaiah, the major portion of the exilic Isaianic tradition, has been under attack. Not only its exilic origin but also the Babylonian setting are questioned, e.g. Christopher R. Seitz, *Zion's Final Destiny: The Development of the Book of Isaiah: A Reassessment of Isaiah 36–39* (Minneapolis: Fortress Press, 1991), pp. 205-207; R.E. Clements, 'Beyond Tradition-History: Deutero-Isaianic Development of First Isaiah's Themes', *JSOT* 31 (1985), pp. 95-113 (110); Philip R. Davies, 'God of Cyrus, God of Israel: Some Religio-Historical Reflections on Isaiah 40–55', in Jon Davies, Graham Harvey and Wilfred G.E. Watson (eds.), *Words Remembered, Texts Renewed: Essays in Honour of John F.A. Sawyer* (JSOTSup, 195; Sheffield: JSOT Press, 1995), pp. 207-25 (210-25). However, H.G.M. Williamson, 'First and Last in Isaiah', in Heather A. McKay and David J.A. Clines (eds.), *Of Prophets' Visions and the Wisdom of Sages: Essays in Honour of R. Norman Whybray on his Seventieth Birthday* (JSOTSup, 162; Sheffield: JSOT Press, 1993), pp. 95-108, upholds the traditional exilic Babylonian setting.

1. *Exilic Passages*

At a glance, the exilic רוח passages are easily divided into two categories: futuristic and non-futuristic passages. Two non-futuristic passages are discussed first, followed by the discussion of three futuristic passages, although sometimes, especially in 42.1-4, the categorization is ambiguous due to the nature of the passage.

> 40.12-14
> 12 Who would measure the waters in the hollow of his hands,
>> Or measure the heavens with a span,
>> Or contain the dust of the earth in the measure,
>> Or weigh mountains on scales,
>>> or hills in a balance?
> 13 Who would measure Yahweh's spirit,
>> Or instruct him as his counselor?
> 14 Whom would he consult for his enlightenment,
>> Or to teach him in the way of justice,
>> Or to teach him knowledge,
>> Or to show him the path of understanding?

The occurrence of רוח יהוה (the spirit of Yahweh) is found amid a sharp and incisive declaration (40.12-31), which follows a joyful opening proclamation of restoration (vv. 1-11). Smart argues that the prophet anticipates opposition from the realists and their skepticism pitted against his faith in a speedy return as described in vv. 1-11.[4] Confronting this spiritual foe, the writer carefully argues that Yahweh is not only able to save (vv. 12-26), but in fact he is willing to perform another miraculous redemption (vv. 27-31).[5] In this polemic against idols, the prophet asks a series of rhetorical questions. The scene is definitely of creation, particularly in contrast to the human creation of idols. However, the intention is not so much a cosmological argument as an assertion to Yahweh's supremacy over all deities.[6] Motyer and

---

4.   James Smart, *History and Theology in Second Isaiah: A Commentary on Isaiah 35, 40–66* (Philadelphia: Westminster Press, 1965), p. 55.

5.   Bruce D. Naidoff, 'The Rhetoric of Encouragement in Isaiah 40.12-31: A Form-Critical Study', *ZAW* 93 (1981), pp. 62-76 (67). Also Roy F. Melugin, 'Deutero-Isaiah and Form Criticism', *VT* 21 (1971), pp. 326-37 (336-37); Claus Westermann, *Isaiah 40–66: A Commentary* (OTL; trans. David M.G. Stalker; Philadelphia: Westminster Press, 1969), pp. 50-51.

6.   Christopher R. North, *The Second Isaiah* (Oxford: Clarendon Press, 1964), p. 13.

Hanson assume as the cognitive background the Babylonian mythology where Marduk consulted with Ea, the all-wise, in his creation.[7]

Views on the identity of the רוח are diverse. Westermann sees the רוח יהוה here as the power of God which works miracles, especially miracles connected with salvation,[8] which is a common meaning of the רוח in the Old Testament tradition. However, his suggestion of the parallelism between v. 13a and v. 13b does not provide a decisive clue, although this interpretation fits into the wider context of vv. 12-26, where Yahweh's saving power is argued against the idols.

The LXX rendering of 'mind' (νοῦν) is shared by numerous scholars.[9] North and Neve contend that the use of the qal form of the verb תכן (direct) in Proverbs (16.2; 21.2; 24.12) provides a clue.[10] Proverbs 24.12, 'Yahweh measures hearts [לבות]', and Prov. 16.2, 'Yahweh measures minds [רוחות]', prove the exchangeability of the two terms. Even though used in its piel form, the meaning is not different.[11] In addition, all the verbs, 'consult', 'taught' and 'show' with their objects certainly have a better reference to the wisdom and intelligence of Yahweh than to his creative power. Even v. 13b, if it is in parallel with v. 13a, offers a similar impression.

7.   J. Alec Motyer, *The Prophecy of Isaiah: An Introduction and Commentary* (Downers Grove, IL: InterVarsity Press, 1993), p. 303; Paul D. Hanson, *Isaiah 40–66* (Interpretation: A Bible Commentary for Teaching and Preaching; Louisville, KY: Westminster/John Knox Press, 1995), p. 28.

8.   Westermann, *Isaiah 40–66*, p. 50. Also J. Muilenburg, 'The Book of Isaiah, Chapters 40–66', *IB*, V, pp. 382-773 (437), 'God sends forth his spirit as an active and life-giving force to do his work and achieve his purpose'.

9.   J. Skinner, *The Book of the Prophet Isaiah Chapters XL–LXVI* (Cambridge Bible for Schools and Colleges; Cambridge: Cambridge University Press, rev. edn, 1917), p. 9; R.J. Clifford, 'The Function of Idol Passages in Second Isaiah', *CBQ* 42 (1980), pp. 450-64 (457); North, *The Second Isaiah*, p. 83; *idem, Isaiah 40–55* (Torch Bible Commentary; London: SCM Press, 2nd edn, 1964), p. 45.

10.   North, *The Second Isaiah*, p. 13; Neve, *The Spirit of God*, pp. 99-100, where the analogy of Egyptian god Horus who weighed the hearts of the dead before Osiris, the judge, is to be noted.

11.   R.N. Whybray, *The Heavenly Counsellor in Isaiah xl 13-14: A Study of the Sources of the Theology of Deutero-Isaiah* (SOTSMS, 1; Cambridge: Cambridge University Press, 1971), p. 15. However, John L. McKenzie, *Second Isaiah* (AB, 20; Garden City, NY: Doubleday, 1968), p. 20, translates 'direct', following G.R. Driver, 'Hebrew Notes', *VT* 1 (1951), pp. 241-50 (242-43). Contra, LXX renders the verb as ἔγνω 'understood'.

However, the opening questions of v. 12 involve more than Yahweh's intelligence and wisdom. If v. 13 links the previous verse with the following, it may be reasonable to conclude that the רוח refers to God's infinite power and wisdom in the context of creation.[12] Whybray concurs by identifying God's רוח with his mind which includes 'both his purpose and his practical intelligence and ability'.[13] Similarly, D.W. Watts considers that it includes 'mind, purpose, and plans, but moves beyond them to include motivation and implementation'.[14] The message is clear, that is, no one can 'judge' (or 'measure', 'weigh') God's spirit, but rather Yahweh, as God and creator, weighs human hearts.

The notion of רוח יהוה as the intelligence and wisdom of Yahweh is a usage unusual in the Old Testament. Although 30.1 links God's רוח with his wisdom in a non-creation setting, there is no close parallel elsewhere. One can detect the influence of wisdom tradition here as well as in 30.1.[15]

34.16-17[16]

16 Seek from the book of Yahweh and read,
   not one of these is missing,
      none lacks its mate
   For the mouth has commanded,
      and his spirit has gathered them;
17 He has cast the lot for them
      his hand has portioned it out to them with the line;
   They shall possess it forever
      from generation to generation they shall dwell in it.

---

12. Montague, *The Holy Spirit*, p. 50; John D.W. Watts, *Isaiah 34–66* (WBC, 25; Waco, TX: Word Books, 1987), p. 86, argues that 'mind' is too restrictive and passive in comparison with 'spirit' with its active and dynamic resonance, although the latter includes the former. Youngblood, *The Book of Isaiah*, p. 114, identifies its context with Yahweh's majesty and power. John Scullion, *Isaiah 40–66* (OTM, 12; Wilmington, DE: Michael Glazier, 1982), p. 26, notes that, unlike Ugaritic and Mesopotamian cosmogony, in the prophetic claim there is no motif of struggle in God's creation.

13. Whybray, *Heavenly Counsellor*, p. 10.

14. Watts, *Isaiah 34–66*, pp. 90-91.

15. Whybray, *Heavenly Counsellor*, pp. 26-27, denies wisdom influence here.

16. Regarding the unit division, commentators are divided. For this division, see Otto Kaiser, *Isaiah 13–36: A Commentary* (OTL; trans. R.A. Wilson; London: SCM Press, 1974), p. 359; Wildberger, *Jesaja 28–39*, p. 1326. However, for vv. 5-17 see Duhm, *Das Buch Jesaja*, p. 216; and for vv. 9-17 see Cheyne, *The Prophecies of Isaiah*, I, p. 198. This passage is closely attached to the entire chapter.

Chapters 34 and 35 are regarded by many as reflecting the exilic or even postexilic sentiment.[17] The apocalyptic feature is apparent; a world catastrophe and the end of history is something not seen among earlier prophets. Even the 'Day of Yahweh' idea of Amos 5.18-20 and Isaiah 2–5 does not have so fully a developed concept as here, although the language used is cosmic in scope.[18]

The passage forms the concluding part of a series of judgment oracles (34.1-4, 5-17). Verses 16 and 17 reinforce the certainty of the announced judgment upon Edom. The logic is found in vv. 16b-17, introduced by כִּי, 'for'.

In spite of the ambiguous identity of some creatures inhabiting the desolate land,[19] the overall picture of vv. 1-15 is rather clear. Edom, a representative of the nations who used to stand against Israel and its God, is going to be destroyed. The land will be subsequently repopulated with a varied assortment of animals usually found in the wild or desolate countryside. The repopulating of a land by wild animals (e.g. Hos. 2.12) and the wooded forest (Mic. 3.12b) are traditional pictures of desolation. There is a strong impression that the writer is employing the overall idea and language first applied to the destruction scene of

17. For a close relation of chs. 34–35 to chs. 40–55, see Marvin Pope, 'Isaiah 34 in Relation to Isaiah 35, 40–66', *JBL* 71 (1952), pp. 235-43 (343); Clements, *Isaiah 1–39*, p. 272. O. Kaiser assigns the passage to a much later postexilic time, *Isaiah 13–36*, p. 353; and so do Charles C. Torrey, *The Second Isaiah: A New Interpretation* (New York: Charles Scribner's Sons, 1928), p. 53, and Walter Harrelson, 'Isaiah 35 in Recent Research and Translation', in Samuel E. Balentine and John Barton (eds.), *Language, Theology, and the Bible: Essays in Honour of James Barr* (Oxford: Clarendon Press, 1994), pp. 247-60 (251-54). See also Stacey, *Isaiah 1–39*, p. 206; McKenzie, *Second Isaiah*, pp. 6-12. O.H. Steck, *Bereitete Heimkehr: Jesaja 35 als redaktionelle Brücke zwischen dem Ersten und dem Zweiten Jesaja* (SBS, 121; Stuttgart: Katholisches Bibelwerk, 1985), argues that ch. 35 was deliberately composed to link the first two sections of the book, thus reflecting both First and Second Isaiah. In contrast, Williamson, *The Book Called Isaiah*, pp. 214-20, dates ch. 34 later than the composition of Second Isaiah. He notes a particular connection between this chapter and ch. 13. Also Claire R. Mathews, *Defending Zion: Edom's Desolation and Jacob's Restoration (Isaiah 34–35) in Context* (BZAT, 236; Berlin: W. de Gruyter, 1995), p. 27, favors a postexilic date.

18. McKenzie, *Second Isaiah*, pp. 3-12.

19. For instance, Vincent Tanghe, 'Lilit in Edom (Jes 34,5-15.)', *ETL* 59 (1993), pp. 125-33, identifies Lilith as the name of a demon, based on the Assyrian *lilidu*, 'progeny, young animal'. Hence, according to Tanghe, the section depicts the fate of Edom, with a 12-member animal list as its conclusion.

Jerusalem by First Isaiah (32.9-14). There is also an allusion to several older traditions, namely a recollection of the representation in Gen. 2.1; a possible reference to the Gideon narrative for חרב ליהוה (sword of Yahweh; Judg. 7.20) and consequently the Messianic hymn (Isa. 9); the destruction of Sodom and Gomorrah (Gen. 19); and possibly Genesis 1 or Jer. 4.23-26.[20] The ambiguous identity of some animals does not weigh heavily in the clarity of the entire message.

However, with v. 16, there is a sudden change of the subject matter. The two verses (16-17) function to affirm the certainty of the fulfillment of the previous prophecies upon Edom. The identity of the 'scroll' or 'book' has been problematic. Some identify it with the prophecies of Isaiah in which the command to gather certain animals may have been written.[21] A great disadvantage of this interpretation is that nowhere in First Isaiah is any such close parallel found. This leads others to look for comparable passages outside First Isaiah, for example in Isa. 40.26, Mal. 3.16, Ps. 130.16 and Ezek. 39.17.[22] Still others argue for a post-exilic date of the verses based on the apocalyptic language and a tendency toward a religion based on the letter of the scripture (34.6, 16).[23] D.R. Hillers translates ספר as 'covenant-inscription' based on other ancient Near Eastern treaties.[24] He argues for the presence of a treaty between Judah and Edom within the period of the writer, which was later broken by Edom.[25] Watts identifies it with an imaginary judicial transcript containing God's decision about his vengeance against Edom.[26] Seitz identifies it with the ' "book" in which the Noah story appeared'.[27]

20. James Muilenburg, 'The Literary Character of Isaiah 34', *JBL* 59 (1940), pp. 339-65 (363).

21. Neve, *The Spirit of God*, 83; Fohrer, *Das Buch Jesaja*, II, p. 115; Delitzsch, *Prophecies of Isaiah*, I, p. 75.

22. Scott, 'Isaiah Chapters 1–39', p. 358; Kaiser, *Isaiah 13–39*, p. 359. Torrey's textual emendation, *Second Isaiah*, p. 294, followed by Scott, 'Isaiah Chapters 1–39', p. 358, is to be noted, although it is highly unlikely.

23. Kaiser, *Isaiah 13–39*, p. 353.

24. Delbert R. Hillers, *Treaty-Curses and the Old Testament Prophets* (Rome: Pontifical Biblical Institute, 1964), pp. 45-46.

25. Hillers, *Treaty-Curses*, pp. 48-49, obviously assumes Isaianic authorship of the passage.

26. Watts, *Isaiah 34–66*, pp. 7, 14.

27. C.R. Seitz, *Isaiah 1–39* (Interpretation: A Bible Commentary for Teaching and Preaching; Louisville, KY: Westminster/John Knox Press, 1993), p. 237.

For the role of the רוח which is not significantly affected by the identity of the 'scroll', at least two possibilities have been suggested. First, Muilenburg picks up the Noachic allusion and concludes that as the animals were preserved in the ark to reinhabit the earth after the flood, so Yahweh, through his word and spirit, preserves the animals to reinhabit desolate Edom after its complete destruction. He also contends that just as the spirit and the word were active in creation, so they are also active at the 'undoing of creation'.[28] This interpretation seems to ignore the connection of the spirit and the word to the 'scroll' or the previous prophecies. The second argument is closely linked with the 'scroll'. 'His mouth'[29] and 'his spirit' stand close to each other, and this causes some to take v. 16b as parallel.[30] One disadvantage of this interpretation is that the objects do not correspond to each other. 'His mouth' orders the gathering, and 'his spirit' gathers the creatures. Hillers notices that the inhabitance of desert animals is a typical treaty-curse found often in Near Eastern treaties.[31] If he is right, the 'pouring of libation' as the ceremonial conclusion of a treaty and the denial of the involvement of Yahweh's spirit in the treaty (30.1) has an interesting allusion to the present passage.

It seems that the רוח gives expression to the word by executing it; yet they are not separate actions by different agents. Considering also the fact that both the 'mouth' and its parallel 'spirit' and also 'hand' (v. 17) are organs of a person, it is possible to follow Fohrer's contention that 'Er hat es geboten, er hat sie versammelt' ('He ordered it, he gathered them').[32] This certainly agrees with Johnson's argument of 'extension of personality'[33] or rather 'extension of being'. The close proximity of the 'word' of Yahweh which is uttered by moving air (רוח) and Yahweh's רוח should not, by any means, be overlooked. Montague rightly

---

28. Muilenburg, 'Literary Character', p. 345. Also Stacey, *Isaiah 1–39*, p. 210, 'What Yahweh did then he can undo and reorder his creation as he wishes'.

29. MT has פי 'a mouth [or, my mouth]...', while LXX, 'for the Lord has commanded...' (ὅτι ὁ Κύριος αὐτοῖς ἐνετείλατο); 1QIsa[a] (as well as RSV, NIV) reads פיהו 'his mouth', while *BHS*, after a few MSS, inserts יהוה between פי and הוא, 'the mouth of Yahweh that...'

30. Neve, *The Spirit of God*, p. 83, 'a rephrased statement of the same action'.

31. Hillers, *Treaty-Curses*, pp. 44-45.

32. Fohrer, *Das Buch Jesaja*, II, p. 145.

33. Johnson, *The One and the Many*, p. 16.

observes the close association of word and spirit which is also an important theme of the exilic Isaianic tradition.[34]

However, whether the role of the רוח is extended to that of the inspiration of the 'word' in the 'scroll' is questionable, although some have attempted to make that application.[35] The first attempt usually begins with the expanded interpretation of 'her mate' (16) as if it refers to 'items' in the 'scroll'. Leupold interprets the 'not-missing-of her mate' as referring not only to the various types of desert creatures, but also to the entire sweep of the prophecy.[36] However, it is apparent that 'her mate' in v. 16 must be the same as 'her mate' in v. 15b which refers to a certain creature. The identical suffix allows for only that one antecedent; the referents in v. 15b and v.16 are one and the same. The whole argument is that the land will be utterly destroyed and all these animals will have seized possession of Edom, because Yahweh has commanded and gathered them there (cf. Ezek. 39.17). This is affirmed by v. 17 where the measuring and allocating of the land is to be performed by Yahweh himself. The role of the רוח in this passage is, therefore, to execute what has been uttered by Yahweh, rather than to inspire the uttered or written word.

32.15-20[37]

15 Until the spirit from above is poured upon us,
   and the wilderness becomes a fruitful field,
   and the fruitful field is deemed a forest.
16 Then justice will dwell in the wilderness
      and righteousness abide in the fruitful field.
17 And the effect of righteousness will be peace,
      and the result of righteousness, quietness and trust for ever.

---

34. Montague, *The Holy Spirit*, p. 41; Neve, *The Spirit of God*, p. 84.

35. Neve, *The Spirit of God*, p. 84, 'the spirit inspired in the prophet Yahweh's word of command...Maybe רוח is the breath by which the word of command written in the book of the prophecy is uttered.' Yet see Herbert C. Leupold, *Exposition of Isaiah* (2 vols.; Grand Rapids: Baker Book House, 1968), I, p. 533, who extended the role of רוח to the preservation of the prophetic words.

36. Leupold, *Exposition*, I, p. 533.

37. For this unit division, see Wildberger, *Jesaja 28–39*, p. 1273; Duhm, *Das Buch Jesaja*, p. 206; Kaiser, *Isaiah 13–39*, pp. 331-32. For vv. 9-20 as a unit, see T.K. Cheyne, *Introduction to the Book of Isaiah* (London: Black, 5th edn, 1895), p. 186. But for vv. 12-17 as a unit, see Irwin, *Isaiah 28–33*, p. 119; Kirsten Nielsen, *There Is Hope for a Tree: The Tree as Metaphor in Isaiah* (trans. Christine Crowley and Frederick Crowley; JSOTSup, 65; Sheffield: JSOT Press, 1989), p. 179.

18 My people will abide in a peaceful pasture,
   in secure dwellings,
   and in quiet resting place.
19 And it will hail when the forest falls
   and the city will be utterly laid low.
20 Happy are you who sow beside all waters,
   who let the feet of the ox and the ass range free.

An oracle of judgment (32.9-14) is artificially linked with an oracle of salvation (15-20) with the unusual conjunction עד.[38] The frequent parallelism and a careful wordplay highlight the contrast between the sinful state of the people (9-14) and the salvation and its effect in the restored kingdom (15-20). The word שאננות (complacent) in 32.9 is repeated in 32.18 in a positive sense, and בטחות (feel secure) in 32.11 shares the same root with מבטחים in 32.18.[39] 'The righteousness...the fruitful land' (v. 16) has an ABC//C'B'A' construction. The 'water' reference may be an implicit inclusio with the water imagery of the רוח as being poured out (v. 15).

Not only the date of the passage but also where it begins have been matters of scholarly debate. The abrupt continuation with 'until...',[40] and the sudden occurrence of the first person plural denoting the Judahites, have been observed as evidence for a later date for vv. 15-20.[41] Mowinckel notes that the different meter and עד (until) in its inconsistent relation with עד־עולם (14) are further clues that this passage is not directly connected with the preceding one.[42] Therefore, this passage

38. Some argue that v. 15a concludes the previous passage, and v. 15b begins this oracle (e.g. Stacey, *Isaiah 1–39*, pp. 198-99).

39. Robert B. Chisholm, Jr, 'Wordplay in the Eighth-Century Prophets', *BSac* 144 (1987), pp. 44-52 (46).

40. The problematic עד prompts various suggestions: Duhm, *Das Buch Jesaja*, p. 207; Wildberger, *Jesaja 28–39*, p. 1273; Snaith, *Notes*, p. 73; Watts, *Isaiah 1–33*, p. 415. The presence of two adverbial clauses in vv. 14 and 15 makes the best sense only when vv. 15-20 are separated from vv. 9-14.

41. For a later date, see Kaiser, *Isaiah 13–39*, p. 332; Fohrer, *Das Buch Jesaja*, II, pp. 126-27; Mowinckel, '"Spirit" and the "Word"', p. 202. For Isaianic authorship, see Barth, *Die Jesaja-Worte*, pp. 211-12; Briggs, 'Use of *Ruach*', p. 142; Duhm, *Das Buch Jesaja*, p. 207; Montague, *The Holy Spirit*, p. 40; Skinner, *Isaiah, Chapters I–XXXIX*, p. 258. For Josianic origin, see Clements, *Isaiah 1–39*, p. 263.

42. Mowinckel, 'The "Spirit" and the "Word"', p. 202. Those who argue for Isaianic authorship notice the division between 32.9-14 and 15-20, e.g. Skinner, *Isaiah, Chapters I–XXXIX*, p. 258, assigns vv. 9-14 to the early period of Isaiah's ministry, and vv. 15-20 to a much later time.

has been deliberately interpolated by a later hand to tone down the threat of punishment (vv. 9-14).[43]

The argument seems to fit perfectly with the exilic period as the spirit of penitence prevails.[44] This 'we' realizes that Isaiah's prophecy of judgment has been fulfilled, and the city is going to become 'a joy of wild asses and a pasture of flocks'.[45] The language is found again in 34.1-15 where the desolation of Edom is announced. Now the writer encourages the community to look beyond the distress and expect that the period of humiliation will be replaced by a time of salvation, ushered in by the outpouring of the spirit from on high as the source of all the eschatological blessings.

Although the phrase רוח יהוה is not used here,[46] it is difficult to see 'the spirit from on high' as other than the spirit of God, since the 'high' refers to heaven as the dwelling place of God (2 Sam. 22.17; Ps. 144.7; Jer. 25.30; Isa. 33.5; 38.14; 57.15).[47] Besides, the imparting of divine power is described as 'pouring out', denoting that the spirit is given in its fullness and in great abundance as if God empties out his inexhaustible power on the nation.[48] No opposing force can resist the

43. Mowinckel, '"Spirit" and the "Word"', p. 202, 'the clearest case imaginable of spurious interpolation in a prophetic book'. On the other hand, Kaiser, *13–39*, p. 332, assumes that both vv. 9-14 and this passage are composed by one later hand, assuming a direct relation between them. Youngblood, *The Book of Isaiah*, p. 92, however, dates the passage to around the event in 701 BCE.

44. Edgar W. Conrad, *Reading Isaiah* (Minneapolis: Fortress Press, 1991), p. 180, and Katheryn Pfisterer Darr, *Isaiah's Vision and the Family of God* (Literary Currents in Biblical Interpretation; Louisville, KY: Westminster/John Knox Press, 1994), p. 234, identify the first person plural with the surviving 'we', who are repentant. Seitz, *Isaiah 1–39*, pp. 229-30, places the entire chapter around the Assyrian invasion in 701 BCE.

45. Cf. Mic. 3.12b. For a fine discussion on the development of the רוח of Yahweh during the exilic period, see Richard J. Sklba, '"Until the Spirit from on High is Poured out on Us" (Isa 32.15): Reflections on the Role of the Spirit in the Exile', *CBQ* 46 (1984), pp. 1-17.

46. The use of the masculine gender is unusual. Frederick Bush explains that 'often when the verb stands first, agreement is not followed. Though this usually affects number, it can also be true of gender'; personal comment on the passage, 9 May 1996.

47. Kaiser, *Isaiah 13–39*, p. 333. Cf. Youngblood, *The Book of Isaiah*, p. 93, 'the Messiah came to pour out his Spirit…'

48. Neve, *The Spirit of God*, p. 77. The root ערה means 'to be naked, bare'. LXX and Tg have the simple 'come' whereas in Syr. *ye'or*, 'be roused'. Snaith,

unconditional imparting of the spirit. This verb ערה 'poured out' is used in its positive sense for the first time.[49] This negative usage may be due to the mythical negative impression of 'water' as a chaotic force against creation in the pre-exilic and early exilic periods.[50] However, this old theme is used here in a positive sense, to regenerate the nation and its land.[51] The use of the verb is not intended to indicate the nature of the spirit of God as if it were a substance like water. Nevertheless, the רוח has the function of a stream of water, apparently picking up a relationship introduced in Isa. 30.28 in its judgment context ('his רוח... like flood').

Here the רוח is referred to as the transforming power of the history of Israel, bringing an end to the suffering of Israel in history. The 'pouring out' of the spirit is seen as the sign of the beginning of the new age of salvation and also a characteristic of the new age. The primary meaning of the רוח is clearly retained here as a divine force intimately linked with life (cf. Ps. 104.29-30; Isa. 31.3). The רוח יהוה is the only giver of life and bestows new life in every realm of the restored nation. As a consequence of the lavishing 'pouring out' of רוח, nature is to be renewed not only in fertility, but through transformation. Fruitfulness and miraculous increase are a direct contrast to the failure of harvest (32.10) and total desolation of the land (vv. 13-14). The agricultural realism of the hope is depicted in v. 20, indicating that the age of salvation is a time of fruitfulness. This physical or material fruitfulness is closely linked with the righteousness of people in the spiritual realm as is common in the Old Testament (cf. Ps. 72; Isa. 11.1-9).[52] It should be observed that the spirit is not poured upon nature, but upon 'us'. The consequences rather point to the very character of God, and thus the spirit indicates the extension of God's being. The effect of righteousness is described by Kaiser as follows:

Notes, p. 73, suggests that this translation is under the influence of Vg and, possibly, derives from the use of the root in Isa. 53.12 and Ps. 141.8.

49. This usage is a direct contrast to 29.10, where the verb refers to the sending of the spirit of deep sleep, Montague, *The Holy Spirit*, p. 40.

50. Neve, *The Spirit of God*, p. 76.

51. Montague, *The Holy Spirit*, p. 40.

52. The construct singular form of מעשה means 'work' but here more specifically 'effect of working'. Lindblom, *Prophecy in Ancient Israel*, p. 391, writes 'according to ancient Hebrew thought, moral perfection is always accompanied by שלום in the material as well as the spiritual sense'.

...free, and untroubled existence and unhindered progress of men,
animal and fields in all embracing peace and prosperity, *šālōm*, and
secondly in the quiet confidence of men toward their God (cf. 30.15) and
security in the relationship between men and other men, men and
animals, and animals and other animals (cf. Ezek. 34.25ff; Deut. 33.28
and Isa. 11.1-9).[53]

The nation abiding in a peaceful habitation (v. 18, cf. Hos. 2.18b)[54] is
a direct contrast to the judgment pronounced on Jerusalem, 'the joyful
city' (14). The result of the national renewal gives an impression of the
return of paradise with justice, righteousness, peace, quietness and trust
forever. The two subsequent verses reinforce this idea. Although the
precise meaning cannot be drawn with full certainty, v. 19 seems to
refer to Yahweh's mighty theophany of judgment upon the enemy army
and the city, the source of all hostility towards the people of God and
the city of God (cf. 25.1-5; 27.10).[55] Verse 20 offers another marvelous
picture of the coming age. Water will be so abundant that not only will
seed grow in profusion (cf. 30.23-24), but also the draught animals will
not be fed in their stalls but will be allowed to walk across the fields
and pasture there. The picture is certainly beyond the idea of 30.24.
This second creation happens only when the spirit is 'poured out'.

Montague observed that this consequence is the first clear and positive association of the spirit of God with the new ethical life that is part

53. Kaiser, *Isaiah 13–39*, p. 335.

54. The change of the person ('my people') causes Watts, *Isaiah 1–33*, p. 417,
to emend to 'people' without much textual support. Irwin, *Isaiah 28–33*, p. 133,
tries to solve the difficulty by beginning a new unit with v. 18, yet the intimate flow
of the theme makes this less convincing. However, an enigmatic change of person
can also be seen elsewhere (e.g. Isa. 53).

55. וברד is a denominative of ברד in MT as in RV. Many either repoint as a
noun, 'and [there will be] hail in the downfall of the forest', or emend to וירד, 'and
down shall come with a downfall...' as in Syr. and Tg, followed by Wildberger,
Jesaja 28–39, p. 1274, and BHS. Irwin, *Isaiah 28–33*, p. 134, derives ברד from the
Ugaritic root *brd*, 'to cut, to divide' and translates 'with an ax'. Watts, *Isaiah 1–33*,
p. 416, however, rules out the option and retains the repetition of the same root as
'an artistic device contrasting the following pair'. For other options, see J. Reider,
'Contributions to the Scriptural Text', *HUCA* 24 (1952–53), pp. 85-106 (88); G.R.
Driver, 'Isaiah I–XXXIX: Textual and Linguistic Problems', *JSS* 13 (1968), pp. 36-
57 (52); Kaiser, *Isaiah 13–39*, p. 336; NEB, 'It will be cool on the slopes of the
forest then, and cities shall lie peaceful in the plain'. Nielsen, *There Is Hope for a
Tree*, p. 180, views the falling forest as an internal purification as a condition for
the time of salvation.

of the coming salvation.[56] This is not the first occurence of an ethicized understanding of רוח, but in the previous cases, they are used in judgment contexts (Mic. 3.8).

The argument for the presence of human officers and ministers in the coming age is discussed by several scholars. Briggs in fact equates the 'pouring out' of the spirit with the endowment of the people with 'the gifts of government' so that justice and righteousness shall prevail.[57] He certainly reads 32.1-8 into the present passage, where the former presupposes pre-exilic social injustice (32.6-7), namely taking advantage of the powerless. The picture of this future age has more emphasis on a king and rulers (v. 1). A similar expression is found in 1.26-27 that God will restore Jerusalem's judges as at the first and her counselors as in the beginning, the reference is to the idealized Davidic period.[58] However, in vv. 15-20 there is no allusion to any monarchical implication. 'Righteousness' in the field replaces a 'king' who reigns in righteousness (v. 1) and 'justice' in the desert for 'rulers' who rule with justice (v. 1). In fact, the kingly work bringing about security and peace, the elimination of enemies as well as initiating justice and righteousness are all attributed directly to the רוח. There is no human agent present. This points to the antimonarchical attitude in the exilic period as well as to the expectation of Yahweh's direct rulership. If a mediator is present, he is a lofty figure, the 'Servant'. Beyond that, the democratization of the impartation of the spirit is unmistakable.

44.1-5
1   But now hear, Jacob my servant,
        and Israel whom I have chosen.
2   Thus says Yahweh, your maker,
        and your shaper from the womb will help you.
    Fear not, my servant Jacob,
        and Jeshurun, whom I have chosen.
3   For I will pour water on a thirsty land,
        and streams on a dry place.
    I will pour my spirit on your seed,
        and my blessing on your offspring.
4   They shall spring up between blades of grass,
        and like willows by streams of water.

56. Montague, *The Holy Spirit*, p. 40.
57. Briggs, 'Use of *Ruach*', p. 141.
58. Roberts, 'The Divine King and the Human Community', p. 133.

5   This one will say, 'I belong to Yahweh',
        and the other will call out, 'In the name of Jacob',
        and still the other will write on his hand, 'Belong to Yahweh',
        and will entitle himself by the name 'Israel'.

This oracle of salvation forms a sharp contrast with its previous passage by the use of 'but now'. In 43.22-28, the old Jacob/Israel is described as having been rejected as the unfaithful servant, but now in the consolidation message, Jacob is called 'my servant' and 'my chosen'. These two designations show God's sovereign act and gracious will as the basis for the renewal. In that light, the 'servant' refers to the end which Yahweh seeks to achieve by means of Israel's election.[59] God's sovereign act is further shown in two verbs of creation, namely, to 'form' and to 'shape'.[60] It takes God's one-sided creating activity for Israel to be newly born as the servant of Yahweh. This emphasis of creation is in the framework of the election tradition which gives the prophet the assurance of future transformation. Snaith identifies this new Jacob/Israel with the wider group of exiles, that is, the group which elsewhere is the 'we' that have sinned (42.24; 53.46).[61] The 'fear not' cry introduces an urgency that a new situation has come about as the former situation described in 43.22-28 was coming to an end. For the exilic Isaianic tradition, judgment is a prelude of coming salvation. Judgment comes only to cleanse the guilt of the people (43.25), for the ultimate goal of God in his economy is always salvation.

To this new servant Jacob/Israel, or Jeshurun, an unprecedented outpouring of blessing is promised. It is reasonable to say that here the desert is Israel in its barrenness and hopelessness,[62] and does not designate the desert between Babylon and Palestine, which would imply a second exodus. The outpouring of 'my רוח' or 'water' on the thirsty land certainly means more than what Duhm sees, that Cyrus is about to let a handful of exiles return from Babylon to Jerusalem. Smart appears

59. Westermann, *Isaiah 40–66*, p. 135.

60. The two verbs are in fact found in the creation story in Gen. 2.

61. Norman H. Snaith, 'The Servant of the Lord in Deutero-Isaiah', in H.H. Rowley (ed.), *Studies in Old Testament Prophecy Presented to Professor Theodore H. Robinson by the Society for Old Testament Study on his Sixty-Fifth Birthday* (Edinburgh: T. & T. Clark, 1950), pp. 187-200 (196).

62. Smart, *History and Theology in Second Isaiah*, p. 110; Hanson, *Isaiah 40–66*, pp. 82-83.

to be correct in seeing beyond this dekerygmatization of the message. The outpouring of the spirit (cf. 42.1) is God's coming (40.3-5) to transform Israel as the eschatological consummation at the end of the age.[63] It is more than the conferring of certain spiritual benefits upon Israel. Rather, it is the manifestation of Yahweh's רוח as the extension of Yahweh's very personality (e.g. Ps. 139.7; 143.10; Isa. 63.11, 14; Ezek. 1.12, 20, 21; 10.17; Hag. 2.4-5).[64] It is only in this manifestation that Israel becomes capable of producing the far-reaching effect described in Isa. 44.4 and 5.

However, the specific effect of the outpouring of the spirit shows that here the prophet primarily refers to the power of life as a stream in the desert.[65] Such imagery is frequent in Isa. 32.15; Ps. 104.30; Zech. 12.10 and Ezekiel 37, where the dry bones are raised by the life-giving רוח יהוה. Here, a close association of the רוח with water is evident.[66] In fact, 'water/stream' is the source of vitality and life. In v. 3cd 'spirit' is evidently in the parallel position with 'blessing'[67] and they are promised to the future generation. This also makes it clear that the prophet does not here refer to the new exodus which he describes as to be experienced by this generation. Nor does he refer to the prophetic spirit to restore Israel's priestly role as Wilson contends.[68] Rather, the creation language reinforces the life-giving effect of the spirit.[69] This direct association of the רוח//blessing and water//stream is more conclusive than the indirect implication in 32.15. This perhaps indicates that the Israelites are beginning to overcome the negative impression of water found early in Israelite tradition (e.g. Hos. 5.10) and in the Babylonian

---

63. Smart, *History and Theology*, p. 110. Perdue, *Wisdom and Creation*, p. 138, argues that the sending of rain refers to Yahweh's 'providential rule of the natural order'. However, the effect goes beyond the natural realm in this passage.

64. Johnson, *Vitality of the Individual*, p. 33.

65. 'The energy of life', according to Briggs, 'Use of *Ruach*', p. 144; 'Gotteskraft die das physische Leben schafft', P. Volz, *Jesaia: 2. Hälfte, Kap. 40–66* (KAT, 9; Leipzig: Deichertsche, 1932), p. 5, and *idem*, *Der Geist Gottes*, p. 76; or 'die lebenspendende Kraft', Fohrer, *Das Buch Jesaja*, III, p. 73.

66. Montague, *The Holy Spirit*, p. 51; North, *Second Isaiah*, p. 131.

67. Skinner, *Isaiah, Chapters XL–LXVI*, pp. 51-52.

68. Andrew Wilson, *The Nations in Deutero-Isaiah: A Study on Composition and Structure* (Lewiston, NY: Edwin Mellen Press, 1986), p. 85.

69. Koch, *Der Geist Gottes*, p. 121, identifies it with the 'göttlichen *Lebensodem*, der von Jahweh ausgeht, den Menschen zum Leben erweckt und am Leben erhält'.

creation myth. That this is a rather late development is attested by a group of exilic and postexilic רוח passages such as Isa. 42.5; 57.16; Ezek. 37.1-14; Zech. 12.1; Job 27.3; 34.1; Ps. 146.4. Abundance and unlimitedness of the 'emptying out' from the opened window of heaven (cf. Mal. 3.10) is a reflection of the verb, 'pour out'.[70] And 'your seed... your offspring' is another indication of the everlasting nature of the blessing.

The result of the outpouring of the רוח יהוה is described in vv. 4 and 5 in two aspects. Verse 4 obviously means the increase of the people of Yahweh in number, since the antecedent of 'they' (v. 4) is only the descendants and offspring in v. 3. To Israel, which has been faithless and has become few in the exile as expressed by being dry and thirsty, is promised fertility through the power of the spirit. Therefore, it does not refer to vegetation but people.[71] The image of the rapidly growing poplar trees with the intense greenness of its leaves which are found along the 'water courses' (or perhaps artificial irrigation canals fed by a river, cf. Ps. 46.4; Prov. 21.1)[72] should mean more than just numerical growth. The effect in the following verse assumes something of a qualitative aspect, namely influence.[73] However, unlike in 32.15 where the רוח יהוה is closely connected with physical and ethical aspects, here the רוח יהוה has no spiritual force.[74]

The second result of the outpouring of the spirit described in v. 5 has generated two different opinions concerning the identification of the speaker in v. 5. One group sees the speaker as a group of Israelites, that is the reclamation of defaulting Judahites. Torrey argues that in 48.1 and 2, the prophet begins an invective against the faithless sons of Jacob by saying that they have no right to the names of Yahweh and Zion.[75] Snaith, however, interprets this verse with his understanding of Second Isaiah as a strong nationalist, and reaches the same conclusion.[76]

---

70. North, *Second Isaiah*, p. 133.

71. Holland Jones, 'How I Would Use Messianic Prophecy in Advent', *CurTM* 9.6 (1982), pp. 349-59 (357).

72. North, *Second Isaiah*, p. 133.

73. North, *Second Isaiah*, p. 132. Torrey, *The Second Isaiah*, p. 344, contends that 'stream in the desert' always and everywhere must mean spiritual blessings for chosen people. This proves incorrect in the present context.

74. Volz, *Jesaia*, p. 5.

75. Torrey, *Second Isaiah*, p. 433.

76. Norman H. Snaith, 'Isaiah 40–66: A Study of the Teaching of the Second Isaiah and its Consequences', in *Studies on the Second Part of the Book of Isaiah*

For him the speakers in v. 5 are the descendants mentioned in v. 3 and they are Israelites by birth. Watts views here a heightened enthusiasm among the exiles to resist the force of assimilation, such as using Babylonian names, and to belong to Yahweh.[77] This interpretation, however, faces an irreconcilable problem with the second and fourth members of the verse. It is certainly unnatural for any Israelite born to have a need to call himself Jacob, or to add the name Israel to his own. The speakers must be non-Israelites who witness the work of the life-giving spirit within Israel and are convinced by the absoluteness of Yahweh and then turn to him.[78] Even the abrupt connection between vv. 4 and 5 favors this interpretation, since it is unlikely for 'one' or 'another' (v. 5) to be identified with 'they' (v. 4). Again one does not have to see the prophet as a universalist to be able to identify the speakers as proselytes.[79] The real motif here is not necessarily the salvation or conversion of foreigners, but the glorious manifestation of the restored nation Israel among the other nations. The miracle of growth and Yahweh's presence among his people become so evident that those who witness this voluntarily come under the rule of Yahweh. In that sense the prophet is still a nationalist.

This change is described as an individual act rather than any form of mass conversion. They are to come in by ones and twos and indeed the earliest record of this kind is found in Third Isaiah (56.3-8).[80] The ancient world does not have any supra-national or supra-racial faith (cf. 1 Sam. 26.19), as a person's religion is determined by birth. This could

(VTSup, 14; Leiden: E.J. Brill, 1967), pp. 137-264 (184).

77. Watts, *Isaiah 34–66*, p. 144. Also several writers share the nationalistic interpretation, e.g. Motyer, *The Prophecy of Isaiah*, p. 342; Youngblood, *The Book of Isaiah*, p. 117; Wolfgang Roth, *Isaiah* (Knox Preaching Guides; Atlanta: John Knox Press, 1988), pp. 132-33.

78. Among many, Westermann, *Isaiah 40–66*, p. 138; Montague, *The Holy Spirit*, p. 51; Neve, *The Spirit of God*, p. 77; Skinner, *Isaiah, Chapters XL–LXVI*, pp. 52-53; North, *Second Isaiah*, p. 133; Muilenburg, 'Isaiah, Chapters 40–66', p. 503.

79. The rigid interpretation of a universalistic Second Isaiah with the 'proselytes' is the counterpart of a nationalistic Second Isaiah with the 'defaulting Jews', evidenced in Smart, *History and Theology*, p. 113. However, C. Stuhlmüller, *Creative Redemption in Deutero-Isaiah* (AnBib, 43; Rome: Pontifical Biblical Institute, 1970), p. 129 n. 448 and pp. 130-31, identifies the speakers with Gentile proselytes to whom an invitation is extended to come to Jerusalem and worship in the temple.

80. North, *Second Isaiah*, p. 134.

necessitate that the proselytes take a decisive step accompanied by some outward manifestation such as tattooing their hands ליהוה as if a kettle is engraved with למלך (belong to the king) to designate owner-ship (1 Kgs 20.41; Ezek. 9.4; cf. Rev. 7.3; 13.16).[81] The adding of a surname is described as another outward manifestation of their conver-sion.[82] The simple meaning is that the converts will testify by word and other outward manifestations.

In this passage, again the democratizing trend of the 'outpouring' of the רוח יהוה is evident. There is no mediator between Yahweh and the people, the recipients of the רוח. The unconditional, universal and end-less endowment characterizes the future age of salvation which is cer-tainly beyond the second exodus. The close association of the רוח with the image of water and the increase of Israel in number and influence is the suitable picture of its result. However, the inclusion of the Gentile proselytes is a striking significance. As Westermann describes, this represents the breakthrough to a new understanding of the chosen peo-ple as the community which confesses Yahweh.[83]

42.1-4
1   Behold my servant whom I confirm,
        my chosen one in whom my soul delights;
    I have put my spirit on him.
        He extends (the) judgment to the nations.
2   He does not shout nor lift (his voice).
        He does not let his voice be heard in the street.
3   He does not shatter a bruised reed,
        nor put out a flickering wick.
        (Yet) truly he does extend (the) judgment.
4   He does not fail. Nor is he discouraged
        until he establishes (the) justice in the land;
        and coastlands wait for his instruction.

This passage has been much discussed ever since Duhm identified 42.1-4 as the first Servant Song of four which he sees as independent

81. Skinner, *Isaiah, Chapters XL–LXVI*, p. 52, says that tattooing is a civil as well as a religious custom (Lev. 19.28; Ezek. 9.4; Gal. 6.17); and see North, *Second Isaiah*, p. 133. Hanson, *Isaiah 40–66*, pp. 82-83, views both interpretations as viable.
82. An Arabic custom in relation to Arabic *limua*, see North, *Second Isaiah*, p. 133.
83. Westermann, *Isaiah 40–66*, p. 137.

from the 'main body of Second Isaiah'.[84] However, the passage will be discussed mostly in its own right.[85]

In this poem,[86] the Servant is introduced by Yahweh (as in the fourth song, but in the second and third, the Servant is speaking),[87] as he already exists and has been endowed with the רוח. And this endowment has a definite purpose for the future. The Servant is to bring forth משפט ('justice' or 'judgment') to the nations.

The first verse describes the designation of the Servant (1a, b), his equipment (1c) and his mission (1d). With the first two designations, 'my Servant' and 'my chosen', Yahweh introduces his Servant in the same manner as he does Jacob/Israel elsewhere (41.8, 9). With the frequent use of the first person singular pronoun ('I', 'my'), one can easily detect the election motif. In fact, Rowley finds a close parallel between language used in v. 1 for the Servant and that used for Israel

84. Duhm, *Das Buch Jesaja*, p. 227; contra, Muilenburg, 'Isaiah, Chapters 40–66', p. 465, Smart, *History and Theology*, p. 80; and others, who consider that there are no separate 'Servant Songs' at all.

85. For a detailed discussion of various positions on the subject, see Christopher R. North, *The Suffering Servant in Deutero-Isaiah: An Historical and Critical Study* (Oxford: Oxford University Press, 1948), especially pp. 192-219; Snaith, 'Servant of the Lord', pp. 187-200; H.H. Rowley, *The Servant of the Lord and Other Essays on the Old Testament* (London: Lutterworth, 1952), pp. 1-88; J. Lindblom, *The Servant Songs in Deutero-Isaiah: A New Attempt to Solve an Old Problem* (Lund: C.W.K. Gleerup, 1951), pp. 46-51, 102-104; K. Jeppesen, 'Mother Zion, Father Servant: A Reading of Isaiah 49–55', in Heather A. McKay and David J.A. Clines (eds.), *Of Prophets' Visions and the Wisdom of Sages: Essays in Honour of R. Norman Whybray on his Seventieth Birthday* (JSOTSup, 162; Sheffield: JSOT Press, 1993), pp. 109-25. For a survey, see C.G. Kruse, 'The Servant Songs: Interpretive Trends since C.R. North', *Studia Biblica et Theologica* 8 (1978), pp. 3-18. For an updated summary, see G.P. Hugenberger, 'The Servant of the Lord in the "Servant Songs" of Isaiah: A Second Moses Figure', in Philip E. Satterthwaite, Richard S. Hess and Gordon J. Wenham (eds.), *The Lord's Anointed: Interpretation of Old Testament Messianic Texts* (Carlisle: Paternoster Press; Grand Rapids: Baker Book House, 1995), pp. 105-40 (106-19).

86. There are different views on the division of the unit. Many take 42.1-4 and 5-9 as different units; for the different addressees and different use of רוח, see, e.g., Snaith, 'Isaiah 40–66', p. 167; for 42.1-7 as a unit, Ringgren, *The Messiah*, p. 40; Clifford, 'Function of Idol Passages', p. 452; and for 41.1–42.4 as a single poem, see Muilenburg, 'Isaiah, Chapters 40–66', p. 447-48.

87. Karl Elliger, *Deuterojesaja*. I. *Jesaja 40,1–45,7* (BKAT, 11.1; Neukirchen–Vluyn: Neukirchener Verlag, 1978), p. 199, identifies the scene as that of the heavenly 'Thronversammlung'.

elsewhere. For instance, 'chosen' is also found in reference to Jacob/ Israel in 41.8; 'uphold' in 41.10; and רוח in 44.3.[88] Based on this observation, he concludes that at least in the first Song, the Servant is Israel in a collective sense as in the rest of Second Isaiah (41.8-9; 42.19; 43.10; 44.1, 2, 21, 26; 45.4; 48.20).[89] However, for the second song Rowley modifies the Servant into the purified Israel as a future figure.[90] This implies that he demonstrates a certain degree of fluidity in the identification of the Servant throughout the Songs.

On the contrary, many contend that the Servant is an individual.[91]

88. Rowley, *The Servant of the Lord*, p. 49; also Ralph Marcus, 'The "Plain Meaning" of Isaiah 42.1-4', *HTR* 30 (1937), pp. 249-59 (250), 'the Servant concept here is closest to that found in the whole of Second Isaiah'; P.A.H. de Boer, 'Second-Isaiah's Message', *OTS* 11 (1956), pp. 1-126 (80); North, *Suffering Servant in Deutero-Isaiah*, p. 107; Ralph W. Klein, *Israel in Exile: A Theological Interpretation* (Philadelphia: Fortress Press, 1979), p. 119; Jörg Jeremias, '*Mišpaṭ* im erstern Gottesknechtlied (Jes xlii.1-4)', *VT* 22 (1972), pp. 31-42 (40). For Snaith, 'Isaiah 40–66', pp. 170, 173, the first batch of exiles, which was later expanded to include all the exiles. W.E. Barnes, 'Cyrus the "Servant of Jehovah" Isaiah xlii, 1-4(7)', *JTS* 32 (1931), pp. 32-39 (34) sees the first song as heterogeneous from other songs because of the close connection with the rest of Second Isaiah.

89. Collective interpretation is first of all found in H. Wheeler Robinson, *The Cross in the Old Testament* (London: SCM Press, 1955), p. 69; *idem*, *Corporate Personality in Ancient Israel* (Philadelphia: Fortress Press, rev. edn, 1980), especially pp. 37-41; O. Eissfeldt, 'The Ebed-Jahwe in Isaiah xl-lv. in the Light of the Individual, the Ideal and the Real', *ExpTim* 44 (1932–33), pp. 261-68 (266). LXX obviously assumes this identity by adding Ἰακωβ and Ἰσραηλ to the MT reading of v. 1.

90. Robinson, *The Cross*, pp. 50-51; Ellen F. Davis, 'A Strategy of Delayed Comprehension: Isaiah liv 15', *VT* 40 (1990), pp. 217-21 (219); Ann Johnston, 'A Prophetic Vision of an Alternative Community: A Reading of Isaiah 40–55', in Lewis M. Hopfe (ed.), *Uncovering Ancient Stones: Essays in Memory of H. Neil Richardson* (Winona Lake, IN: Eisenbrauns, 1994), pp. 31-40 (33). Anyone subscribing to the collective interpretation, or Israel, has to deal with the second song, one way or the other, where the Servant is described as having a mission to Israel. Some treat ישׂראל as a secondary gloss, e.g. Walther Zimmerli, 'The עֶבֶד יהוה in the OT', *TDNT*, V, pp. 656-77 (666-67). Hanson, *Isaiah 40-66*, pp. 41-44, 223-24, argues that the identity of the Servant is intentionally withheld for ambiguity and that the Servant is to serve as a model for both the individual and the community that are called by Yahweh. Leslie C. Allen, in a conversation (1993), expressed a similar function of the Servant figure.

91. Jeppesen, 'Mother Zion, Father Servant', p. 112; H.-J. Hermisson, 'Israel und der Gottesknecht bei Deuterojesaja', *ZTK* 70 (1982), pp. 1-24.

Mowinckel argues that in Second Isaiah, including the present passage, the Servant is distinguished from Israel in many ways. He particularly points out that Israel is always the passive servant while the Servant is active in accomplishing his mission.[92] It is not easy to draw an accurate picture of the Servant. A servant, however, does not refer to a slave, although de Boer's description of Jacob after the disaster appears attractive as the fate of a servant sold to a foreigner.[93] Rather, the Servant here is, as throughout the Old Testament, a lofty figure. Muilenburg sees that the designation 'my Servant' is derived from court language where the official of the king was known as his servant whose function is to make known the king's judicial decision.[94] In the same sense, Yahweh is the king of Israel and Israel is his servant in Second Isaiah. There is also another major interpretation that is held: it is conceivable that from the beginning the identity of the Servant has been intended to be vague. According to Cook, it is as foolish to ask 'Who is the Servant' as to ask 'Who is the Prodigal Son?'[95] At the same time, it is equally valid to argue that the Servant is obviously known to the hearers during the exile.

Here, the Servant has already been present and has been endowed with the spirit of Yahweh. No such parallel can be found elsewhere, except with a future reference (32.15; 44.3). The nature of God's רוח upon the Servant is intimately related to the mission of the Servant and his figure, whether he is a prophet or a king. Certain features of the endowment with the divine רוח can be singled out regardless of the identity of the Servant. The spirit of God is to inspire the Servant and enable him to accomplish his mission effectively, thereby bringing forth משפט. Although one can perceive the authenticating function of

92. Mowinckel, *He That Cometh*, p. 207.
93. De Boer, 'Counselor', pp. 44-45.
94. Muilenburg, 'Isaiah, Chapters 40-66', p. 464.
95. S.A. Cook, 'The Prophets of Israel', in S.A. Cook *et al.* (eds.), *Cambridge Ancient History* (3 vols.; Cambridge: Cambridge University Press, 1970-), III, pp. 458-99 (492). Harold Schweizer, 'Praedikationen und Leerstellen im 1. Gottes-knechtslied (Jes 42.1-4)', *BZ* 26 (1982), pp. 251-58, also argues that the intentional vagueness is seen as a means of involving the hearer in the account by forcing him or her to fill in what is missing. A similar argument for intentional ambiguity is given by Hans M. Barstad, 'The Future of the "Servant Songs": Some Reflections on the Relationship of Biblical Scholarship to its Own Tradition', in Samuel E. Balentine and John Barton (eds.), *Language, Theology, and the Bible: Essays in Honour of James Barr* (Oxford: Clarendon Press, 1994), pp. 261-70 (262-68).

the spirit, the emphasis is strongly related to the mission. The endowment of a selected leader, king, prophet or judge with the spirit is an old
tradition found in early literature (e.g. 2 Kgs 2.9). In this sense the
present passage is a continuation of the charismatic work of the יהוה
רוח.[96] North tries to see a connection between here and Isa. 11.2 where
the spirit of Yahweh is defined in various aspects.[97]

Another observation is that in this text the רוח יהוה is described as
'resting' upon the Servant, which seems to indicate a permanent endowment. This phenomenon is found exclusively among the kings (1 Sam.
16.13), and not among the prophets or judges. This, however, is not a
decisive support for the conclusion that the Servant is a kingly figure.
Here the main purpose is rather to show the support and guidance of
Yahweh to the Servant. It implies the intimacy of his relation with God,
the identity of the purpose, and the presence of God's power in him.[98]
This is to ensure the fulfillment of the mission in spite of difficulties the
Servant will eventually face as described in the following verses.

משפט, that is the mission of the Servant, is also tied up with the figure
of the Servant. The three occurrences of the term affirm that the sole
mission of the Servant is the establishment of משפט. As an oversimpli-
fication, it seems that those who argue for the kingly figure tend to see
משפט in its primary meaning which is 'justice' or 'judgment'.[99] Watts
identifies the Servant with a heavenly messenger who will bring the
court decisions to the nations.[100] By establishing the 'verdict' in the
nations, the mission of the Servant seems that of a royal figure. On the
other hand, those who see the Servant in the prophetic image argue that
the משפט here means 'right religion'.[101] That the coastlands wait for the
'instruction' (תורה) reinforces this interpretation.

Furthermore, those who perceive the mission of the Servant as universal tend to interpret the term as the latter, while those who see it as

96. Neve, *The Spirit of God*, p. 84. Hanson, *Isaiah 55–66*, p. 44, defines the
spirit as 'the power and wisdom of God' to fulfill a God-given task. However,
Wilson, *The Nations in Deutero-Isaiah*, p. 55, identifies this as 'his [God's] prophetic spirit'.

97. North, *Isaiah 40–55*, p. 61.

98. Smart, *History and Theology*, p. 83.

99. E.g. Ringgren, *The Messiah*, p. 66; Lindblom, *Servant Songs in Deutero-
Isaiah*, pp. 16-18.

100. Watts, *Isaiah 34–66*, p. 119.

101. E.g. Snaith, 'Servant of the Lord', p. 193; Mowinckel, *He That Cometh*,
p. 189.

national are inclined to understand the term as the former.[102] In addition, those who see the passage as the conclusion of the second trial scene insist that the term must have the judicial meaning, especially against the nations and their gods who oppress Israel.[103]

One clue found in the structure of the passage is the parallelism of משפט with תורה (v. 4). Although in all the five instances where תורה occur in the exilic Isaianic tradition, the exact significance is not easily determined, and Jensen assumes that in all these cases, the probable usage is in its broad sense, meaning 'instruction' or 'revelation'.[104] Gottwald also prefers the broad definition as 'the teaching and arbitration of God that will extend to the nations from Israel (Isa. 2.3)'.[105] This is in contrast to the narrow use of the term which refers to the law of Israel. This indicates that the mission of the Servant is mainly religious rather than political in nature and is beyond the boundary of the Israelite religion. Also יוציא (bring out), the verb used with the משפט, almost certainly means 'bring forth' (from the mouth), that is to speak, as in Jer. 15.19; Job 8.10; Prov. 10.8.[106] This means something is preached (cf. 42.2), rather than the executing or the issuing of a decree. However, v. 3 seems to allude to more than just preaching. Therefore, the משפט must have something to do with the principle of the universal kingdom of God, or the order willed by God. This certainly gives preference to the broader interpretation of the משפט. It is frequently quoted that the משפט here is parallel with the Arabic *din* which has the same wide latitude of meaning as ὁδός ('way') in the New Testament.[107]

Up to this point, the discussion seems to lead us to the prophetic role of the Servant rather than to the kingly one. However, for the kingly figure, equally strong arguments have been presented by a large number

---

102. A LXX MS (cI) tends to see the mission as national, adding to v. 3 τὴν (τῶν) Ἰουδαίων ἀσθένειαν 'of Judah's weakness'.

103. W.A.M. Beuken, '*Mišpaṭ*: The First Servant Song and its Context', *VT* 22 (1972), pp. 1-30 (6).

104. Jensen, *Use of* tôrâ *by Isaiah*, p. 23; also McKenzie, *Second Isaiah*, pp. 36-38; Rowley, *The Servant of the Lord*, p. 15.

105. Gottwald, *All the Kingdoms*, p. 236. Also Hanson, *Isaiah 40–66*, p. 42.

106. North, *Suffering Servant in Deutero-Isaiah*, p. 141.

107. North, *Suffering Servant in Deutero-Isaiah*, p. 141; Snaith, 'The Servant of the Lord', p. 193; Muilenburg, 'Isaiah, Chapters 40–66', p. 464; H.W. Hertzberg, 'Die Entwicklung des Begriffes *mšpṭ* im AT', *ZAW* 41 (1923), pp. 16-76 (41); J.P.M. van der Plög, '*Šapaṭ* et *Mišpaṭ*', *OTS* 2 (1943), pp. 144-55 (155); Koch, 'Der Gottesgeist und der Messias', p. 387.

of scholars. Pedersen argues that the endowment mode of the רוח יהוה
directly points to the kingly figure. Yahweh's spirit does not work in
the king with ecstatic violence on particular occasions. The endowment
is present in him as a constant possession, because he is Yahweh's
anointed and Yahweh's son.[108] North also supports the permanent
endowment of the spirit as an evidence of the kingly figure, from the
fact that even the broken Saul is still the anointed of Yahweh.[109]
Ringgren's argument is based on the royal ideology of the ancient Near
East. For instance, although there is no instance in Israel of the king
being elected and called by God, this idea, according to him, belongs to
a common idea in the ancient world. He also notes that any atoning
activity, especially suffering or even death as ideally described in Isaiah
53 and perhaps in 42.4, is the king's role, and not the prophet's. In fact,
Ringgren sees a clear link between the songs and the enthronement
psalms.[110] Westermann also notes that the introductory announcement
of the Servant in v. 1 is more akin to that of the political leader, that is,
the judges (e.g. Gideon in Judg. 6) or the king (Saul in 1 Sam. 9.15-17;
David in 1 Sam. 16).[111] It is true that the call of a prophet is strictly
between God and the prophet, while that of a king requires the presence
of others who witness it. Barnes carries it a step further; for him, this
song is a 'Cyrus Song', and in it he sees the introduction of a con-
queror. Particularly in v. 3, he finds a sure description of Cyrus's com-
passionate policies toward Israel and the gentile nations. Naturally, the
משפט here is perceived as a political or juridical act carried out by
Cyrus.[112] This interpretation is, however, severely weakened by two
considerations. First, it is hard to see that Cyrus teaches תורה to the
coastlands. Secondly, it is also difficult to believe that v. 4ab, the
description of suffering, is intended to refer to any part of Cyrus's
career.

The strongest argument in favor of the prophetic figure is that the

108. Pedersen, *Israel, Its Life and Culture*, III–IV, pp. 52, 56, 86.

109. North, 'Hebrew Kingship', p. 16.

110. Ringgren, *The Messiah*, pp. 39-42.

111. Westermann, *Isaiah 40–66*, pp. 93-94.

112. Barnes, 'Cyrus', p. 35. Also Antti Laato, *The Servant of YHWH and Cyrus: A Reinterpretation of the Exilic Messianic Programme in Isaiah 40–55* (ConBOT, 35; Stockholm: Almqvist & Wiksell, 1992), p. 267, argues that the appointment of the Servant is given in 'the form of a YHWH prophecy using terminology derived from the royal ideology', hence, the text is a royal poem.

Servant is a mediator between God and people through the ministry of the word. In particular, the teaching of the תורה is never done by a king, but by either prophets or priests. Furthermore, the religious nature of the mission itself points to this figure. The prophet is also endowed with Yahweh's spirit, called from his mother's womb (cf. 49.2; Jer. 1.5) and called a servant (Isa. 20.3; 44.26; 2 Kgs 9.7; Jer. 7.25; 25.4; 26.5; 29.19; 35.15; Amos 3.7, etc.). The suffering of the Servant can be more easily countenanced with the prophetic picture rather than with the kingly one.

However, every objective observer would agree that neither of these two figures fits perfectly in the description of the Servant. Although many agree that he seems to be more a prophet than a king, it is likely that the writer combines something of the functions of both and he is not to be placed in either category to the exclusion of the other.[113] Even his mission cannot be explained in terms of one figure to the exclusion of the other. Although the Servant seems to be a new ideal of prophecy, he also possesses certain, but not decisive, features of a king, or rather of a judge. Samuel or Moses, or even Abraham may fall in this category as he demonstrates both prophetic and political leadership, as the ruler of Israel or a clan. The open claim for the endowment of God's spirit is a feature that survives in the royal tradition (cf. Isa. 11.1-5). The less royal feature for the future king was also observed in ch. 11. The Servant, then at least in this passage, is an agent of God along the royal tradition, but his non-royal and more prophet-like work is further developed.

In this passage the effect of the resting of the רוח יהוה upon the Servant becomes clearer. Just as the old leaders experienced, the presence of God's spirit serves two traditional functions: authentication and equipment. Whoever the Servant may be, his closeness is reinforced with the endowment of the spirit. However, unlike the ancient leaders for whom God needed to show to the human world their election into leadership, the Servant is introduced by God himself. Hence, he does not require any authenticating measure. At the same time, unlike the ancient heroes who demonstrate superhuman ability as a mark of the spirit-endowment, the Servant is going to have non-heroic features. The proclamation of the spirit presence will ensure the authenticity of the Servant's election. Secondly, it is the רוח יהוה which enables him to

---

113. E.g. North, *Isaiah 40–55*, p. 62; Mowinckel, *He That Cometh*, p. 219.

preach the מִשְׁפָּט to the neglected as well as to the nations, even to the coastlands. It is also the רוּחַ יהוה which will sustain the Servant in a long period of future suffering and cause him to carry on the task persistently.[114]

The close connection of the רוּח with מִשְׁפָּט indicates that the spirit of Yahweh acquires an ethical aspect. The underlying trait of the passage is the continuation of the old tradition, that is, the endowment of extraordinary supernatural strength and ability to the chosen leaders of Israel. There is the additional aspect of spirit-originated ability upon the Servant, the ability to endure suffering, and not to demonstrate destructive strength. This old idea is thus applied in two new ways.

2. *God's* רוּח *in the Exilic Isaianic Theology*

There are at least two questions as one discusses Isaianic exilic matters. The first is to determine what is the nature of Second Isaiah which makes up the major portion of the exilic Isaianic theology. The exact formation of Second Isaiah is an unsettled scholarly matter.[115] Nevertheless, it is almost certain that the anonymous prophet addresses the immediate spiritual crisis of his fellow citizens. He particularly points

114. The pointing in v. 4 is debated. The MT reads יָרוּץ from רוּץ 'to run' (BDB, p. 930), while *BHS* points יֵרוֹץ from רצץ 'crush' after LXX (θραυσθήσεται). Various translations are suggested: Syr. 'he is extinguished'; Tg יִלְאֵי 'he will become tired'. *BHS* and LXX readings are still favored by many commentators and translations. The bottom line is that the spirit will enable the servant to do his mission and also to endure suffering.

115. Scholars are divided into three groups of opinion: (1) Oracles were delivered independently and later collected. See, e.g., Mowinckel, *He That Cometh*, p. 188; also *idem*, 'Die Komposition des deuterojesajanischen Buches', *ZAW* 49 (1931), pp. 87-112, 242-60. (2) A unified literary work from the beginning. See, e.g., Muilenburg, 'Second Isaiah, Chapters 40–66', pp. 384-86. (3) Both elements are found. See, e.g., Westermann, *Isaiah 40–66*, pp. 27-30.

For studies of smaller units, see, e.g., Menahem Haran, 'The Literary Structure and Chronological Framework of the Prophecies in Is. xl–xlvii', in *Congress Volume: Bonn 1962* (VTSup, 9; Leiden: E.J. Brill, 1963), pp. 127-55; Antti Laato, 'The Composition of Isaiah 40–55', *JBL* 109 (1990), pp. 207-28; John Goldingay, 'The Arrangement of Isaiah xli–xlv', *VT* 29 (1979), pp. 289-99; Yehosua Gitay, *Prophecy and Persuasion: A Study of Isaiah 40–48* (Forum Theologiae Linguisticae, 14; Bonn: Linguistica Biblica, 1981), pp. 5-33; *idem*, 'Deutero-Isaiah: Oral or Written?' *JBL* 99 (1980), pp. 185-97. Williamson, *The Book Called Isaiah*, p. 241, denies the existence of Second Isaiah as a separate book.

to his audience who long to do away with foreign rulers and wait for the restoration of Zion in the midst of their serious theological crisis.[116] The second question is whether the theology of Second Isaiah and that of other Isaianic passages found outside Second Isaiah share a similar, if not identical, theological concern.

The theological significance is found in their historical circumstances, however vague its evidence may be. In the uncertain exilic period,[117] a severe theological doubt can reasonably be assumed, particularly from the fall of Jerusalem and the temple. The theological crisis stemmed from two opposing factors: faith in Yahweh reinforced by the prophetic promises, and their exilic reality. It is possible that one sector maintained the expectation of a speedy restoration which could have stemmed from the messages of Jeremiah and Ezekiel. Yet, the promises unfulfilled for half a century could have caused some, if not the majority, to settle down and give up the hope of restoration. Also the presence of a powerful ruler could have caused them to doubt the supremacy of Yahweh[118] and the validity of their special relationship with him.

2.1 *Yahweh*

Against the serious question of the capability of the God of Israel, especially against the nations, their rulers and their gods, the exilic Isaianic tradition depicts the greatness and absoluteness of Yahweh in various ways.

One remarkable theme is Yahweh as the creator. No parallel is found to this emphasis in any other prophets including First Isaiah.[119] Yahweh

116. Arvid S. Kapelrud, 'The Main Concern of Second Isaiah', *VT* 34 (1982), pp. 50-58 (50).

117. Peter R. Ackroyd's two books, *Israel under Babylon and Persia* (Oxford: Oxford University Press, 1970) and *Exile and Restoration* (OTL; London: SCM Press, 1968), provide necessary details. See also Klein, *Israel in Exile*.

118. The emphasis on Cyrus within the exilic tradition seems to reflect the difficulties the Judahites had in accepting him as God's chosen tool. The Cyrus Cylinder describes Cyrus as, in his own words, chosen by Marduk to restore the god to his rightful place, against Nabonidus's neglect of Marduk in favor of the moon-god Sin (*ANET*, pp. 321-38). Throughout *The Servant of YHWH and Cyrus*, Laato attempts to establish an intimate relationship between the servant of Yahweh and Cyrus.

119. With a possible exception of Amos 4.13, if an eighth-century date for the text can be established, see, e.g., North, *The Second Isaiah*, p. 13.

is the one who orders heaven and earth (Isa. 40; 44.24), and also the sole controller of the universe (45.8, 18; cf. 51.5). He is the first and the last, enduring until the very end of existence (41.4b). God's רוח is intimately linked with the creation, as God's spirit planned in wisdom and proceeded in power (40.13).

This creative activity of God's רוח is extended in Isa. 34.16.[120] The spirit is to carry on what the mouth of God declared and repopulates Edomite territories with wild beasts. With the strong allusion to the creation accounts, the act of the רוח of God is a work of re-creation. This understanding is possible only under the assumption that רוח יהוה is actively involved in creation.

The creation references, however, are found in the context of the birth of the nation Israel.[121] It is Yahweh who determines the history of Israel and the nations. Yahweh's challenge to the gods of the nations (41.21-29) to bring proof of their ability to predict, or to bring about, future events (41.22-24) is a clear contrast to Yahweh as the creator and controller. Yahweh's creative power, with his רוח deeply involved in the entire process (Isa. 40.13), is a proof of his supremacy over the gods.[122] He not only reveals the course of future history, but also brings about events which have been proclaimed through his prophets.[123] Therefore, to the prophet, the appearance and success of Cyrus is nothing but an example of God's absoluteness and universality. In fact, Yahweh is the only God and there is no one else. To Morgenstern, even the repeated proclamation of אני יהוה/אנכי (43.11; 44.24; 45.5-7, 18, 21, 22) has no other meaning but that of the exclusive divinity of the universal God.[124] Lee also argues that the verb ברא is used in chs.

---

120. Jacques Vermeylen, 'Le motif de la création dans le Deutéro-Isaïe', in F. Blanquart (ed.), *La création dans l'Orient ancien* (Paris: Cerf, 1987), pp. 183-240, considers that creation involves the king, emergence of a people and establishment of a moral order. All these are found in Second Isaiah.

121. Johnston, 'Prophetic Vision', p. 37, argues that chs. 40–55 forms a chiastic structure with 44.21–45.19 at the center. Thus Yahweh's re-creation of Israel is understood as the central message of Second Isaiah. She also lists at least five verbs used for Yahweh's creative act: יצר, נטה, רקע, ברא and עשׂה (p. 36).

122. Perdue, *Wisdom and Creation*, p. 326.

123. S.H. Blank points out the significance of the role of the prophets in court scenes in 'Studies in Deutero-Isaiah', *HUCA* 15 (1940), pp. 1-46 (3).

124. Julian Morgenstern, 'Deutero-Isaiah's Terminology for "Universal God"', *JBL* 62 (1943), pp. 269-80 (269), '...the second member [of the phrase] has lost in large measure its original connotation as the proper name of the national God and

40–55 with an exclusive reference to Yahweh's supreme power.[125] This emphasis is consistent, according to Lee, both in Yahweh's creation of 'the ends of the earth' (40.28; 45.18-19) and the creation, thus the re-creation, of Israel (43.1-7). Elliger argues that the creation language is used to indicate God's repeated intervention including His restoration of Israel from the foreign oppression.[126] One can say that this is a most exclusive kind of monotheism.

However, the most prominent theme in the book is the exodus tradition (43.19-20; 48.21; 52.11-12).[127] This is another feature about which the pre-exilic Isaianic traditions are silent.[128] As mentioned above, the creation emphasis can be understood only in the birth of Israel, which is the exodus event. The motif goes further back to Abrahamic (51.2-3) and Noachic covenant (54.9). Even before the Hebrews knew Yahweh as the creator, he was known as their redeemer and deliverer from Egypt. The creation doctrine is first applied to the creation of the nation Israel rather than to the creation of the universe. In that sense, von Rad's point appears correct that ברא and גאל are almost synonyms in Second Isaiah.[129] The new saving acts of Yahweh are described in the form of another exodus, but this time, much more

has instead become the prophet's characteristic designation of the universal God'.

125. Stephen Lee, 'Power not Novelty: The Connotations of ברא in the Hebrew Bible', in A. Graeme Auld (ed.), *Understanding Poets and Prophets: Essays in Honour of George Wishart Anderson* (JSOTSup, 152; Sheffield: JSOT Press, 1993), pp. 199-212 (200), contends that the thrice-repeated paired words, יעף, 'to faint', and יגע, 'to grow weary' (40.28-31), are the focus of the message, and provide the clue for the power reference.

126. Elliger, *Deuterojesaja*, I, p. 293.

127. Von Rad, *Old Testament Theology*, II, p. 239; Kapelrud, 'The Main Concern', p. 51. R.J. Clifford, 'The Unity of the Book of Isaiah and its Cosmogenic Language', *CBQ* 55 (1993), pp. 1-17 (3), again counts 40.1-11; 41.17-20; 42.10-43.8; 43.16-21; 46; 49.1-11; 51.9-11; 55.12-13; and ch. 35 for the exilic references. The latter is compared with 4.5; 10.24; 11.11, as pre-exilic passages.

128. Clifford, 'The Unity', p. 3.

129. Von Rad, *Old Testament Theology*, II, p. 241. See *idem*, 'The Theological Problem of the Old Testament Doctrine of Creation', in *idem*, *The Problem of the Hexateuch and Other Essays* (London: SCM Press, 1966), pp. 131-43 (136), where he argues that the connection between creation and redemption is made only in Second Isaiah. However, Westermann, *Isaiah 40–66*, pp. 24-25, contends that two originally separate creation traditions, the creation of human beings (Gen. 1–11) and that of the universe (Psalms and Second Isaiah), are brought together by Second Isaiah. Clifford ('The Unity', p. 8) supports von Rad's position.

wonderful and marvelous. This exodus combines the creation motif of
רוח יהוה; both motifs include a process to overcome a chaotic force.
Ezekiel experiences the re-creative work of God's spirit for the nation
(Ezek. 36).

In the exilic evidences, Yahweh as king assumes a very different
character than in the pre-exilic passages. In the latter, Yahweh works
primarily through the earthly king as long as he is obedient. However,
for the exilic mind, Yahweh stands in front of the new exodus, recalling
Yahweh as warrior in the ancient traditions. His glory is to be revealed
(40.3-11). The voice of the herald is approaching and the entire universe joins in the rejoicing (52.7). Even the last verse (55.13) seems to
say that the sacred way across the desert will be kept in perpetuity as a
commemorative.[130] The רוח of Yahweh takes no role in this process.

Yahweh's direct rule over Israel and the universe is evident throughout the exilic tradition. First of all, the prominent royal figure, a frequent eschatological feature in the pre-exilic tradition, is almost missing. The two likely candidates in the exilic tradition are the Servant and
Cyrus, if the two are not identical. The Servant is not an entirely royal
figure. In fact, he exhibits more evidence of prophetic features than
royal. Even though the spirit of Yahweh is given to him, it is not to
perform the traditional royal or leadership function as found among the
judges and the kings as described in Isa. 11.1-5. Cyrus, although hailed
as the liberator, is not expected to 'rule' over the people; his role ends
as the exiles return. The lack of any human agent for Yahweh's rule is
an entirely new development. Secondly, expressions such as אני יהוה
ואין עוד, 'I am Yahweh, there is no other' (Isa. 43.11; 44.6; 45.5, 6, 14,
21, 22; 46.9) reinforce God's supremacy not only over the idols and
gods, but also over human rulers. He is going to be the sole ruler over
Israel and over the nations. There will be no regent or king who will
represent Yahweh's rule in the world. He rules sovereignly and directly.

The redemption of God, however, is more than just the physical
deliverance from the foreign ruler and a second exodus. The concept
gains a more spiritual and inward meaning in the exilic Isaianic tradition. It is signified by the wiping out of sins and forgiveness (43.25;
44.22; 54.8). Also prominent is a physical aspect of Yahweh's blessing. Agricultural prosperity and security are directly attributed to the
outpouring of the spirit (32.15-16). With another agricultural imagery,

130. North, *The Second Isaiah*, p. 17.

44.1-5 describes the numerical increase of the restored community and its influence on the Gentiles. These are again viewed as a direct result of the presence of God's רוח upon the people of God.

2.2 *Israel*

In two passages, for the first time, Israel is promised to receive the outpouring of God's רוח (32.15 and 44.1-5). In both cases, the water image portrays the abundant outpouring of the spirit. The democratizing development of the tradition makes everyone in the restored community the recipient of this blessing. However, it is difficult to determine which previous spirit tradition is applied here. The functional consequence of the spirit presence precludes several options. First, through the spirit, God intended neither to authenticate Israel's election, nor empower them for a given task. Secondly, there is no prophetic activity resulting from the pouring out of רוח יהוה. Neither does the spirit function as God's emissary (as seen in 1 Kgs 22.22-23), since the spirit does not assume personality. The רוח of God will simply be upon his people, and in both cases the effect is seen in their agriculture (32.15-20) and national surroundings (44.1-5). The spirit is not poured upon the land, but upon the people, and still the effect is realized not only in their lives, but also in their land and surroundings.

Out of three covenant traditions that are present in the exilic Isaianic tradition,[131] not only the Sinaitic tradition, but also the Davidic tradition are specifically applied to Israel as a whole: the promise of the throne of David (2 Chron. 6.42) is applied to the whole nation. In this 'democratizing' process, 'Israel is to become the sovereign ruler [נגיד] of the peoples' (55.4).[132]

Israel was once separated temporarily from God and his land because of its sin (Lam. 1.8-9).[133] It received from Yahweh's hand 'twice-over for all her sins' (40.2; 51.17). However, the basis of the forgiveness and restoration is not Israel's 'pay-off' of her sin, but Yahweh's love (49.15-16) and promise (54.11-14), because 'no decent husband could disown the bride of his youth' (45.6). Consequently, they will return home and rebuild the cities with unprecedented prosperity (49.14-21).

131. Von Rad, *Old Testament Theology*, II, p. 239.
132. Von Rad, *Old Testament Theology*, II, p. 240.
133. Norman K. Gottwald, *Studies in the Book of Lamentations* (London: SCM Press, 1954), p. 115, 'the Book of Lamentations was one of the major sources of Deutero- and Trito-Isaiah'.

Israel is to be the witness of the true deity of Yahweh in the challenge between the witness of the gods and Israel, witness of Yahweh (43.9). Israel will be informed of things to come in advance (48.6) and she is to declare it to the nations and they will know not only that Yahweh alone is God, but that he is with Israel. In that sense, Israel is called the servant of Yahweh, but a passive one, with its consequence beyond her own restoration and glorious future. This day of restoration will be inaugurated by the pouring out of the רוח from above (32.15).

2.3 *Zion*

The centrality of Zion in Israel's faith could have contributed significantly to the theological and religious crisis. Zion was the Holy City which was often accompanied by the presence of the glory (כבד) of Yahweh (e.g. 1 Kgs 8.10-11; Isa. 6.1-4). The Davidic covenant is also tied up with Zion as the seat of the everlasting kingship. Israel's false expectation of the Day of Yahweh was pointed out repeatedly by the prophets, and it finally came into a historical reality. The erosion of the Davidic covenant resulting from Israel's unfaithfulness weakened Zion's claim as the seat of the everlasting kingship. Therefore, the destruction of Zion means the cessation of all cultic and religious practices and this leaves an unprecedented socio-religious vacuum.

However, after more than half a century of desolation, Second Isaiah begins to predict the return of the glory of Yahweh upon Zion. The ruined city with its destroyed temple is seen through the eyes of the prophet as a city destined to be rebuilt, which is guaranteed by Yahweh himself (41.19; 49; 54.11-17). Zion will no longer be a city belonging to David. Rather this will be the future home of God's sacred people and even of the Gentiles (49.22-23; 45.14). The old Zion covenant begins to refer not only to the sacred place, but also to its inhabitants, and ultimately to God's people as a body (41.27; 46.13; 49.14; 51.3, 11, 16; 52.1, 7, 8).

As Clifford argues, all three main theological themes of Second Isaiah, which easily represent the exilic Isaianic tradition, are closely associated with Zion.[134] The expectation of an exodus from captivity with conquest and the restoration has Zion as its goal. The creation theme serves a dual purpose: to complement the exodus and conquest tradition (41.17-20; 42.13-17; 43.16-21; 49.8-12), and to describe the victory over the enemy and the building of Zion, the temple city. Cyrus,

134. Clifford, 'The Unity', p. 3.

by defeating Babylon and building Zion, becomes Yahweh's king, replacing the Davidic dynasty.

According to Spykerboer, the restored Zion is described as a paradisiacal city completely transformed. The abundance of water, wine, milk and fatness (22.1-5) characterizes the lavish provision of Yahweh (e.g. 32.15; 44.1-5). In truth, coming to 'the water', or Jerusalem is same as 'going to Yahweh'.[135]

2.4 *Universalism*

This unique exilic feature is achieved by the Isaianic tradition in four ways: (1) through the introduction of a surprise servant, Cyrus, as Yahweh's anointed; (2) as Israel assumes a 'missionary' call for the nations; (3) by Yahweh's salvation plan which includes the nations; and (4) by asserting Yahweh's lordship over the universe.

The introduction of Cyrus as God's chosen servant for the liberation of the exiles is a bold theological venture. Historically, this interpretation is conceivable as Cyrus is going to destroy the Babylonian power which ruined Jerusalem and the temple. It is rather common to expect Yahweh to use a nation to bring judgment on another due to its oppression of God's people. Assyria brings judgment upon Ephraim and Syria which attacked Judah (Isa. 7.17-20). Centuries later, Babylon was used by Yahweh to destroy Assyria. Nebuchadnezzar, summoned by Yahweh to bring judgment to the nations including Israel, is called 'my servant' by Jeremiah (25.9; 27.6; 43.10). However, nowhere is Yahweh's tool of judgment explicitly called 'my anointed' (cf. Isa. 45.1), aroused 'in (God's) righteousness', nor does it bring true liberation to the people of God (45.4, 13). Cyrus falls short only in that the spirit of God is not present. This is the result of a radical shift in the exilic theological thinking. Whether this shift reflects the democratizing move of the Davidic covenant is not clear.

The call of Israel as a people of God includes their task to proclaim Yahweh as the lord of heaven and earth; that is, the call is for service.[136] The Isaianic tradition points repeatedly to the failure of the servant Israel (41.27-30; 42.6-7). That is why the new servant, whoever that

135. H.C. Spykerboer, 'Isaiah 55.1-5: The Climax of Deutero-Isaiah, an Invitation to Come to the New Jerusalem', in Jacques Vermeylen (ed.), *Le livre d'Isaïe: Les oracles et leurs relectures unité et complexité de l'ouvrage* (BETL, 81; Leuven: Leuven University Press, 1989), pp. 357-59.

136. Wilson, *The Nations in Deutero-Isaiah*, p. 8.

may be, is going to fulfill the unfulfilled mission toward the nations
(42.1, 4). It takes the equipping of רוח יהוה to accomplish God's מֹשׁפּט
in a lowly and humble manner particularly as he faces difficulties. In
the restored age, Israel will finally fulfill this 'missionary' call, not by
its active pursuit, but by being a recipient of Yahweh's blessing and his
spirit (44.1-5). As a consequence, the Gentiles will come to their recognition of, and submission to, Yahweh's supreme lordship.

However, it would be far-fetched to say that Israel has an active mission to go out to the nations and convert them to Yahweh religion. Nor
does this mean that the universality of Yahweh necessarily applies to
the Israelite understanding of its future mission,[137] in spite of the universal effect of the restoration of Israel and its witness to the nations, as
seen in 45.22-23. The message is merely that through the redemption
of Israel, the manifestation of God will have such a dazzling effect
throughout the nations that the Gentiles will come in humble, subser-
vient awe.[138] In a sense, the exilic Isaianic tradition, including Second
Isaiah, reflects strong nationalistic orientation.[139] This motif is also seen
in God's plan for some nations such as Edom destined for destruction
(ch. 34), for not all the nations are to participate in Israel's salvation.

Closely related to the foregoing discussion, the exilic Isaianic tradition pays more attention to the fate of the nations. It is not new that the
nations are sometimes viewed as objects of Yahweh's blessing. This
occurs mostly in judgment contexts upon Israel (e.g. 5.26-30a). Often
judgment on Israel and blessing to the nations occur simultaneously. In
the same way, blessing to Israel often coincides with God's judgment
upon the nations. In this traditional pattern, רוח יהוה is viewed as the

137. 'A virtual unanimity of opinion about universalism in the conception of
God and the task of Yahweh's Servant' (de Boer, 'Second-Isaiah Message', p. 84).
For the (mis)translation of אור גוים (42.6; 49.6) as 'a light to the Gentiles' rather
than the real meaning 'a light of the Gentiles', see de Boer, 'Second-Isaiah
Message', p. 92. For עם ברית as 'a covenant of the people' (42.6; 49.8), see, e.g.,
Snaith, 'Servant of the Lord', p. 157, and *idem*, 'Isaiah 40–66', p. 155. Contra,
Wilson, *The Nations in Deutero-Isaiah*, pp. 329-32, argues for an active missionary
call to Israel.

138. Snaith, 'Isaiah 40–55', p. 156.

139. Not in the sense in which Lindblom argues that Second Isaiah regards the
pagan nations only as objects of doom, *Prophecy in Ancient Israel*, p. 366. Second
Isaiah is a nationalist, because the main concern is the restoration of Israel, and the
conversion of the Gentiles still serves to express the glory of Israel in the vindication and abundant blessing of its God (e.g. 42.1-4; 44.4-5).

executing faculty of God (34.16), as it is closely paralleled to the mouth of God. An apparently new development in the exilic Isaianic tradition, however, is that God's salvation plan includes both Israel and the nations. As observed above, the primary recipient of Yahweh's salvation is Israel, while the nations enjoy the secondary effect. In this process, the רוח of God plays a definite role (44.1-5).

Yahweh's claim to universal rule is drastically reinforced in the exilic tradition in several ways. Second Isaiah opens his message by proclaiming Yahweh's power and supremacy (40.3-20) which concludes with a strong denunciation of the idols which the nations worship and rely upon (vv. 19-20). Their inability to measure Yahweh's רוח, or his wisdom and power, in the process of creation, recalls his supreme wisdom against the wise men in the court and his power against Egyptian military might (30.1-5; 31.1-3). The creation imagery not only portrays his ownership of the nations but also treats them as insignificant. The sheer comparison between the ocean and a bucketful of water (40.12) highlights Yahweh's supremacy. Yahweh's return to Zion is closely linked with his increasing kingship over the earth in 52.7-10. Spykerboer argues that the invitation issued in 55.1-2 is for the nations 'to come to the new Jerusalem where Yahweh reigns and to share in its wealth'.[140] The establishment of the universal rulership of Yahweh over Israel and the nations marks the climax of the exilic Isaianic eschatology. Yahweh is about to reign over Israel as King (41.21-29; 43.15; 44.6-8; 52.7), and he is also prominent in the new age of eschatological times as the unique and incomparable God, King Yahweh. However, his kingship is primarily his authority rather than the realm of his rule. Redemption, salvation, creation and judgment are royal acts of Yahweh as King.[141] The nations' pilgrimage to Zion, the seat of Yahweh's kingship (Isa. 45.14-15; 49.14-21, 22-23; 52.1-2) certainly indicates the fullness of Yahweh's kingship over the nations.

2.5 *The Servant of Yahweh*

In the exilic Isaianic tradition, there are two agents of Yahweh who will accomplish his plan: the Servant and Cyrus. Cyrus is viewed as God's anointed to liberate God's people from the Babylonian captivity. In a

140. Spykerboer, 'Isaiah 55.1-5', p. 358.
141. Dirk H. Odendaal, *The Eschatological Expectation of Isaiah 40–66 with Special Reference to Israel and the Nations* (Nutley, NJ: Presbyterian and Reformed Publishing, 1970), p. 95.

sense, his role corresponds to that of Moses. Once the people are liberated, however, Cyrus's role does not continue, and it is Yahweh himself who will lead the exodus march.

The Servant figure, as discussed above (pp. 88-96), is a divine agent very different from traditional leaders. In spite of much debate over uncertainties in many aspects of the songs,[142] it is reasonable to assert that the exilic theologian reckons the Servant with other elements of restoration. In the absence of a human royal figure expected after the return, this figure is commissioned to bring forth משפט to the nations (42.1-4). The task was originally entrusted to Jacob/Israel, but it failed.

The extreme ambiguity of this figure, at least to modern readers, was either intended from the beginning, or the identity was commonly known and assumed. It is possible that from the beginning a certain degree of flexibility or fluidity was intended in the identification and the mission of the Servant in each song.[143] The Servant's expected role in the immediate future, especially in contrast to Jacob/Israel, occupies an important place in the exilic Isaianic theology. The Servant's mission is described as possible only because of the רוח of Yahweh.

2.6 *Eschatology*
Almost all the theological themes in the exilic Isaianic period are eschatological. The community perceives itself as standing at the dawning of the new era, standing between (to borrow a New Testament expression) fulfillment of judgment ('already') and still anticipating restoration ('not yet'). Lindblom aptly describes the book:

---

142. E.g. I. Engnell, 'The Ebed Yahweh Songs and the Suffering Messiah in "Deutero-Isaiah"', *BJRL* 31 (1948), pp. 54-93 (62), who states that the very different results of studies are sufficient evidence that the separation of the 'songs' from the rest of Second Isaiah is problematic. Other questions continue to evolve around the nature of the 'songs', the identity of the servant, the nature of his mission, the authorship of the 'songs', and so on. For a full discussion of the history of the study, see North, *Suffering Servant in Second Isaiah*, pp. 6-103; and Harold H. Rowley, 'The Servant of the Lord in the Light of Three Decades of Criticism', in *idem*, *The Servant of the Lord*, pp. 3-57. For a recent argument with a good survey, see Laato, *The Servant of YHWH and Cyrus*.

143. E.g. Torrey, *Second Isaiah*, pp. 135-36.

> If one considers eschatology to be hope for a new era, in which all rela-
> tionships are radically changed, Deutero-Isaiah in that sense is from its
> beginning to its end an eschatological book.[144]

There are a number of characteristics of the eschatological perception in the exilic Isaianic tradition.

2.6.1 *Imminent Realization*. Truly the exilic tradition is conscious of its place at the junction of a new departure in the history of Israel. According to the exilic understanding of history, the final stage of the history of Israel and of humankind is about to occur. Contrary to the pre-exilic prophets whose message is predominantly of judgment, in the exilic Isaianic voice the judgment has already occurred to Israel (40.1-2; 51.17-20) as well as to some nations (34.16), and the time of salvation is imminent (40.3-5; 51.17-20).

The expectation of final events is explicit, and they are taking place. A second, and more wonderful exodus is about to take place (43.14-21; 48.20-21; 51.10-11; 52.11-12; 55.12), and Yahweh's 'shepherd', Cyrus, has already appeared (44.28; cf. 45.1-3; 48.3). This will usher in a host of events: the rebuilding of the Temple (44.28); Yahweh's reign as King of Zion (52.7-8) in a kingdom of security and salvation (51.3; 54.13-14); the destruction of enemies (47; 51.23); Yahweh's eternal covenant with Israel based on Yahweh's promise of mercy given to David (55.3); and a universal hope of salvation extended to the nations through the mission of the Servant (42.1-4; 6-7). The tension between the 'former things' and the 'new things' is so great that the day of the 'new things' is described in almost other-worldly and paradisiacal words (43.22–44.4; 57.1-21; 59.1-21, etc.).

This expectation of immediate restoration differs from the promise of salvation in earlier prophets. In those prophets, salvation is expected in a distant future, whereas in the exilic prophecy eschatology is something to be experienced as a present reality. Therefore, most prophetic

---

144. 'Wenn man aber unter Eschatologie die Hoffnung auf ein neues Zeitalter versteht, wo alle Verhaeltnisse in etwas ganz anderes verwandelt sind, so ist das Buch Deuterojesaja vom Anfang bis zum Ende ein eschatologische Buch' (J. Lindblom, 'Gibt es eine Eschatologie bei den alttestamentlichen Propheten?', *ST* 6 [1953], pp. 79-114 [106]). In slightly different ways, see Muilenburg, 'Isaiah, chapters 40–66', p. 399; Volz, *Jesaia*, p. xx; and Smart, *History and Theology*, pp. 34-37.

utterances are not to be seen as prediction, but rather as the announcement of salvation and restoration.[145] Even the Servant is described as already present and endowed with the spirit of Yahweh (42.1).

The description of the coming salvation in terms of creation (41.20; 45.8; 48.7) is part of the exilic Isaianic eschatological logic. It may go along with Gunkel's idea of *Urzeit und Endzeit* (beginning and end time).[146] Furthermore, it should not be overlooked that all of nature is involved in the final events (40.4; 44.23; 55.12). This is seen as the establishment of the paradisical condition, rather than the occurrence of an apocalyptic cosmic catastrophe.

2.6.2 Yahweh's Direct Reign. There are two human agents present in the exilic eschatology, the Servant and Cyrus, provided that the two do not refer to each other. However, they do not have royal roles. This is a drastic contrast to the pre-exilic expectation of the ideal ruler (e.g. 11.1-5), which was already substantially 'deroyalized'. With all the restored orders the community is about to experience, the Davidic king who will rule the restored community is nowhere alluded to.

This sets the stage for Yahweh's direct involvement. His personal and direct intervention is seen in the second exodus. He, not a human agent such as Moses, is to lead the exiles. When he marches across the desert, instead of the traditional route, the mountains, hills and valley cooperate with God's will (40.3-4). This is well linked not only with the kingly rule of God, but also with his lordship over the universe as creator.

The establishment of the universal rulership of Yahweh over Israel and the nations marks the climax of the exilic Isaianic eschatology. It is accompanied by Yahweh's triumph over the gods of the nations. Yahweh is the true king of Israel (41.21-29; 43.15; 44.6-8; 52.7). Redemption, salvation, creation and judgment are royal acts of Yahweh as King.[147] The nations' pilgrimage to Zion, the seat of Yahweh's kingship attests to the fullness of Yahweh's kingship over the nations (Isa. 45.14-15; 49.14-21, 22-23; 52.1-2).

This contrasts radically with the realistic view of pre-exilic eschatology which assumes that the existing order and system will continue.

145. Jenni, 'Eschatology of the OT', p. 131.

146. H. Gunkel, *Schöpfung und Chaos in Urzeit und Endzeit* (Göttingen: Vandenhoeck & Ruprecht, 1895), p. 367.

147. Odendaal, *The Eschatological Expectation*, p. 95.

The exilic eschatology anticipates drastic changes to mark the end of the present age. At the same time, the coming age and its accompanying events are viewed as taking place in the continuing realm of present history. This eschatology is an expression of the prophet's faith in God's sovereignty over the world and its history.[148] God works in the realm of present history.

3. *Concluding Observations*

3.1 *The* רוח *in the Traditions*

The most obvious development in the רוח יהוה tradition is the sudden emergence of the spirit as the agent of creation and life. The exilic environment provides a fertile ground for the development. A strong and rich creation tradition in Mesopotamia may have a part in this development. The idea of creation appears to have gone through a substantial evolution by the exilic period. The Isaianic tradition in this period includes three rich facets of creation: initial creation (40.13; cf. Gen. 1.2); re-creation (43.16; cf. Ezek. 36); and prosperity in physical and spiritual senses (32.15; 44.1-5). In all the stages, the spirit of God plays a definite role. One should also remember that 34.16 has a strong allusion to the creation theme.

The leadership רוח is present in 42.1-4 upon the Servant, with more of a spiritual emphasis. As reviewed above (pp. 89-96), the exact nature of the Servant is fluid and ambiguous and so is the nature of the spirit. The spirit, however, seems to function along the typical idea of leadership: to reinforce God's election; and to enable the Servant to accomplish the given task. The task, however, is more prophet-like than kingly. This is probably due to the further deroyalization of God's leader, if not king, toward the exile. With the historical failure of the human king, and with the Deuteronomistic sentiment for God's direct rule (1 Sam 8.4-8), the new Servant, not the king, assumes a hybrid character. This tradition still maintains its exclusivity.

Isaiah 34.16 and 40.13 bring the idea of the divine רוח a step closer to God's personhood; in these passages, the spirit works as God's direct agent. This is in marked contrast with the fact that, in the other passages examined, the spirit is always directed to a person (42.1-4) or a group of people (32.13-15; 44.1-5). It almost replaces God himself. In

---

148. Smart, *History and Theology*, p. 30.

34.16, the impression is stronger as 'his spirit' (רוחו) is juxtaposed with his 'mouth' (פי). In a true sense, the רוח refers to the 'extension of God's personality'.[149] On the other hand, this aspect of God's רוח can easily assume a separate personality as seen in 1 Kings 22. The idea of the messenger (מלאך) could be a further development of this aspect.

However, not every tradition is present or reshaped by exilic theologians. For instance, there is no reference to רוח יהוה as the source of prophetic inspiration in this period. Probably even at this time the negative impression of the pre-exilic ecstatic nabiism is still so prevalent that the exilic Isaianic tradition is hesitant to apply רוח יהוה to any individual figure.[150]

3.2 *Characteristics of the* רוח יהוה *in the Exilic Tradition*
There are a number of characteristics that the רוח יהוה concept exhibits within the exilic Isaianic tradition. Reinterpretation of the old tradition is common in this period.

3.2.1 *Further Refinement*. As already noted in the pre-exilic material, the leadership רוח יהוה continues to be refined. The רוח endowed to the Servant becomes highly advanced from the violent charismatic prowess in the earlier tradition. The spirit will, as in the old tradition, equip the Servant to succeed, and, this time, to endure hardships. The Servant's manner is described as gentle and compassionate, and here is an entirely different picture of a spirit-equipped leader. This portrait is in contrast to that of Cyrus (especially in 44.28–45.4) who is described as a successful military man. This leader, to whom often many royal titles and attributes are unreservedly granted, is never presented as having God's רוח.

It is also noticeable that ethicizing is one trend in modification, for the more prophet-like feature reinforces this development. In addition, the creation of an ideal environment is directly attributed to the coming of the רוח יהוה (32.15). The old tradition of justice and righteousness (Isa. 11.1-5; 28.6) continues in the role of the spirit. But this time, the realization of the ideal society is due to everyone in the restored community having Yahweh's רוח. It is a striking development from the

---

149. Johnson, *The One and the Many*, p. 16.

150. Mowinckel, '"Spirit" and the "Word"', pp. 199-227, most prominently argues for the case. However, Arvid S. Kapelrud does not fully agree with Mowinckel (see Kapelrud, 'The Spirit and the Word', pp. 41-47).

pre-exilic notion of the ideal king from whose righteous rule the paradisiacal peace will be experienced. Perhaps the theological reflections
of the exiles caused them to change to the concept of permanent moral
power infusing the entire community, preparing it for the future.

3.2.2 *Democratization.* Democratization of the concept is prominent. It
will be upon 'us', the members of the restored community, and upon
Jacob/Israel, again the community restored in Zion. This democratization of the divine spirit, however, is restricted to the creation-life רוח in
this time. Also noted is the emphasis on the community rather than
individuals. The coming of the divine spirit may find its precedence in
the 70 elders (Num. 11.17, 25, 26) and some prophetic guilds (1 Sam.
10.10; 19.20-21), but nowhere is an entire nation viewed as having the
outpouring of the divine spirit.

3.2.3 *Creation/Life Connection.* As discussed above at length, the
spirit's involvement in Yahweh's creation, particularly of the nation,
demonstrates an intense theological activity during the exilic period.
One of them is Yahweh as creator. The covenant/election tradition is
easily fused into this new theological thinking (see especially 44.1-5).
It is plausible to assume that this usage is connected with the development of the Priestly theology evidenced in Gen. 1.2. Sklba detects a
reappropriation of some old Israelite traditions, and even some foreign
ones.[151]

Related to the creation tradition is the frequent association with water
imagery. Water, first of all, is viewed as an indispensable element for
prosperity. The imagery is all positive and so are the verbs associated
with it. This may indicate the state of exilic Judahite theology which
becomes stable enough to free itself from the negative image of the
chaotic water in the Babylonian myths.

3.2.4 *More Active and Direct Eschatological Role.* In 32.15-20 and
44.1-5, the coming of the רוח יהוה is promised unconditionally to the
members of the restored community. In 42.1-4, although the endowment of the spirit is said to be a completed event, the full effect of it is
moved to the future. Isaiah 32.15 is clear evidence that the exilic tradition understands the new age to be closely connected with the coming

151. Sklba, ' "Until the Spirit" ', p. 13.

of רוח יהוה. The pouring out of the divine spirit inaugurates the new restored era. It is also the main active force which will bring an increase in physical and material realms (32.15-20 and 44.1-5). The appearance of the Servant also is a mark of the new age. His success is attributed to the divine spirit.

3.2.5 *Other Features.* There are other features which appear already in the pre-exilic Isaianic traditions. The reference of the רוח יהוה to a certain aspect, if not the person, of Yahweh began with 31.3. In 34.16 and 40.13, the רוח יהוה represents the divine being. The presence of the יהוה רוח is the presence of Yahweh himself. The influence of the wisdom tradition found in earlier tradition (11.1-5; 30.1) continues in 40.13.

Chapter 3

POSTEXILIC ISAIANIC SPIRIT TRADITION

During the pre-exilic and exilic periods, the idea of the רוח of Yahweh
has undergone a significant change within the Isaianic tradition. This
change came about to meet the unique spiritual and social needs of the
people in the given social and historical situation. During the postexilic
era, the process of development observed in the previous chapters was
expected to continue. This dynamic plays a crucial role as the prophetic
tradition finds itself in a new pastoral circumstance within the reduced
and suffering Judean community.

1. *Passages*

59.15b-20

[15]...When Yahweh saw, it displeased him, that there was no justice.
[16]When he saw that there was no one, he wondered that no one inter-
vened. His own arm wrought victory, and his righteousness upheld it.
[17]So he put on righteousness as a breastplate and a helmet of salvation
on his head. And he put on clothes of vengeance as his uniform, and
draped himself in violent fury as a mantle. [18]Measured by deeds, so he
repays: wrath to his adversaries, a reproach to his enemies. To the
coastlands he makes full payment with a deed. [19]And they from the west
fear the name Yahweh. And they from the rising sun his glory. For he
comes like a rushing stream. The spirit of Yahweh is the driving force in
him. [20]But he comes to Zion (as) a redeemer and to those repenting of
rebellion in Jacob. Oracle of Yahweh.

This passage is an oracle of salvation, which follows a community
lament acknowledging the lack of משפט and צדקה (59.9-11) and the
consequences of their shortcomings (vv. 12-15a). Verse 9, in particular,
makes it clear that the mounting guilt is the theological reason for the
delayed salvation, which is the major motif of postexilic Isaianic

theology.[1] Sins are both against God (v. 13a) and against neighbor
(v. 13b). The change of the person in vv. 14-15 is to recapitulate the
lament before the following oracle of deliverance. The frequent change
is observed in person from the second to the third and then to the first
person. A similar change of tone is observed in 59.1-20. This strongly
implies that several sayings are put together as a communal lament,
probably for cultic use.[2]

The passage, according to Westermann, is originally part of an old
epiphany: 'God's advent to punish his foes which takes place before the
eyes of the whole world which is terrified at his sovereign power (e.g.
Isa. 33.3)'.[3] Yahweh is often described as the divine warrior bringing
judgment on the enemies of Israel, but deliverance for his people
(Exod. 15.1-18, especially v. 3; Deut. 33.2-5, 26-29; Judg. 5.4-5; Ps.
68; Hab. 3.2-15, etc.). This old tradition with references to external
enemies, however, is 'twisted' to be applied to the current crisis.[4] This
time the enemies are within, unfaithful ones of the Judeans (also Isa.
63.10).[5]

Yahweh comes to establish his lordship over Judah and over the
world (v. 19ab), but Yahweh's coming to Judah is, first of all, as its
judge. The absence of מִשְׁפָּט (justice) is a clear mark that there is a
complete breach between God and his people (v. 15b), and the lack of
מִשְׁפָּט, in the Isaianic tradition, is displayed in social injustice. The
remoteness of God leaves his people helpless, and it is well expressed
by the fact that there is no one who will or can intervene for them. So

---

1. Von Rad, *Old Testament Theology*, II, p. 280.
2. Blenkinsopp, *A History of Prophecy in Israel*, p. 270.
3. Westermann, *Isaiah 40–66*, p. 349.
4. Elizabeth Achtemeier, *The Community and Message of Isaiah 56–66: A Theological Commentary* (TC; Minneapolis: Augsburg, 1982), p. 71; Westermann, *Isaiah 40–66*, pp. 349-50.
5. Muilenburg, 'Isaiah, Chapters 40-66', p. 695, treats the enemies as those from without. However, many commentators consider them as those within: D.J. Kendall, 'The Use of *Mišpaṭ* in Isaiah 59', *ZAW* 96 (1984), pp. 391-405 (399-400); S. Sekine, *Die tritojesajanische Sammlung (Jes 56–66) redaktionsgeschichtlich untersucht* (BZAW; 175; Berlin: W. de Gruyter, 1989), p. 133; Volz, *Jesaia II*, p. 236; R.N. Whybray, *Isaiah 40–66* (NCBC; London: Marshall, Morgan & Scott; Grand Rapids: Eerdmans, 1975), p. 226. However, P.A. Smith, *Rhetoric and Redaction in Trito-Isaiah: The Structure, Growth and Authorship of Isaiah 56–66* (VTSup, 62; Leiden: E.J. Brill, 1995), p. 124, identifies the enemy as both the 'apostate Jews and the gentile nations'.

Yahweh himself has to deliver his people out of his gracious love (v. 16). The prophet both begins and ends the accusation by stating that the people do not know (the way of) שָׁלוֹם (v. 18).[6]

Verse 19 is problematic as found in the *BHS* reading. The key to the solution, according to Kendall, is רוּחַ, which LXX omits.[7] But whether the רוּחַ is to be seen as 'spirit' or 'wind' is an equally divided matter. The overall context of judgment,[8] the use of רוּחַ in its parallel passage as a purifying force (57.13), and the reference to the 'rushing stream' in the same verse appear to favor 'wind'—a natural phenomenon—rather than 'spirit'.[9] The LXX reading, according to Rofé, takes נהר צר as meaning:

> ...a river enclosed in a narrow bed, therefore flowing in a rush. Accordingly, רוח יהוה נססה בו should be construed as an additional attribute to נהר: (a river) driven forward by a fierce wind (YHWH functioning as a superlative).[10]

However, a careful examination shows that the other rendering is equally plausible. Since the writer likens the coming of Yahweh to the 'rushing stream', the 'stream' cannot influence the identification of רוּחַ. In addition, the context is more than judgment; it is the powerful and glorious presence of God as the sole lord of the world. This is particularly true in v. 19, where his coming is described with his 'name' and 'glory'. Moreover, the first half of v. 19 refers to the nations not as enemies but as witnesses to Yahweh's action described in v. 18.[11] Briggs takes the middle ground by defining רוּחַ as the 'hard breathing

---

6. Kendall, '*Mišpaṭ*', p. 400.

7. Kendall, '*Mišpaṭ*', p. 401.

8. The storm and the wind (רוח) describe how God comes in judgment, according to Muilenburg, 'Isaiah, Chapters 40–66', p. 695.

9. Peter D. Miscall, *Isaiah* (Sheffield: JSOT Press, 1993), p. 135; Westermann, *Isaiah 40–66*, p. 344, and Norman H. Snaith, *The Distinctive Ideas of the Old Testament* (London: Epworth Press, 1944), p. 153. Muilenburg, 'Isaiah, Chapters 40–66', p. 695, refers to the רוח as the mighty wind of Yahweh which drives on a pent-up stream to break through its channels, as paralleled in Isa. 30.27-28.

10. Alexander Rofé, 'Isaiah 59.19 and Trito-Isaiah's Vision of Redemption', in Jacques Vermeylen (ed.), *Le livre d'Isaïe: Les oracles et leurs relectures unité et complexité de l'ouvrage* (BETL, 81; Leuven: Leuven University Press, 1989), pp. 407-10 (407).

11. George A.F. Knight, *Isaiah 56–66* (ITC; Grand Rapids: Eerdmans, 1985), p. 38; Whybray, *Isaiah 40–66*, pp. 227-28.

of God through the nostrils in anger'.[12] This is strongly reminiscent of Exod. 15.8 where a distinction is not clear between the east wind and God's spirit. S. Mowinckel also favors the 'spirit' as Yahweh's activating emotion.[13] In either translation, the term is closely linked with the 'all powerful' nature of Yahweh.[14]

In the old warrior imagery of God, the spirit is often associated with a man whom God uses as a weapon (e.g. Judg. 6.34, 'The spirit of Yahweh clothed, that is, armed itself with Gideon', and also Zech. 9–13). Human agents are present in the previous Isaianic material. In the pre-exilic material, a king (Isa. 11.1-5) and judges (28.6) are promised God's spirit, while in the exilic period it is his Servant. However, in this postexilic passage, there is no human agent involved. W. Brownlee correctly observes the distancing tendency of God away from human involvement:

> When in post-exilic literature apocalypticism makes its appearance, more and more the element of theophany is played up; and frequently God is thought of as a lone Warrior... The so-called Trito-Isaianic materials picture Yahweh as acting alone (also 63.1-6; cf. Joel 3.9-12; Zech. 14).[15]

The writer expects that God will act directly to intervene in the affairs of his people.[16] The basis of hope is the one-sided nature of God's acts of grace and faithfulness in spite of the unfaithfulness of his people.[17] The historical absence of a definite political or military figure after the exile may contribute to the theophanic appearance. The passage concludes with the expectation of Yahweh's coming as a redeemer for those in Zion who have awaited his salvation.

What, then, is the spirit? One should be aware of the uncertainty in the meaning of this passage. If the traditional rendering is taken, the רוח

---

12. Briggs, 'Use of *Ruach*', p. 133. Also Torrey, *The Second Isaiah*, p. 263.

13. Mowinckel, ' "Spirit" and the "Word" ', p. 204.

14. Snaith, 'Isaiah 40–66', p. 153.

15. William H. Brownlee, 'From Holy War to Holy Martyrdom', in H.B. Huffmon, F.A. Spina and A.R.W. Green (eds.), *The Quest for the Kingdom of God: Studies in Honor of George E. Mendenhall* (Winona Lake, IN: Eisenbrauns, 1983), pp. 281-92 (284-85).

16. In this sense, the translation of Motyer, *The Prophecy of Isaiah*, p. 492, is illustrative, 'When an adversary comes streaming in, the Spirit of the Lord lifts a banner against him'. However, this traditional Jewish exegesis is rejected for grammatical reasons: see Rofé, 'Isaiah 59.19', p. 407.

17. Smart, *History and Theology*, p. 256.

is a force which drives a rushing stream, in which case it is close to the 'wind' as a natural force, since the imagery has a definite emphasis on the forcefulness. However, if צר is taken as the subject, then the rendering of רוח takes on a more personal notion, acting as Yahweh's representative.[18] This can assume the more traditional warrior image, as in the book of Judges. Rofé's rendering is an example:

> ...for an envoy will come as light
> the spirit of the Lord waves him as a flag.[19]

Here, the רוח takes a radically different meaning. As Yahweh 'waves' the envoy, the nations shall revere the name and glory of God. So, the spirit is going to 'lift up' the Servant as God introduces him (42.1). However, this usage is not found anywhere in the Old Testament. Caution should be exercised, therefore, against coming to any firm conclusion in an uncertain passage such as this.

48.16b; 61.1-3
  (48.16b)
    And now, the Lord Yahweh
    has sent me and his spirit!

Isaiah 48.16b is treated along with 61.1-3, not only because of its apparent postexilic date, but also because of its affinity with the latter. The passage presents at least three difficult problems in maintaining a unity with the preceding and following verses. The sudden change of the person in v. 16b interrupts the utterance of Yahweh and surprisingly interjects the utterance of the prophet himself.[20] In fact, if just v. 16b is removed, the entire passage from v. 12 to v. 22 flows undisturbed.[21] A more serious difficulty, however, is in v. 16b itself: 'and his spirit' (ורוחו) is awkwardly added to 'and now Yahweh God has sent me' (ועתה אדני יהוה שלחני) with no grammatical relationship. The last question is the identification of the 'me' whom Yahweh has called.

To solve the first problem, many omit 'and his spirit' as a later

---

18. Rofé, 'Isaiah 59.19', p. 409, emends צר to ציר, thus reading 'envoy' instead of 'stream' and takes it as the subject. See also Motyer, *The Prophecy of Isaiah*, p. 492.

19. Rofé, 'Isaiah 59.19', p. 409.

20. LXX and Vg omit 'the Lord Yahweh'.

21. Julian Morgenstern, *The Message of Deutero-Isaiah in its Sequential Unfolding* (Cincinnati: Hebrew Union College Press, 1961), p. 68. He traces it to Zech. 4.9b; 6.15aβ.

addition,[22] and some treat the entire verse as a gloss.[23] Others try to divide vv. 12-19 into several smaller units, which justify the changing rhythm and the sudden change of the speaker, and even a mutilated fragment like v. 16.[24] Still others make wild emendations of v. 16b, so that the entire verse can be an utterance of God.[25] Franke treats the verse as an example of enjambment since an expected announcement is missing.[26] However, the best solution might be to leave v. 16a as it stands, and to see v. 16b as a later insertion. North contends that the Trito-Isaianic circle is responsible for the addition, based on its affinity with 61.1 where the speaker is less reticent than his exilic counterpart appears to have been.[27]

The grammatical ambiguity of 'and his spirit' prompts various arguments. Unless the phrase is eliminated as 'a gloss within the gloss',[28] basically three options emerge. The first is to take רוחו as a second subject, which will in turn produce a translation, 'Yahweh God and his spirit have sent me'.[29] This presents a problem, however, because in the Old Testament, the spirit is understood to be sent, but never sending.[30] The second option is to take the word as another object, so that the phrase would read, 'and now the Lord Yahweh has sent me, and his

22. For instance, Torrey, *Second Isaiah*, p. 378; Duhm, *Das Buch Jesaja*, p. 328; Morgenstern, *The Message*, p. 70; Muilenburg, 'Isaiah, Chapters 40–66', p. 561.

23. E.g. NEB. However, Chris Franke, *Isaiah 46, 47, and 48: A New Literary-Critical Reading* (Biblical and Judaic Studies from University of California, San Diego, 3; Winona Lake, IN: Eisenbrauns, 1994), p. 224, rules out the possibility due to the problematic nature of the passage, while A.S. Herbert, *The Book of the Prophet Isaiah: Chapters 40–66* (CBCOT; Cambridge: Cambridge University Press, 1975), p. 84, dismisses the option, claiming 'it explains nothing'. *BHS* proposes either אשלחנו לארחו or שלח אני בחירי.

24. For example, Snaith, 'Isaiah 40–66', pp. 197-98.

25. Edward Kissane, *The Book of Isaiah* (2 vols.; Dublin: Browne & Nolan, 1941–43), II, p. 177, emends as 'And now, I Yahweh have sent deliverance'. Also Albert Condamin, *Le livre d'Isaïe* (Paris: Libraire Victore le Coffre, 1905), p. 294.

26. Franke, *Isaiah 46, 47, and 48*, p. 225.

27. North, *The Second Isaiah*, p. 181.

28. Schoemaker, 'Use of "Ruach" ', p. 27.

29. JB; Smart, *History and Theology*, p. 149; Torrey, *Second Isaiah*, p. 378; U.E. Simon, *A Theology of Salvation: A Commentary on Isaiah 40–55* (London: SPCK, 1953), p. 160.

30. North, *The Second Isaiah*, p. 181; Franke, *Isaiah 46, 47, and 48*, p. 224.

spirit' (RV),[31] or 'with his spirit' (NIV).[32] Nonetheless, this does not resolve the problem satisfactorily. There is no other case in the Old Testament in which God sends his servant and his spirit, as if the latter stands alongside a persona as an entity on the same level.[33] It is also argued that the separation of the spirit from God as an independent entity is an idea wholly unacceptable in Old Testament thought.[34] Moreover, 'send me and his spirit' cannot justifiably be equated with '[God] sends me with his spirit'. This leads some to suspect either a verb or a word has been lost, for example, 'upon me'.[35] This would place 'his spirit' in parallel with 'Yahweh God'. In fact, 61.1 appears to be the closest parallel to this, especially if v. 16b indeed came from the postexilic Isaianic tradition.

Then, as to the identification of 'me', the reference of the original utterance (61.1) is to prophetic inspiration which has virtually disappeared from the mouth of the prophets.[36] Gitay argues that the prophet is about to make a public announcement about new things.[37] However, by placing v. 16b in its present context, which deals with Cyrus, 'a friend of Yahweh', the postexilic hand further affirms that Cyrus is Yahweh's chosen liberator of his people.[38] Hence, the spirit here can be seen as the warlike spirit given to him.[39] This concept goes back to the earliest days of Israel when the judges were claimed to have been possessed by the רוח of Yahweh (Judg. 6.34; 11.29; 13.25; 14.6, 19; 15.14). The result of the endowment with the רוח of Yahweh is

31. North, *The Second Isaiah*, p. 181.

32. Skinner, *Isaiah Chapters XL–LXVI*, p. 93.

33. It may be argued that in 1 Kgs 22, the spirit assumes a distinct personality in the divine court. Whether this is a literary device or an actual scene, the spirit is sent alone to 'entice' humans (Ahab's prophets).

34. Snaith, *Distinctive Ideas*, p. 158. At this point, the 'spirits' in 1 Kgs 22 should be treated as a separate category. They are much closer to the idea of angels.

35. Snaith, 'Isaiah 40–66', p. 188.

36. For the 'prophetic inspiration', see Alphonsus Benson, *The Spirit of God in the Didactic Books of the Old Testament* (Catholic University of America, Studies in Sacred Theology, Second Series, 29; Washington: Catholic University of America Press, 1949), p. 76; Briggs, 'Use of *Ruach*', p. 142; de Boer, 'Second-Isaiah's Message', p. 52; Simon, *A Theology of Salvation*, p. 160.

37. Gitay, *Prophecy and Persuasion*, p. 220.

38. Antoon Schoors, *I Am God your Saviour: A Form-Critical Study of the Main Genres in Is. XL–LV* (VTSup, 24; Leiden: E.J. Brill, 1973), p. 279.

39. Condamin, *Le livre d'Isaïe*, p. 249; Watts, *Isaiah 34–66*, p. 178.

primarily the presence of extraordinary might on the chosen heroes, who in turn deliver Israel from foreign rulers. This corresponds to the role of the spirit in this passage. It is a drastic application of the previously higher regard of prophecy to the old 'lower' role of the spirit.[40] Still other options for the identity of the prophet have been put forward: Israel as God's prophet, Israel as God's servant, or Israel as the Lord's word personified.[41]

(61.1-3b)

1 The spirit of my Lord Yahweh is upon me,
      because Yahweh has anointed me
      to bring good news to the poor, he has sent me;
   to bandage those with broken hearts,
      to proclaim liberty to captives,
      and a releasing to those imprisoned,
2 to proclaim the year of Yahweh's favor
      and our God's day of vengeance,
   to comfort all mourners,
3 to assign (rights) to Zion's mourners.
   And to give them a wreath of flowers
      instead of ashes,
   oil of gladness
      instead of mourning,
   a mantle of praise
      instead of a spirit of fainting.

Form-critically speaking, the passage cannot exactly be identified with any existing literary genre. Yet, its close affinity to a pre-exilic prophetic call has been noted.[42] The presence of various literary elements leads some to call it 'a hybrid genre of different forms'.[43] The appearance of the call-like oracle in the middle of a series of promises

40. Briggs, 'Use of *Ruach*', p. 142.
41. Miscall, *Isaiah*, p. 116.
42. Mic. 3.8 is often pointed out in this regard; see, e.g., Montague, *The Holy Spirit*, p. 53. However, Micah's prophetic call is to proclaim judgment, whereas in Isa. 61.1-3b the call is to introduce an oracle of salvation. Westermann, *Isaiah 40–66*, p. 365, contends that the affinity is not to a vocational call as seen in Isa. 6 and Jer. 1 (and even Isa. 40.6-8), but to the Servant Songs. He also compares the the passage Micah passage and concludes that a pre-exilic stereotypical form, originally connected with salvation oracles, is taken over and used in a call setting.
43. Donald E. Gowan, 'Isaiah 61.1-3, 10-11', *Int* 35 (1981), pp. 404-409 (406), argues that the present form is different from the herald formula, royal hymn of self-glorification or Servant Songs, and claims prophetic authority (e.g. Mic. 3.8).

for Zion (chs. 60–62) without either an introduction or a conclusion seems to support the 'hybrid' nature. As frequently argued, this passage, along with chs. 61 and 62, might also be a prophetic liturgy which was originally used by a prophet in a cultic context.[44] A series of seven infinitives (vv. 1c-3), all dependent upon the verb 'sent' (שׁלח), describes the sevenfold task of the speaker.[45]

In this call-like self-declaration of divine authority, an old connection between the endowment of the divine spirit and the anointing is revived (for Saul in 1 Sam 10.1-13, and for David in 1 Sam. 16.13; cf. 2 Sam. 23.1-7). At first, only kings and high priests were anointed, although Elisha was anointed by Elijah as a prophet (1 Kgs 19.16).[46] The prophetic inspiration of the spirit of God throughout the Old Testament is for the preaching of Yahweh's word (e.g. Num. 24.2; Mic. 3.8; Ezek. 11.5; Zech. 7.12; Joel 3.1-2; 2 Sam. 23.2; Neh. 9.30; 2 Chron. 15.1; 20.14).[47] Although the anointing here is with the spirit rather than with oil as in the case of the kings, Snaith argues that the anointing may not necessarily involve an actual anointing with oil.[48] By this time, the 'anointed' (משׁח) was rather broadly understood as one chosen by God for a particular purpose.[49] In particular, the historical reality that the postexilic community does not have any royal figure seems to strengthen the case. As a consequence, the speaker is seen primarily as a prophetic rather than a royal figure, even a non-eschatological and non-messianic one.[50] He functions mainly as a spokesman for Yahweh.

44. Wilson, *Prophecy and Society*, p. 260.

45. Achtemeier, *Community and Message*, p. 89, compares the sevenfold nature of the task with the sevenfold spirit in Isa. 11.2.

46. Its metaphorical use is evidenced in 1 Kgs 19.16; see Grace I. Emmerson, *Isaiah 56–66* (OTG; Sheffield: JSOT Press, 1992), p. 75.

47. T.C. Vriezen, *An Outline of Old Testament Theology* (Oxford: Basil Blackwell, 1958), p. 250, argues that all the references, including this passage, are from later times.

48. Snaith, 'Isaiah 40–66', p. 199; Whybray, *Isaiah 40–66*, p. 241.

49. Duhm, *Das Buch Jesaja*, p. 413, regards the anointing here as 'no more than a rather loftier expression for sending'. Also Lindblom, *Prophecy in Ancient Israel*, p. 192; Westermann, *Isaiah 40–66*, p. 366; Whybray, *Isaiah 40–66*, p. 258; W. Zimmerli, *Old Testament Theology in Outline* (trans. David E. Green; Edinburgh: T. & T. Clark, 1978), p. 100.

50. Among many are A. Joseph Everson, 'Isaiah 61.1-6 (To Give Them a Garland Instead of Ashes)', *Int* 32 (1978), pp. 69-73 (70); Kissane, *Book of Isaiah*, II, p. 35; McKenzie, *Second Isaiah*, p. 181; Mowinckel, ' "Spirit" and the "Word" ',

However, Eaton and others find strong evidence for a royal figure, for the anointing and putting on of the spirit of God can be found only in the royal rite.[51] He further argues that the passage reflects the royal duty in the New Year Festival,[52] where the king's function, as the festal proclaimer of Yahweh's victory and glad tidings, fits with a series of effects described in 61.2-3.[53] In particularly, the releasing of captives[54] and the 'day of vengeance' appear to have strong royal and political elements. In fact, much of what the speaker says about himself is used elsewhere of kings (cf. Isa. 11.1-5), and some of his tasks are elsewhere attributed to God alone ('bind up the brokenhearted', cf. Job 5.18; Ps. 147.3; Isa. 30.26; Ezek. 34.16; Hos. 6.1).

The diverse interpretations of the 'year of favor' continue to fuel disagreements as to the identity of the speaker. Eaton, on one hand, pairs the 'day' and the 'year' as an expression of Yahweh's victory over the enemies for his people.[55] On the other hand, Zimmerli contends that the 'year' reflects the sabbatical or jubilee year or new year's day, with which the proclamation of liberty to the captives is associated (Lev. 25).[56] The 'day of vengeance' is part of the holy war tradition

p. 203; James D. Newsome, Jr, *The Hebrew Prophets* (Atlanta: John Knox Press, 1984), p. 173.

51. John H. Eaton, *Festal Drama in Deutero-Isaiah* (London: SPCK, 1979), p. 90; also *idem*, 'The Isaiah Tradition', in R. Coggins, A. Philips and M. Knibb (eds.), *Israel's Prophetic Tradition: Essays in Honour of Peter Ackroyd* (Cambridge: Cambridge University Press, 1982), pp. 58-76 (70). Mettinger, *King and Messiah*, pp. 25-26, argues for the royal nature by the proclamation of דרור (cf. Jer. 34.8, 15, 17) as well as the royal anointing.

52. Eaton, *Festal Drama*, p. 90. G. Widengren, *Sakrales Königtum im Alten Testament und im Judentum* (Stuttgart: W. Kohlhammer, 1955), pp. 57-58; Ringgren, *The Messiah*, p. 33.

53. Eaton, *Festal Drama*, p. 90.

54. Ringgren, *The Messiah*, p. 33 calls attention to the Assyrian and Egyptian texts in which the release of captives is a standard practice at the accession of a new king. However, the Hebrew verb פקח means to 'open', and both the opening (of eyes) and the releasing (of prisoners) are possible. LXX's reading ἀνάβλεψιν, 'recovery of sight [to the blind]' is followed by Lk. 4.18. Accordingly, LXX reads τυφλοῖς (= עורים or סנורים). But MT has the Qal passive plural participle of אסר and this is supported by 1QIsaᵃ, Tg and Vg.

55. Eaton, *Festal Drama*, p. 90.

56. W. Zimmerli, 'Das Gnädenjahr des Herrn', in Arnulf Kuschke and Ernst Kutsch (eds.), *Archäologie und Altes Testament: Festschrift für Kurt Galling z. 8.*

(Amos 5.18-20; Isa. 2.12-17; Zeph. 1.1-2.4; Jer. 46.2-12) from which von Rad finds the origin of the Day of Yahweh concept.[57]

This military and royal idea, however, has been modified to refer to a non-royal and non-military work of the prophet. Mendenhall correctly points out that its 'imperium rather is the ground for the events most needed by those who are in the greatest misery: the poor, the broken-hearted, the captives, and the grief-stricken'.[58] Here it becomes evident that the two different traditions are used with some modifications to picture the coming days of salvation.

The presence of both prophetic and royal elements recalls the first (42.1-4) and other Servant Songs (especially 49.1-6). The similarity in language is so unmistakable[59] that Snaith even calls the passage a secondary Servant Song.[60] The prophet appears to identify himself with the Servant of 42.1-3 as fulfilling the mission of the Servant Songs.[61] It is possible that this later prophet may be laying a claim to the song as its heir. Given this, it is not unnatural for the speaker of this passage to display prophetic as well as royal elements of his task as in the first Servant Song. As Westermann observes, the disparate items of old offices, that is, royal and prophetic, are 'accumulated into a baroque and artificial picture, having lost their old connotations'.[62] The claim is

Jan. 1970 (Tübingen: J.C.B. Mohr, 1970), pp. 321-32. See also Gowan, 'Isaiah 61.1-3, 10-11', p. 607.

57. Gerhard von Rad, 'The Origin of the Concept of the Day of Yahweh', *JSS* 4 (1959), pp. 97-108.

58. George E. Mendenhall, *The Tenth Generation: The Origins of the Biblical Tradition* (Baltimore: The Johns Hopkins University Press, 1973), p. 100.

59. The endowment of the spirit of Yahweh (42.1; 61.1); proclamation of freedom (42.7; 61.1; cf. 49.9); announcement of the favor of Yahweh (49.8; 61.21) to those who mourn (cf. 49.13; 61.2) and who are of a faint spirit (42.3; 61.3) and the building of the desolate heritage (cf. 49.8; 61.4) display the connection, according to Achtemeier, *Community and Message*, p. 88. One evident difference is between the speakers: God in the first Servant Song, and the prophet himself here.

60. Snaith, 'Isaiah 61.1-3, 10-11', p. 119. Some identify the speaker with the servant, e.g. Schoemaker, 'Use of "Ruach"', p. 27; Vriezen, *Outline*, p. 216.

61. McKenzie, *Second Isaiah*, p. 181. Hanson, *Isaiah 40–66*, pp. 223-24, believes that the servant figure provides a model for those who are called by Yahweh.

62. Westermann, *Isaiah 40–66*, pp. 365-67. However, the prophetic voices of the postexilic era are not in complete agreement with one another. See how other postexilic prophets such as Haggai and Zechariah uphold the traditional royal and priestly offices.

'something new and daring, a strikingly bold affirmation which equates the work of the prophet with the saving work of God himself'.[63] This does not only mingle traditions, but also breaks and goes beyond the traditional boundaries. The ideal role of a prophet has changed since the exile, particularly in a situation where no visible royal figure exists any longer.[64]

The main task of the speaker is to preach restoration, transformation and liberation from broken-heartedness, captivity,[65] lost property and status, and mourning.[66] He portrays himself and his mission predominantly with a prophetic color.[67] The prophet in the postexilic time is more than a prophet in its conventional definition: he is the announcer and introducer of the time of salvation.[68] However, with the royal element still appearing, as Eaton argues forcefully, one may see him in a kind of hybrid office as in the Servant (Isa. 42.1-4).

Accordingly, there may be two old יהוה traditions behind the passage: the prophetic (Num. 24.2; 2 Sam. 23.3) and royal endowment of the spirit of Yahweh (1 Sam. 16.13; 2 Sam. 23.1-7). These old traditions set the chosen ones apart from ordinary people and elevate them close to the realm of the divine world.[69] The presence of a prophet in the

63. Gowan, 'Isaiah 61.1-3, 10-11', p. 406.

64. Whether this passage represents an actual prophetic call or an idealized role of a prophet is not clear. Considering other claims, the latter seems to be more convincing. For instance, the servant, even though introduced in the present tense, is an expected and idealized figure rather than a present reality. The fact that no historical postexilic prophets, such as Haggai and Zechariah, make a similar claim reinforces the argument.

65. With the prophetic emphasis, Westermann, *Isaiah 40–66*, p. 366, contends that the captives are not the exiles, but people put in prison for debt and the like as in 58.6. The economic difficulties in the postexilic period are well attested, e.g. Ezra 3.3; Hag. 1.5-6, 9-11; 2.16-17.

66. Watts, *Isaiah 34–66*, p. 303, makes an observation that the speaker's task here is in contrast to those tasks of 11.2-5 where the ruler is pictured as a powerful figure.

67. Gowan, 'Isaiah 61.1-3, 10-11', p. 407, observes that 'every line except "to proclaim liberty to the captives and the opening of the prison to those who are bound" speaks of the emotional effect of the day which is good news, comfort, gladness, and praise'.

68. Montague, *The Holy Spirit*, p. 54.

69. H.H. Rowley, *The Faith of Israel* (London: SCM Press, 1956), p. 85, 'He not merely has the command of God laid upon him. He may be lifted in some measure into the very personality of God.'

divine council (e.g. Isa. 6; 1 Kgs 22.19-22) further strengthens this argument, although in the Israelite tradition (unlike the surrounding cultures, particularly the Egyptian), no one is identified with or elevated to divinity. Here, the 'extended personality of Yahweh'[70] enables the chosen one to proclaim the restoration and liberation to his people. He is a herald who announces the dawn of the age of salvation which is closely related to the messages of Second Isaiah. The prophet is well aware of his mediatory role as commonly seen in Isa. 11.1-3 and 42.1-4. In a similar way, the king is viewed as Yahweh's specially chosen. In the Israelite tradition, when a king is chosen by God himself, God's spirit is present (1 Sam. 10 for Saul and 1 Sam. 16 for David), and success as a king, therefore, is closely associated with God's spirit. Its ideal description is found in Isaiah 11, and some elements are also found in this present passage.

63.10-14

10 But they rebelled
    and grieved his holy spirit.
  Therefore he turned to be their enemy,
    and himself fought against them.
11 And [they] remembered the days of old,
    of Moses, and of his people.
  Where is he who brought [them] up out of the sea?
    The shepherd of his flock?
  Where is he who put in the midst of them
    his holy spirit?
12 Who caused his glorious arm
    to go at the right hand of Moses,
  who divided the waters before them
    to make for himself an everlasting name?
13 Who led them throughout the depths?
    As horses in the desert they did not stumble,
14 As cattle go down into the valley,
    the spirit of Yahweh brought them to rest.
  So you did lead your people,
    to make for thyself a glorious name.

An affinity of 63.7–64.11 to the community lament in Psalms is widely recognized.[71] To the lament, a prophetic oracular response is

70. Johnson, *Vitality of the Individual*, pp. 2-3.

71. Hanson, *Isaiah 40–66*, pp. 81-100; Westermann, *Isaiah 40–66*, p. 368; Artur Weiser, *The Old Testament: Its Formation and Development* (trans. Dorothea

added, whose form is 'a typical cultic sermon containing historical surveys of past history, moral admonitions and instruction in cultic affairs'.[72] Some scholars call the entire passage (vv. 7-14) a prophetic intercessory liturgy or a sermon-prayer.[73] Westermann observes, however, that this particular section (63.7-14) differs most significantly from a communal lament. The recitation of the saving deeds of God which normally forms an introductory part of the communal lament is expanded to such an extent that it appears almost to be an independent historical psalm such as Psalms 89 or 44.[74] Also, unlike in a lament, God is referred to in the third person.

The motif of the historical review is similar to the Deuteronomistic trend. The confession of guilt for the fall of the temple and Jerusalem is unmistakable. The recitation of the past history, especially in a cultic setting, is more than remembrance:

> Actualization of God's gracious deeds is equivalent to an appeal to that gracious will which once upon a time wrought these deeds, and is now entreated to perform them afresh.[75]

In vv. 7-9, God's gracious deeds in the past are characterized by the piling-up of words like חסד 'gracious deeds, goodness' (twice in v. 7), רב־טוב 'rich in goodness' (v. 7), רחם 'mercy' (v. 7), אהבה 'love' (v. 9), and חמלה 'pity' (v. 9). One half of the covenant formula, 'They are my people' (אך־עמי המה, v. 8, cf. Exod. 6.7; Jer. 31.33), recalls God's loving relationship with his covenant people. His abiding presence not only assures and protects them, but it actively saves them (e.g.

M. Barton; New York: Association Press, 1961), p. 207, noting its affinity with Lamentations and no relation with Second Isaiah, dates the passage earlier than Second Isaiah.

72. Lindblom, *Prophecy in Ancient Israel*, p. 271

73. Aubrey R. Johnson, 'The Psalms', in H.H. Rowley (ed.), *The Old Testament and Modern Study* (repr.; Oxford: Oxford University Press, 1961), pp. 162-209 (179). Also Watts, *Isaiah 34–66*, p. 329. Muilenburg, 'The Book of Isaiah, Chapters 40–66', p. 729, asserts that the prayer was composed for a special occasion, most likely a day of prayer for people. However, Hanson, *Isaiah 40–66*, p. 238, concedes that the voice is that of those oppressed by the leaders of the community.

74. Westermann, *Isaiah 40–66*, p. 386. Also Achtemeier, *Community and Message*, p. 113. But H. Odeberg, *Trito-Isaiah: A Literary and Linguistic Analysis* (Uppsala Universitets Arsskrift, Teologi, 1; Uppsala: Lundeqvist, 1931), p. 18, contends that vv. 7-14 are a hymn reminiscent of Pss. 44; 66; 68; 78; 89; 105; 106; 107.

75. Westermann, *Isaiah 40–66*, p. 387.

'redeemed...carried...' [v. 9], cf. 46.3-4; Deut. 32.7, 11-12). The strong corporate consciousness and the appeal to the exodus events are apparent. In response to the חסד of Yahweh, however, the people of Israel (see the emphatic 'they') reject his love and rebel against him. The effect of their rebellion is to grieve the holy spirit of God.

The spirit (v. 10) is conceived of as 'a representative or manifestation of Yahweh on earth'.[76] The holy spirit is not identified with the angel.[77] The statement, 'Neither envoy nor messenger (מלאך)—he himself saved them' (v. 9), rules out any identification of the 'holy spirit' with angels. It is more akin to the פנים, which reinforces this nature of the spirit.[78] Although in some cases פנים is associated with the wrath of God,[79] here רוח is used to indicate the intimacy between God and his people. In fact, פנים and רוח often appear side by side: as in Ps. 139.7, 'Where can I go from your spirit? From your presence (פנים) where can I flee?' Similar usages are also found in Ps. 104.29 and 51.13. Like 'the angel of his presence (פנים)', 'his holy spirit' (רוח קדשו) is God's medium of providential leading, salvation and redemption.[80]

The verb to 'grieve' (עצב) has prompted some scholars to conclude that the passage implies the personality of the spirit.[81] However, a

76. Lindblom, *Prophecy in Ancient Israel*, p. 413. But Edward R. Dalglish, *Psalm Fifty-One in the Light of Ancient Near Eastern Patternism* (Leiden: E.J. Brill, 1962), p. 159, contends the grieving of his holy spirit is the rejection of the prophetic ministry, which is inspired by the holy spirit. On the contrary, Mowinckel, '"Spirit" and the "Word"', p. 204, interprets the spirit as 'his mind and plan'.

77. Contra Briggs, 'Use of *Ruach*', p. 144, who identifies the spirit with the theophanic angel who led Israel in the wilderness. R.C. Cripps, 'The Holy Spirit in the Old Testament', *Theology* 24 (1932), pp. 272-80 (278) argues that the spirit is something apart from, but parallel to Yahweh's angel.

78. The spirit is never identified with God himself, even in an expression like 'Where shall I go from your spirit?' (Ps. 139.7). Contra Helmer Ringgren, *Israelite Religion* (trans. David E. Green; Philadelphia: Fortress Press, 1966), p. 93. More accurately, the spirit is associated with the presence of God.

79. W.F. Albright, *Yahweh and the Gods of Canaan: A Historical Analysis of Two Contrasting Faiths* (University of London; Winona Lake, IN: Eisenbrauns, 1968), p. 135.

80. Watts, *Isaiah 34–66*, p. 332. The contention of Cripps, 'The Holy Spirit', p. 278, that the spirit here is the 'life-giving principle for Yahweh', appears to be incorrect.

81. For instance, Skinner, *Isaiah Chapters XL–LXVI*, p. 222, claims that the passage exhibits the 'highest degree of personification of the spirit attained in the

careful examination of the use of the verb reveals that the intended meaning, especially in its piel form, is to 'impose one's will' or to 'oppose one's will' against another's (e.g. 1 Kgs 1.6; 1 Chron. 4.10; Ps. 56.5; cf. Job 10.8 and Jer. 44.19 in a physical sense).[82] The accurate use of the verb can be expressed by 'opposed' or 'resisted' rather than 'grieved'.[83] Yet the surprising use of the verb may be an indication, as Muilenburg contends, of the trend that moves in the direction of the personification of God's spirit as found in the Wisdom of Solomon.[84] It is a rebellion against his חסד and guidance. The holiness of God is almost always present in association with the theophany of his פנים. It is the danger of destruction if one comes too close or sins (cf. Exod. 19.21-24; 33.20).[85] It is his holiness, not his goodness, that is put to grief,[86] and as a result, God turns on them like an enemy (v. 10). The grieving of his holy spirit not only makes God withdraw his protective favor from them, but also exposes them to experiencing the hostilities of life.

This passage (vv. 10-14) is tangled with many difficult textual problems.[87] Since a textual problem is often interrelated with other textual

Old Testament', and Delitzsch, *Prophecies of Isaiah*, II, p. 456, views the spirit here as 'an existence capable of feeling and therefore not a mere force'.

82. Neve, *The Spirit of God*, p. 129, shows an intensive survey of the use of the verb in different forms. The verb עצב is a transitive verb denoting an action against one's emotion. The niphal form carries the original meaning, to 'grieve something' as David did for Absalom (2 Sam. 19.2), or even to 'feel physical pain' (Eccl. 10.9). On the contrary, nowhere in the Old Testament does either the qal, the piel or the hiphil carry such a meaning.

83. Neve, *The Spirit of God*, p. 129.

84. Muilenburg, 'Isaiah, Chapters 40–66', p. 733. Also Whybray, *Isaiah 40–66*, p. 258, '[the spirit is] personified more clearly... and is on its way to its later full development as a distinct hypostasis in late Jewish and in Christian thought'.

85. Montague, *The Holy Spirit*, p. 57.

86. Westermann, *Isaiah 40–66*, p. 388, argues that rejecting his goodness is to put his holiness to grief 'very characteristic of Old Testament thought'.

87. Verse 11 is extremely uncertain. The subject of v. 11a is not clear. Watts, *Isaiah 34–66*, p. 324, and RSV read 'he' (ויזכר), referring to God, but Whybray, *Isaiah 40–66*, p. 258, refers to the people of Israel. The latter translation poses a problem as the precedent of the third person singular masculine pronoun is plural in v. 10. B. Childs, *Memory and Tradition in Israel* (Naperville, IL: Allenson, 1962), p. 37 n. 45; Robert Koch, 'La théologie de l'esprit de Yahvé dans le livre d'Isaïe', in J. Coppens, A. Descamps and E. Massaux (eds.), *Sacra Pagina: Miscellanea biblica: Congressus Internationalis Catholici de Re Biblica* (2 vols.; Gembloux:

problems in the passage, it is unreasonable to reach a firm conclusion based on this fragile text.

The historical reality of misery makes them remember the glorious 'day of old' and ask where is the God who acted so mightily. The past work of deliverance becomes the basis on which his people can expect a deliverance in the present. Although 'in his midst' may refer to 'in the midst of Israel', the spirit of Yahweh is never bestowed upon the entire nation, but only upon selected leaders: in this case, Moses and the 70 elders. Joel's promise is yet to be fulfilled. The presence of Moses with the powerful manifestation of God's reality is later regarded as the presence of 'his holy spirit' in the midst of the people. This 'holy spirit' is, as in v. 10, an awesome power linked to the divine presence, which Johnson correctly calls the 'extension of his personality'.[88] The emphasis on power and might is well described by such phrases as 'his glorious arm', 'the right hand' and 'divided the waters' in v. 12.[89]

The existence of a medium for the work of the spirit ('[who will] cause his glorious arm to go at the right hand of Moses') is evident. The obvious focus of Moses as the national leader in the exodus event is clear. Moses, as an ideal national leader, may have significance in the postexilic society which longs for full restoration. Considering the growing importance of the Torah during the exilic and postexilic period, the focus on Moses is also to be expected. The protective and guiding presence of Yahweh in the wilderness journey is directly attributed to 'his holy spirit'.

However, the spirit does not participate in the struggle against the

Duculot, 1959), I, pp. 419-33 (424); Muilenburg, 'Isaiah, Chapters 40–66', p. 733; Westermann, *Isaiah 40–66*, p. 385 read 'they' (ויזכרו). Then the next line is read either 'Moses and his people', by inserting ו before עמו (*BHS*), 'Moses of his people' (1QIsaᵃ, Tg and Vg); or more radically 'the savior of his people' as by Torrey, *Second Isaiah*, p. 463. Westermann, *Isaiah 40–66*, p. 385, emends to עבדו, 'his servant' following some Syr. MSS. The object of 'brought up' is not clear. MT has the 'shepherd of his flock' as the object with את as the sign of the direct object, while Tg has אן, 'where'. However, MT has a pronominal suffix, 'them', while *BHS*, 1QIsaᵃ, two Hebrew MSS and Syr. omit it. Even the reading of the 'shepherd' is uncertain. MT has the plural construct form, רעי, followed by 1QIsaᵃ and Vg, while LXX (τὸν ποιμένα) and Tg (כרעיא, 'as the shepherd of') have a singular form.

88. Johnson, *Vitality of the Individual*, p. 33 n. 1. See also his *The One and the Many*, pp. 14-15, 22.

89. Mowinckel, '"Spirit" and the "Word"', p. 204; Volz, *Jesaia*, pp. 270-71, calls 'the power that operates in Israel's history'.

sea, although it is tempting to see v. 11e as a reference to Exod. 15.8
and 10.[90] The work of the spirit is reserved only for action in human
beings.[91] Holiness, unlike in v. 10, is more linked with the formidable
power of God. Likewise, the 'holy spirit' here is basically the same as
in v. 10, but they have different emphases: Yahweh's inner nature in v.
10, and his active outward deeds here.[92]

The 'spirit of Yahweh' in v. 14 is the same spirit that inspired Moses
to manifest the power of God (63.11). Mowinckel defines it as 'the
organ of his solicitous leading of Israel'.[93] The spirit delivered the
Israelites from the 'great depth' and this guidance is compared with
Yahweh's initial creation, binding the chaotic waters (Gen. 1.2; Isa.
11.15; 51.9, 10).[94] The completion of the wandering and the entering
into the promised land is attributed to the spirit of Yahweh.[95] With the
shepherd imagery, the writer highlights that Yahweh, with his holy
spirit, has protected and guided them all through the wandering until he
gave them rest.[96] The spirit here 'almost appears in the guise of a
guardian angel'.[97] The section comes to an end with the appearance of
the second person which prepares for the following prayer. In his
pastoral motif, the prophet affirms that the same spirit will accomplish
the full restoration after the exile.[98]

The peculiar expression of 'his holy spirit' (רוח קדשׁו) in vv. 10 and
11 has prompted numerous discussions among scholars. It is reasonable

90. Neve, *The Spirit of God*, p. 90.
91. Lys, *'Rûach'*, pp. 155-56.
92. Achtemeier, *Community and Message*, p. 115.
93. Mowinckel, ' "Spirit" and the "Word" ', p. 204.
94. Achtemeier, *Community and Message*, p. 115; Muilenburg, 'Isaiah, Chapters 40–66', p. 734.
95. Snaith, 'Isaiah 40–66', p. 237, contends that the prayer is offered by a small
group of people that has been rejected from the main stream of the community. The
memory of the Joseph tribes entering into the land of Canaan under Joshua reflects
their situation and hope. In v. 14, MT takes the verb as hiphil imperfect of נוח 'he
gave us rest'. LXX ('he led') and Vg ('he guided') assume נחה for the root.
Westermann, *Isaiah 40–66*, p. 385, and Whybray, *Isaiah 40–66*, p. 259, prefer the
former for the fitting context and its parallel in Exod. 33.14.
96. Smart, *History and Theology*, p. 269, suggests an emendation of the verb to
'give' into to 'lead' because of the difficulty with which horses find their way in a
desert.
97. Ringgren, *Israelite Religion*, p. 93.
98. Smith, *Rhetoric and Redaction*, p. 45, argues that the prophet assures the
presence and activity of the same spirit in the midst of the people.

to assume that the emphasis of the holiness of Yahweh in the Isaianic tradition (especially ch. 6 and the 'Holy One of Israel' throughout the book of Isaiah) leads to the description of his presence by the 'holy spirit'. R. Koch also suggests that this can be a replacement of the formula רוח יהוה or רוח אלהים because of the reverence for the tetragrammaton.[99] However, the fact that Psalm 51 has the only other occurrence of the term in the Old Testament outside this passage, does not support Koch's contention.

Psalm 51 appears to be of pre-exilic origin, with a definitely later hand turning this penitential psalm to a communal lament. Even the lament-like prayer of Isaiah 63 seems to stem from around or right after the fall of Jerusalem in 587 BCE.[100] In addition, the concept of the holiness of God in the confession of sin is similar in both cases. His holiness cannot be present where there is impurity and sin, for sin has a direct effect on his 'holy spirit' either by 'grieving' it or causing it to be taken away. The 'holy spirit' in both passages is an expression of the highly developed idea of God's transcendence. However, the principal difference between these two is the nature of the 'holy spirit' itself. The 'holy spirit' in Ps. 51.11(13) is the divine spirit or power of the good within an individual, whereas that of Isaiah 63 is the presence of God which leads his people throughout history. The 'holiness' of the psalm has an ethical import while the Isaiah text has the implication of sacredness. Therefore, the same expressions do not warrant the dependency of one passage on the other.[101] Moreover, the psalmist seems to be a selected person who can claim the holy spirit resident within him. Unlike the prophets who received the spirit only intermittently (e.g. 2 Kgs 3.15; 1 Chron. 12.19; 2 Chron. 15.1; Ezek. 11.5), the psalmist could be a king, the only official in Israel who has permanent possession of the spirit of Yahweh.[102]

In the Isaianic passage, the 'holy spirit' is a substitution for the direct revelation of God himself to his people. This expression 'holy spirit' may have been a basis for the later tradition where the expression becomes a technical term as seen in Tg.

---

99. Koch, 'La theólogie de l'esprit', p. 424 n. 1.

100. Westermann, *Isaiah 40–66*, p. 386.

101. Moses Buttenwieser, *The Psalms, Chronologically Treated with a New Translation* (Chicago: University of Chicago Press, 1938), pp. 191-92.

102. North, 'Hebrew Kingship', p. 16; Pedersen, *Israel, its Life and Culture*, III–IV, p. 86.

59.21
'As for me, this is my covenant with them', says Yahweh:
  'My spirit which is upon you,
    and my word which I put in your mouth
  Shall not cease from your mouth, nor from that of your seed,
    nor that of their offspring', says the Lord,
  'from now onward,
  even for ever'.

Most commentators agree that the passage does not belong to the larger section of 59.1-20, and its later origin is also generally argued by many.[103] The argument is basically twofold: the lack of logical connection to the preceding verses as seen in the change of person and unmetrical and prosaic character; and the clue to a different audience.[104] The introduction of a new theme and the presence of a concluding formula (20b) for 59.1-20a are also noticeable.[105] Several scholars pay attention to the different notion of the 'word' here. J. Scullion, after Keller, argues that the passage is 'from a time when the "word" was understood no longer in a prophetic but a nominal sense'.[106] Odeberg even narrows it down to a time after Ezra's reform when the yoke of the Law was accepted by the community.[107] However, the nominal interpretation of the 'word' is subject to question.

As to the function of the passage, however, there is less unanimity. Achtemeier is convinced that the verse forms the conclusion to the first part of the book (chs. 56–59) which was assembled by the 'Levitical-prophetic' community.[108] McKenzie, on the other hand, views this as an expansion of the preceding passage by a later hand. Scullion sees it bridge between chs. 58–59 and 60–62 by offering the final answer to 59.1 and introducing ch. 60;[109] while Westermann transposes it to between 66.20 and 22.[110]

---

103. Among others, e.g. Duhm, *Das Buch Jesaja*, p. 406; Mowinckel, ' "Spirit" and the "Word" ', p. 204; Odeberg, *Trito-Isaiah*, p. 197; Emmerson, *Isaiah 56–66*, p. 74. However, Watts, *Isaiah 34–66*, p. 285, treats the verse as the conclusion of vv. 15b-20.

104. Odeberg, *Trito-Isaiah*, p. 197.

105. McKenzie, *Second Isaiah*, p. 171.

106. Scullion, *Isaiah 40–66*, p. 168.

107. Odeberg, *Trito-Isaiah*, p. 197.

108. Achtemeier, *Community and Message*, p. 72.

109. McKenzie, *Second Isaiah*, p. 169. Also Kendall, '*Mišpaṭ*', p. 404.

110. Westermann, *Isaiah 40–66*, p. 352.

The literary allusion to and interdependency with the Priestly document in the Pentateuch (Gen. 9.8, 9; 17.4)[111] is observed by Duhm.[112] Also '[the law] out of your mouth' echoes Jer. 31.36; Josh. 1.8 (D) (cf. Exod. 13.9; Deut. 6.6, 7; 30.14).

In this prose form, God, for the first time, is the speaker, for Yahweh identifies the prophetic word with his own (cf., e.g., Jer. 1.9; 5.14).[113] The promise is given to a wider circle than a single prophet as in 61.1-3. The word and the prophetic spirit will be found in 'the mouth of your seed' and 'the mouth of your seed's seed'. Lindblom points out that it is only because the prophets are among the people that the people as a whole are thought of as being in possession of the prophetic spirit. [114]

On the contrary, Duhm, with several others mentioned above, contends that the 'word' is not of the prophet, but the presentation of the ideal of legalism: 'the covenant is the law'. As a consequence, the spirit is not 'the spirit that is at work in the Servant, nor the prophetic spirit, nor the spirit that leads Israel: it is probably the spirit of obedience'.[115] His case rests on three observations: First, the Priestly style of the passage; secondly, a declaration of the complete reliability of the word of God (e.g. 31.2; 34.16; 37.36; 40.26; 45.19; 48.16; 49.2; 55.10-11);[116] and thirdly the relatively late date of the passage.

However, another argument against the nominal interpretation of the 'word' and the 'spirit' is the use of the two concepts in chs. 60–62. The 'word' of God is not used in the nominal way referring to Torah. Also,

---

111. Also Torrey, *Second Isaiah*, p. 443.

112. Duhm, *Das Buch Jesaja*, p. 406.

113. 'As for me', used in a prophetic declaration (e.g. Mic. 3.8), is directly applied to this divine speech. Whybray, *Isaiah 40–66*, pp. 228-29, argues that the expression is in the priestly style, while the rest of the verse is reminiscent of Deuteronomic thought.

114. Lindblom, *Prophecy in Ancient Israel*, p. 276. Also Kendall, '*Mišpaṭ*', p. 404; Smart, *History and Theology*, p. 252; Whybray, *Isaiah 40–66*, p. 229; Emmerson, *Isaiah 56–66*, pp. 74-75.

115. Duhm, *Das Buch Jesaja*, p. 406. Some older commentators consider the spirit as the spirit of postexilic law-based piety: G.H. Box, *The Book of Isaiah* (London: Pitman & Sons, 1908), p. 310; K. Marti, *Das Buch Jesaja* (KHAT, 10; Tübingen: J.C.B. Mohr, 1900), pp. 380-81; Cheyne, *Introduction to the Book of Isaiah*, p. 336. It is true that hereditary succession is not practiced among the prophets.

116. Douglas R. Jones, 'The Cessation of Sacrifice after the Destruction of the Temple in 586 BC', *JTS* 14 (1963), pp. 12-31; Scullion, *Isaiah 40–66*, p. 168.

since this passage has the definite function to link the preceding passages with the following chapters, the writer would not normally intend a meaning other than that used in chs. 60–62. It is God's revelation communicated through his word, which has been placed in the mouth of his people. This verse declares that Yahweh will make a (new) covenant with the people, the redeemed Zion, and the redemption is a covenant that is described in the following chapters.[117] The late date of the passage does not exclude the prophetic notion, as is clearly seen in Joel 3.1-3.[118] What the passage intends is well represented by Kendall:

> In fact, v. 21 says that as long as Israel exists, (active) prophecy will never cease to be. It is an aspect of the longed for salvation. The people are the bearers of the prophetic gift, though the nation as a whole is not considered Yahweh's spokesman.[119]

The addressee may not be the prophet but the people. But the people are thought of 'as being in possession of the divine word while they have the prophets in their midst'.[120]

There is a strong emphasis on the perpetuation of prophecy in this verse. It is in contrast with Joel 3.1-3, stressing not only the perpetuation, but also the universality of the prophetic gift. At any rate, both texts indicate that the democratization of the spirit to the people is a known trend in the exilic literature (e.g. Isa. 32.16-20; 44.3) and postexilic literature (e.g. Joel 3.1-3). Becker contends that the theoretical transfer of prophecy to the entire nation (Joel 3.1-3; Isa. 61.1-3) is by analogy with the transfer of kingship to the nation or the people of Israel.[121] Although there is no eschatological notion, unlike the Joel passage, the writer is aware of the fact that he and the people are in the dawn of the age of salvation.

The passage also displays some affinity to the first Servant Song (42.1-4). The addressee is a single individual, and Yahweh's spirit and

117. Based on the statement 'I have put my words in your mouth' in 51.16, Emmerson, *Isaiah 55–66*, p. 74, identifies the addressee with personified Zion.

118. The postexilic date of Joel is still a debated matter: e.g. Allen, *Joel, Obadiah, Jonah and Micah*, pp. 19-25.

119. Kendall, *'Mišpaṭ'*, p. 402. However, Achtemeier, *Community and Message*, p. 73, argues that the passage does not refer to a 'hereditary continuation of the prophetic gift...but to the perpetual remembrance of the prophets' word'.

120. Lindblom, *Prophecy in Ancient Israel*, p. 111.

121. Becker, *Messianic Expectation*, pp. 51, 68-69.

words have already been given to the addressee. However, the similarity ends there. The promise in this passage will continue through generations. For this reason, the reference is more to the prophetic than royal nature of the gift. Possible democratization can be more easily applied to the prophetic gift than to the royal one.

Why is the prophet or prophecy closely connected with the age of salvation? According to Lindblom, the existence of prophecy and prophets is a privilege to Israel (Num. 23.23; Deut. 18.15-22). The disappearance of prophets, therefore, serves as a typical sign of punishment and judgment, and God's distancing of himself from his people (Amos 8.11-12; Ezek. 7.26; Ps. 74.9; Lam. 2.9).[122] Consequently, the coming age of salvation is envisaged as a time when prophecy is given to everyone in the community.

The association of the spirit and the words of God is also noted.[123] Among the pre-exilic prophets, the claim of the spirit of God as the source of prophetic inspiration is scarce.[124] The only exception is Mic. 3.8. Instead, the expression 'the word of Yahweh' seems to occupy the place of the 'spirit of God' idea. It is only after the fall of Jerusalem that the idea receives a revived emphasis as seen in Ezekiel. The idea is applied even to the community (Ezek. 37.1-14; Zech. 12.10; Joel 3.1-3, etc.).

It is generally assumed that the words of God gain increasing significance in the absence of the temple service and sacrifice.[125] Isaiah 59.21 may suggest that the spirit is not to be separated from the word. The presence of the spirit assures that the promise declared up to v. 20 will come true.[126] This relation between the spirit and the word recalls Isa. 34.16 where the fulfillment of the 'word' is achieved by the spirit. In this 'summit of the book's theology of the spirit',[127] the covenant is a

122. Lindblom, *Prophecy in Ancient Israel*, p. 202.

123. E.g. Montague, *The Holy Spirit*, p. 60, 'a perfect coincidence of spirit and word'.

124. For a discussion on the matter, see Kapelrud, 'Spirit and the Word', pp. 40-47, and Mowinckel, '"Spirit" and the "Word"', pp. 199-227; and *idem*, *JBL* 56 (1937), pp. 261-65.

125. Muilenburg, 'Isaiah, Chapters 40–66', p. 696.

126. Neve, *The Spirit of God*, p. 82. However, Gowan, *Eschatology*, p. 75, argues that 'the effect of the gift of covenant and spirit is an internalizing of the divine word' which he seems to identify with 'the statutes and ordinances of the Lord'.

127. Montague, *The Holy Spirit*, p. 59.

firm assurance that prophecy by the spirit of Yahweh and words will perpetually exist in Israel (see, e.g., Joel 3.1-3). Therefore the covenant is not a new covenant as in Jer. 31.31-34 (also Ezek. 36.27), but the fulfillment of an old covenant (e.g. Hag. 2.4-5).

Having said that, one should be reminded that the addressee issue is not completely solved. There is a strong possibility that the writer has a prophetic circle in his mind rather than the people as a whole. The passage is either a fragment or an independent stand-alone oracle.

4.2-6

[2]In that day, the branch of Yahweh will become a beauty and glory. And the fruit of the land will become a majesty and honor to the remnant of Israel. [3]And it will be that the remnant in Zion and the separate in Jerusalem will be called holy. All who are written for life in Jerusalem. [4]When the Lord washes away the filth of the daughters of Zion, he cleanses the bloodstains of Jerusalem from her midst with the spirit of judgment and with the spirit of burning. [5]And Yahweh will create upon all the establishment of the mount Zion and over all her assembly, cloud by day and smoke and glow of fire. Indeed over all glory. [6]It will be canopy and a booth for a shade from heat by day, for a shelter and concealment from thunder-shower and from rain.

This 'proto-apocalyptic' passage is introduced by a familiar eschatological language 'in that day' (ביום ההוא). There have been numerous discussions regarding the interpretation of צמח יהוה. LXX takes the Aramaic word צמחא 'brightness' as its root word and renders ἐπιλάμψει ὁ Θεος 'God will shine forth'.[128] However, the traditional view takes the word as a royal symbol (e.g. 11.1). This usage is evident among exilic and postexilic passages (Jer. 23.5; 33.15; Zech. 3.8; 6.12). Although it is premature to assign the messianic reference to the term,[129] during the postexilic period the term frequently refers to the expected ruler.[130] The eschatological feature is reinforced by the presence of the remnant (vv. 2, 3). On the other hand, a literal interpretation gains its support primarily from its parallel reference. The 'fruit of the land' (פרי הארץ) can be best interpreted as the bountiful product of the

---

128. John Gray, *The Legacy of Canaan* (VTSup, 5; Leiden: E.J. Brill, 1957) quoted by Wildberger, *Isaiah 1–12*, p. 165. See also J. Ziegler, *Das Buch Isaias* (Würzburg: Echter Verlag, 1948), p. 107.

129. Wildberger, *Isaiah 1–12*, p. 116.

130. Conservative scholarship assigns the term to the messiah, e.g. Young, *The Book of Isaiah*, I, p. 173; Youngblood, *The Book of Isaiah*, p. 37.

land,[131] for agricultural bounty is a regular feature of the restored Zion (e.g. Isa. 32.15-20). In that case, taking the 'branch of Yahweh' as 'whatever Yahweh allows to sprout'[132] is not difficult. Yet the passage as a whole has the non-material aspect of the restored community as its emphasis.[133]

The passage is positive in its nature, although judgment is part of the message. It can be easily assumed that the passage has been inserted by later hands, possibly in the postexilic period, to balance out the message of judgment with the present message of salvation.[134] However, the judgment is not historical in which Yahweh uses a nation, but spiritual in which the spirit is the means.[135]

The text portrays fully restored Zion with majesty (גאון) and glory (תפארת and כבוד). This time will be marked by Yahweh's direct intervention and his rule. Even the presence of a 'branch' will be part of God's full restoration,[136] but the 'branch' is not described as participating in God's rule. God's rule in restored Jerusalem will be specifically expressed in his cleansing and protection. Because of Yahweh's direct involvement, the remnant of Zion will be holy (קדוש, v. 3). The

131. Wildberger, *Isaiah 1–12*, p. 166; Seitz, *Isaiah 1–39*, p. 42. Miscall, *Isaiah*, p. 29, and Seitz, *Isaiah 1–39*, p. 42, seem to take both literal agricultural and metaphorical messianic meanings.

132. Wildberger, *Isaiah 1–12*, p. 162.

133. Watts, *Isaiah 1–33*, p. 49 rejects the narrow messianic or agricultural interpretation and views the pair—the 'branch' and the 'fruit'—as referring to 'Yahweh's plans and purpose in their entirety'.

134. The postexilic origin of Isa. 4.2-6 is strongly supported by a number of commentators, e.g. Clements, *Isaiah 1–39*, p. 53; Fohrer, *Das Buch Jesaja*, I, p. 71; Kaiser, *Isaiah 1–12*, p. 85; Watts, *Isaiah 1–33*, p. 51; Eichrodt, *Theology of the Old Testament*, II, pp. 63-64. Nielsen, *There Is Hope for a Tree*, p. 180, assigns the passage to the exilic period, while Wildberger, *Isaiah 1–12*, p. 165, argues that 'at least a core ...could have come from Isaiah himself'. See also Jensen, *Use of* tôrâ *by Isaiah*, pp. 85-89; Yehoshua Gitay, *Isaiah and his Audience: The Structure and Meaning of Isaiah 1–12* (Studia Semitica Neerlandica; Assen: Van Gorcum, 1991), pp. 39-41; B. Wiklander, *Prophecy as Literature: A Text-Linguistic and Rhetorical Approach to Isaiah 2–4* (ConBOT, 22; Lund: C.W.K. Gleerup, 1984), p. 181, who assigns chs. 2–4 to 734–622 BCE. For a survey of the issue, see Williamson, *The Book Called Isaiah*, pp. 146-54.

135. Wildberger, *Isaiah 1–12*, p. 170.

136. Wildberger, *Isaiah 1–12*, p. 166, correctly points out that the 'branch of Yahweh' asserts the sovereign divine act, in comparison with Isa. 11.1, 'a scion from the stump of Jesse'. See also Watts, *Isaiah 1–33*, p. 49.

holiness, however, is attained only through the removal of filthiness and cleansing of guilt. Cleansing is viewed as prerequisite for God's restoration (v. 4): 'the splendor of restoration requires the destruction, the refining away, of the wicked, the dross'.[137]

The passage refers to the spirit of judgment and the spirit of burning (4.4).[138] An identical expression (רוח משפט) appears in Isa. 28.6 with a similar setting. Both passages project the future restored community, and in both cases the spirit functions positively. However, the role of the spirit is quite different. In 4.4, the spirit of judgment and the spirit of burning are given to cleanse the filth of Zion. In 28.6, the spirit is given to those who are going to judge the envisaged restored remnant community. The result of the spirit's activity is cleansing (בער), a ritually purifying work (Ezek. 40.38; 2 Chron. 4.6). Thus the spirit of judgment or justice and the spirit of burning have an immediately negative role in the purifying judgment of Yahweh,[139] in spite of the ultimately positive result.[140] Miscall notes that the passage alludes to Gen. 1.1 by ברא and to Exodus by the 'cloud' and 'fire'.[141]

The spirit is God's impersonal power to bring judgment and salvation

137. Miscall, *Isaiah*, pp. 29-30.

138. N.H. Tur-Sinai, 'A Contribution to the Understanding of Isaiah I–XII', *Scripta Hierosolymitana* 8 (1951), pp. 154-241 (164), emends רוח to דוח 'to purge'. He also emends משפט 'judgment' to משטף 'ablution' ('A Contribution to the Understanding', p. 164). 'Burning' בער is emended to סער 'storm wind' in 1QIsaᵃ after Exod. 1.4; 13.11, 13; Ps. 107.25; 148.8. Wildberger, *Isaiah 1–12*, p. 163, takes the secondary meaning of בער 'consume', 'utterly remove'; cf. BDB, p. 129.

139. NAB translates as 'blast of his searing judgment'.

140. Miscall, *Isaiah*, p. 30, aptly describes the two extreme functions of רוח: 'It denotes both life and death...[it] animates and invigorates (11.2-4; 28.6; 32.15; 42.5; 44.3; 61.1); it burns, desiccates and destroys (4.4; 11.15; 40.7; 49.10); it blows away (17.13; 41.16; 49.10)'. Although he treats the diverse meanings of רוח together, it is here that both the negative and the positive functions come together.

141. Miscall, *Isaiah*, p. 30. Also John F.A. Sawyer, *Isaiah* (2 vols.; DSB; Philadelphia: Westminster Press, 1984), I, p. 45 calls this a new creation and new Exodus. However, v. 5 has a textual uncertainty. MT reads וברא 'and he will create', while LXX renders καὶ ἥξει assuming ובא 'and he will come'. Wildberger, *Isaiah 1–12*, p. 163, also points out the unusual expression that Yahweh 'creates' a cloud and smoke. *BHS* supports LXX reading. Thus LXX, followed by *BHS*, reads καὶ ἔσται, and so reads 'And he will come and will be...' However, Watts, *Isaiah 1–33*, p. 48, maintains the MT reading arguing that the motif here is not theophany but the divine protection.

to his people.[142] The spirit here does not have a human agent, but functions as God's agent to effect people or the 'daughters of Zion'. As far as its function is concerned, Sawyer likens the spirit of judgment to the exterminating angel in Exodus 12.[143] The imagery, then, is that of the wind which blows away the chaff from the threshing floor and burns it.[144] The reference here is entirely impersonal, and the spirit is viewed as a divine force to execute Yahweh's purifying will. The strong emphasis of Zion theology with theophanic language is unmistakable. The positive nature of the passage, but with a purifying judgment, is in accordance with the postexilic spiritual climate.

2. *God's* רוח *in Postexilic Isaianic Theology*

The largest amount of the postexilic Isaianic material comes from Third Isaiah. Diverse theories have been presented as to its origin and nature, which is mainly due to the diverse nature of the message. Other than those who accept the unity of chs. 40–66,[145] there are two main schools in regard to the nature of chs. 56–66: those who maintain unity, and those who reject it. Duhm, who for the first time separated the last 11 chapters from Second Isaiah, argues for a single author with a few later additions.[146] Elliger also argues for a single author. The author is believed to be a disciple of Second Isaiah and among the first generation returnees. This individual is also responsible, according to Elliger, for collecting and editing his master's work.[147] His assessment is based on a linguistic and stylistic analysis. Hanson, with his 'contextual-typological method' and literary analysis, concludes not only the affinity of

142. Wildberger, *Isaiah 1–12*, p. 170; Baumgärtel, 'Spirit in the OT', pp. 362-63.

143. Sawyer, *Isaiah*, I, p. 45.

144. Montague, *The Holy Spirit*, p. 38; Sawyer, *Isaiah*, I, p. 45. Also 'scorching judgment' by Stacey, *Isaiah 1–39*, p. 31.

145. E.g. Smart, *History and Theology*.

146. Duhm, *Das Buch Jesaja*, pp. xv, xx, 389. The triple division of the book of Isaiah has not been accepted by conservative scholars like Young, *The Book of Isaiah*, I–II; Oswalt, *Isaiah Chapters 1–39*; Motyer, *The Prophecy of Isaiah*.

147. Karl Elliger, *Die Einheit des Tritojesaja* (Stuttgart: W. Kohlhammer, 1928); *idem*, *Deuterojesaja im seinem Verhältnis zu Tritojesaja* (BWANT, 63; Stuttgart: W. Kohlhammer, 1933); *idem*, 'Der Prophet Tritojesaja', *ZAW* 49 (1931), pp. 112-41.

Third Isaiah to Second Isaiah, but also the clear unity of chs. 56–66.[148]

However, the complex literary nature of chs. 56–66 gives a strong impression that these chapters are a collection of materials composed by different individuals in different periods.[149] Even the linguistic and stylistic coherence is not consistent on close examination. Any literary or thematic unity can be maintained, therefore, only with artificial connections. At best, one can only detect evidences that materials from diverse origin have been compiled and arranged around a number of themes.[150]

2.1 *Delayed Salvation and Required Judgment*
In many ways, the postexilic tradition continues the exilic Isaianic tradition. The announcement of impending salvation is the most observable similarity (chs. 60–62, particularly 61.1-3).[151] Schramm argues that Third Isaiah serves 'to develop and clarify the theme of Second Isaiah'.[152] The very beginning of Third Isaiah reaffirms that the day of Israel's salvation has come (56.1; cf. 60.1). The prophet stresses the validity of the old promises, which is well expressed by the fact that God identifies the word of the prophet with his own (59.21). Thus, unlike the exilic tradition, the messages of impending salvation are juxtaposed with the messages of necessary judgment as the precondition for salvation.

2.1.1 *Frustration*. The return from the exile is prompted by the expectation of imminent restoration, a glorious second exodus led by Yahweh in person, the glory of Zion and the like. In fact, on the con-

---

148. Paul D. Hanson, *The Dawn of Apocalyptic: The Historical and Sociological Roots of Jewish Apocalyptic Eschatology* (Philadelphia: Fortress Press, rev. edn, 1979), pp. 41-46.

149. For example, Lindblom, *Prophecy in Ancient Israel*, p. 270; Westermann, *Isaiah 40–66*, pp. 296-300. But contra, for 'a single period, by different authors', McKenzie, *Second Isaiah*, p. xxi; and for 'a unified product of the Isaianic school', Achtemeier, *Community and Message*, p. 16.

150. Eissfeldt, *The Old Testament*, p. 344; Otto Kaiser, *Introduction to the Old Testament* (trans. John Sturdy; Minneapolis: Augsburg, 1975), pp. 270-71.

151. The complexity of chs. 56–66 makes it difficult to discuss the message of 'Third Isaiah' because there is more than one voice.

152. Brooks Schramm, *The Opponents of Third Isaiah: Reconstructing the Cultic History of the Restoration* (JSOTSup, 193; Sheffield: Sheffield Academic Press, 1995), p. 80.

trary, the postexilic Judean community experiences frustration in every area of life. Ackroyd points out a number of facts that contribute to the frustration: (1) a rather moderate 'second exodus'; (2) the temple is not fully restored; (3) political obstacles from within and without; and (4) economic difficulties.[153] Thus the partially fulfilled restoration, or delayed salvation, becomes a reality which the community has to reckon with. This 'poor and disorganized'[154] community realizes that the reality is far from being the fulfillment of Second Isaiah's glorious prophecy, and that the day of salvation is delayed. Thus, as the community struggles with the delay of salvation,[155] numerous theological inquiries arise: Why is salvation delayed, and who will (or will not) be included in salvation? These are the main characteristics of postexilic Judaism including Third Isaiah.[156]

2.1.2 *Yahweh.* Yahweh's loftiness is a continuing theme. He is the 'high and holy God, who lives forever' (57.15), and he also inhabits 'a high and holy place' (57.15). The emphasis on God's holiness which appears consistently throughout the entire Isaianic traditions reinforces this emphasis. He is the one 'whose name is holy' (57.13).

However, there are some changes in specifics. First of all, the description of God and his act does not reach the grandeur seen in the exilic texts. In spite of the transcendent emphasis, his immanence with the meek and lowly implies this change (57.15, 18). In addition, the holiness of Yahweh finds a contrast between the exilic and postexilic times. In the former, God's holiness is shown in his power to restore his people from humiliation and subjugation by foreign powers (hence by foreign gods). In the latter, however, the understanding of God's holiness is similar to that of the pre-exilic concept. Its presence cannot permit the iniquity and sins of the people. Therefore, his holiness is expressed in his judgment, but with a strong purging motive. The

153. Ackroyd, *Israel*, p. 172, and Whybray, *Isaiah 40–66*, pp. 40-41. A succession of poor harvests (Hag. 1.9-11; 2.15-17) leaves many without adequate food and clothing (Hag. 1.6). For more discussion, see John Bright, *A History of Israel* (Philadelphia: Westminster Press, 3rd edn, 1981), pp. 365-68; and for the political situation, see Ackroyd, *Exile and Restoration*, pp. 138-44, which covers the 'first stage of the restoration'.

154. McKenzie, *Second Isaiah*, p. xix.

155. Hans-Joachim Kraus, 'Die ausgebliebene Endtheophanie: Ein Studie zu Jesaja 56–66', *ZAW* 78 (1966), pp. 317-32.

156. Schramm, *The Opponents*, p. 82.

concept of holiness is more than sacredness and separateness, both of which contribute to the transcendence of God.

For the postexilic community, the exodus events are analogous to the exilic Judean community. The description of the work of God's spirit in the wilderness is that of tender care and protective guidance. This concept is evident throughout the postexilic Isaianic tradition. The rejection of God's חסד is to 'grieve' his holy spirit (63.10). Here, for the first time, the holiness of God is associated with his spirit. In spite of the shortcomings of the people, God has been patiently postponing the judgment 'for a long time' (57.11). In fact, God makes himself available to be sought out and found by those who did not seek him and spreads out his hands all day long (65.1-3). This is not only because of his special relationship with Israel, but also because of the fact that his spirit abides among his people. Thus the combination of judgment and salvation is characteristic of the postexilic prophetic tradition. However, his grace not only sets limits to judgment on his people (57.16), it also makes judgment distinctly a purge.

Another significant feature, continuing the former Isaianic traditions, is Yahweh's sovereignty. Yahweh is the 'high and lofty One' (57.15); he alone is God. The postexilic tradition is a faithful heir of the exilic Isaianic theology of Yahweh's supremacy (e.g. אני יהוה ואין עוד, 'I am Yahweh, there is no other', 43.11; 44.6; 45.5, 6, 14, 21, 22; 46.9). In 4.2-6, Yahweh's faithfulness and sovereignty is the initiating force to bring first purging judgment and then glowing salvation to Zion. The spirit is God's instrument of purification. God's one-sided grace is well expressed in 63.7-9. 63.10-14 reveals that the holy spirit of God abides with Moses, thus residing in the midst of the people. Yet, the Israelites rebel, and as a result Yahweh becomes their enemy. However, Yahweh will ultimately fulfill his will through his spirit (v. 14). There is an implication here that Yahweh is a warrior who is ready to intervene to rescue his suffering people, although it is from their sins and iniquity (59.19, cf. vv. 1-6).

2.1.3 *'Enemies'*. There are sufficient indications that the postexilic community is divided into two groups: the oppressors and the oppressed, the spurious Israel and the genuine Israel, or the opposing and pious groups. For Second Isaiah, the enemy is clearly the Babylonian empire, but for Third Isaiah, with the vague identity of the group, the enemy is found within.[157] Achtemeier argues that the identity of the oppressed group is crucial in determining the motif as well as the identity of Third Isaiah, if there is such a prophet. Hanson argues that the conflict is between the 'visionary disciples of Second Isaiah' who are proponents of the restoration program described in Isaiah 50–62 and the Zadokite priests who are devoted to the restoration program described in Ezekiel 40–48.[158] The conflict is, in other words, between the prophetic and priestly groups.[159] Among the oppressed priests, according to Achtemeier, one unifying voice emerges to express the lament of suffering. This is the Isaianic school in the early restoration period, and this oppressed group includes foreigners and eunuchs among its members (56.1-8).[160] In spite of Hanson's strong argument, his reconstruction of the postexilic situation is seriously marred by the vagueness of the evidence.[161] Contrary to Hanson and Achtemeier, Schramm argues that the enemies are 'traditional, syncretistic YHWHists…whose religious practices had a long history in the [pre-exilic] kingdoms of Israel and Judah'.[162] They are Pentateuchal ritualists.

Regardless of the exact identity of the enemies, two religious groups are in conflict over religious practices as well as community life. As the community is divided, it is then no longer the entire community which will experience the restoration. Whereas in Second Isaiah, the entire community is called 'Jacob/Israel', the same term is no longer used.

---

157. J. Fischer, *Das Buch Isaias* (2 vols.; Bonn: Peter Hanstein, 1937–39), II, p. 170, and Muilenburg, 'Isaiah, Chapters 40–66', p. 695 argue for the external foe. Smith, *Rhetoric and Redaction*, pp. 124-25, argues for both external and internal foes. See also Fohrer, *Das Buch Jesaja*, III, p. 222; O.H. Steck, 'Jahwes Feinde in Jesaja 59', *BN* 36 (1987), pp. 51-56; K. Pauritsch, *Die neue Gemeinde: Gott sammelt Ausgestossene und Arme (Jesaja 56–66): Die Botschaft des Tritojesaia-Buches literar-, form-, gattungskritisch und redaktionsgeschichtlich untersucht* (AnBib, 47; Rome: Biblical Institute Press, 1971), p. 101.

158. Hanson, *Apocalyptic*, p. 12.

159. Joseph Blenkinsopp, 'The "Servants of the Lord" in Third Isaiah: Profile of a Pietistic Group in the Persian Epoch', *Proceedings of the Irish Biblical Association* 7 (1983), pp. 1-23 (6), identifies the 'servants' with the prophetic minority.

160. Achtemeier, *Community and Message*, pp. 16-18. Similarly Snaith, 'Isaiah 40–66', pp. 135-264, views the chapters as the product of a polemic between the Samaritans or 'proto-Samaritans' and the returned exiles.

161. For a short criticism, see Emmerson, *Isaiah 55–66*, pp. 85-94; and for a detailed criticism, see R.P. Carroll, 'Twilight of Prophecy or Dawn of Apocalyptic?', *JSOT* 14 (1979), pp. 3-35.

162. Schramm, *The Opponents*, p. 181.

There is a clear indication that collective designations are avoided.[163] True Israel within the historical Israel is apparent in the postexilic Isaianic tradition (57.13, 21; 59.2-8; 65.1-16a; 66.3-4, 5, 17).

The offenders are called the 'sons of the sorceress' and 'offspring of the adulterer and the harlot' (57.3), 'children of transgression' and 'the offspring of deceit' (57.4). It is not clear whether all these descriptions are to be taken literally or figuratively. The piling up of their guilt and the intense description of the suffering by the faithful highlights the distinction between the true and false Israel. Although such a distinction is not known to Second Isaiah, the differentiation between a spiritual remnant and a historical one exists in the Isaianic tradition (Isa. 37.30-32).[164]

2.1.4 *Sins.* The 'enemies' are often attacked as prime offenders. One area of Israel's infidelity is in its religious practices. The postexilic Isaianic tradition shares the old prophetic heritage which asserts the vanity of cultic practices (Jer. 7.1-15; Hos. 6.4-6; Amos 5.21-24). Although the temple itself is not yet completely restored, there are indications that some forms of religious practice have been restored by the returning exiles; increased cultic interest is obvious during this time (56.1-2; 58.1-12, 13-14; 66.1-4). Nevertheless, the Sabbath, which becomes a distinguishing mark of religious piety (56.4), is not properly observed (56.1-2; 58.13-14). One may argue for economic difficulties that forced the common people to work for their daily living. However, that others do things for pleasure on the Sabbath implies that the negligence of the Sabbath is a general practice in the community. The wrong attitude to fasting is attacked, too (58.3-7). It is reasonably assumed that fasting finds its place after the fall of Jerusalem, and becomes a standard religious practice during the exilic and postexilic periods (e.g. Zech. 8.18-19). But the fasts soon become a means to demonstrate outward religious piety without a corresponding commitment of the heart to Yahweh and fellow-citizens. In several places, superstitious practices are attacked (57.3-13; 66.1-7, 11-12, 17). What the exact nature of the superstitions is cannot be identified, but the problem echoes the pre-exilic practice of idolatry which accepted the Canaanite gods and cults. The destruction of idols (57.5, 7, 9, 13) and

163. Schramm, *The Opponents*, p. 182.
164. Hasel, *The Remnant*, p. 315.

child sacrifices (57.5) presuppose that idolatry is still a common problem even in this postexilic community.

The next area of the prophetic condemnation is nothing new to the community. The lack of righteousness and mercy is the strongest accusation of First Isaiah.[165] Yahweh demands a right relationship among his people rather than a display of cultic piety (58.5-7). There are everyday sins (59.3) committed by hands, fingers, lips and tongues. They tell lies (57.4) and take prostitutes (57.8). The judicial system is corrupted (57.4), and pleasure-seeking (58.3) is the lifestyle of the rich minority. Oppressing workers, quarreling, fighting and hitting with the wicked fist (58.4) well describe the unorganized society and the exploitation of the situation by the powerful minority. Thus they bind people with 'chains of oppression and yoke of injustice' (58.6). The fasting is condemned because there is no corresponding compassion and generosity (58.1-12).[166] As a result, they completely forget Yahweh (57.11).

Some accusations are addressed particularly to the ruling leaders of Israel. The negligence of the leaders is well described with the use of shepherd imagery. They are appointed to guard and protect his people like watchmen and their watchdogs (56.9-10). They are to lead and guide the people in a righteous way like a shepherd (56.11). Yet they not only neglect their duties, but also seek after their own gain, by taking advantage of their leadership positions (56.11). There is no exception, and 'one and all' are doing wrong. The strong drink they enjoy gives them a false contentment, as expressed in 'Tomorrow will be like this day' (56.12). Consequently, they lack truth (59.15) and walk in darkness and silence like the blind and the deaf (59.10). As they deny Yahweh himself (59.13) there is no righteousness and justice (59.9, 14). Righteousness and justice form a pair of key words that occur throughout the entire book of Isaiah and become the key words in

---

165. Most judgment messages are attributed to the pre-exilic period for their origin, and it is argued that they are incorporated into the message of Third Isaiah by the final editor(s), e.g. Westermann, *Isaiah 40–66*, pp. 296-308.

166. James L. Crenshaw, *Old Testament Story and Faith: A Literary and Theological Introduction* (Peabody, MA: Hendrickson, 1992), p. 3, notes this as 'by far the most radical teaching'. Weiser, *The Old Testament*, p. 207, observes that the use of צדק is illustrative: in Second Isaiah, the concept includes 'the whole of divine salvation', whereas in Third Isaiah, it mainly refers to human uprightness including religious fidelity.

the depiction of the ideal age (e.g. 11.1-9; 32.15). Throughout the Isaianic traditions, the ethical demand has its religious root. In spite of God's gracious patience and invitation, Israel continues to wound God's holiness, that is, it grieves 'his holy spirit' (63.10). Yahweh's holiness demands the removal of the sins and the iniquities of the people so that the delayed salvation can be brought about.

The combination of idolatry and immorality (57.5-10) is strongly reminiscent of the pre-exilic situation. As Westermann argues, the indictment can be of pre-exilic origin and initially is meant to be interpreted literally.[167] As the material is reused for the postexilic community, however, it may be intended to be taken more figuratively.

2.1.5 *Judgment.* Judgment which is found in the postexilic Isaianic tradition is something unknown to the exilic promises, and still is different from that of the pre-exilic traditions. The pronounced judgment is not upon the nation as a whole, but upon a select group of people. Theologically, the nation has already experienced the eschatological judgment in the exile. The limited judgment in this period is God's intervention to bring about the day of full salvation (59.1-20). Therefore, its scope is limited to the 'wicked' who are responsible for the delay of the eschaton (59.1-2). The coming judgment is understood as final and as a means of purging and purifying (65.13-16; 4.2-6). But for idolatry, both the idols and idolaters (57.1, 13) will be judged.

The coming judgment is imminent (57.1, 13), swift and sure (ch. 64). It is described as prolonged death which will remain as monuments to the judgment of Yahweh (66.15, 22). Although they understand that the eschatological judgment is past, the coming judgment is described with eschatological and even apocalyptic features.

The role of the רוח of Yahweh in judgment is an old tradition. This is closely associated with God's breath in his anger or a scorching wind as an agent of God. Isaiah 4.2-6 clearly shows that the spirit of fire and justice is God's power of judgment upon his people. The רוח is also the judgmental power of God which takes away the idols which the unfaithful rely upon (59.19).

2.1.6 *Salvation.* The announcement of judgment (65.13-16) is immediately followed by a new act of creation (65.17). The long-awaited salvation is described as light and healing (58.8); sure protection of

167. Westermann, *Isaiah 40–66*, pp. 321-22.

Yahweh (58.8-9); the provision of abundant food and restoration of ruin (58.10-12); prosperity (65.8-10); and life of peace and joy, a life long and full of abundance (65.17-25). It is also the time when the remaining dispersed will return (60.4) with abundance and wealth (vv. 5-9). Sacrifice and joyful song which are characteristics of the worship of Yahweh will be offered in the celebration of salvation.

There is a distinct emphasis on material prosperity, which reflects the pastoral need of the people.[168] At the same time, there are a number of passages that indicate the piety of the poor that is a feature of postexilic Judaism.[169] Reference is made explicitly in 7.15; 61.1-3; 66.2 and implicitly in 56.9–57.2, 3-13; 58.1-12; 59.1-20; 65.1-7, 11-16; 66.5, 15-16, 24. This also exhibits the polarity of a society where the 'wicked' are mainly the rich ruling class and the 'faithful' are the poor.

As with the judgment, the salvation will come suddenly (66.7-9) as soon as the obstacles are removed. The reoccurring construction of 'only if you...' and 'then...' (58.9b-10a and 10b-12; 58.13 and 14) signifies that judgment is not the only way to deal with the sins, but God invites his people to correct and repent of their wrongdoings. At the same time, the postexilic announcement of the 'imminent' salvation is distinguished from the exilic proclamation of the day of deliverance. Here the 'distinctive explanatory device is that "soon"'.[170] The post-exilic voice assures that the day of salvation, delayed as it is, is a genuine and extraordinary event (56.1; 58.8, 10-11; 62.1-3, 11, etc.) which is like the creation of a new heaven and a new earth (65.17; 66.22).[171] The promise of salvation is the result of Yahweh's grace (66.10-14) and is sealed by his covenant (59.21). Yahweh, as the creator, is the only source of every person's life, because his spirit, the breath of life, makes each one exist. Human existence is entirely dependent upon his life-giving רוח (57.16).

Another reason why the coming salvation is certain is because of the past salvation history. In the cultic setting, Israel confesses the faith that the great deliverance and its subsequent journey was under the

168. Weiser, *The Old Testament*, p. 206.

169. McKenzie, *Second Isaiah*, p. lxx.

170. R.P. Carroll, *When Prophecy Failed: Cognitive Dissonance in the Prophetic Traditions of the Old Testament* (New York: Seabury, 1979), p. 153.

171. Jenni, 'Eschatology', p. 131, contends that the expression is not meant to describe the cosmologically anchored apocalyptic doctrine of the destruction of the old world and the coming of the new aeon (*1 En.* 91.16-17; Jub. 1.29; cf. Rev. 2.11).

guidance, protection and provision of the 'holy spirit' of Yahweh (63.11). The journey was successfully completed as the same holy spirit granted the rest (v. 14).

2.2 *Eschatological Hope*

2.2.1 *Restoration*. As in the exilic tradition, Zion occupies the central position in the expectation of restoration, although the exilic and postexilic viewpoints are different.[172] It is particularly true in chs. 60–62, that is called the 'nucleus of Third Isaiah'[173] or the 'Zion poem'.[174] Jerusalem will be the recipient of Yahweh's grace. New names will be given for the city (62.1-5, 12), and God's glory will fill Jerusalem (60.1-2). The city will be the 'crown of beauty' and a 'royal diadem' to God (62.3), and the 'shoot of Yahweh' and 'the fruit of the land' shall be beauty, pride and glory (4.2-6). Although the reference to the city wall cannot be taken literally, the wall is anticipated to be rebuilt and Jerusalem is to 'be thrilled and rejoice' (60.5, cf. 61.10; 62.5). In fact 'mother Zion' will be astonished by the abundance of her children (66.7-8, cf. 49.21).[175] This is a celebratory mood different from Second Isaiah's.

The restoration of the city naturally means the return of God's favor to his people. In fact, God intentionally preserves a remnant (4.2-3) for the future restored community. In a sense, they are 'the latter day saints'! The sense of election is further strengthened by the distinction between the true and false Israel within the community.

Along with the restoration of Zion, the full restoration of cultic worship is a natural consequence. The frequent emphasis on the observance of religious practices is part of this expectation. Foreigners and even eunuchs will be accepted into worship at Zion and some even take part in cultic practices. Nations will turn to Yahweh and submit their wealth to the temple in Jerusalem (Isa. 11.10; 17.7-8; 18.7; 19.18-25;[176] Jer. 3.7; 12.15-16; 16.19; Zech. 2.11[2.15]; 8.20-23; 14.16). This stress on

---

172. According to von Rad, *Old Testament Theology*, II, p. 281, Zion is the climax of eschatological restoration in Second Isaiah, while in Third Isaiah, unredeemed Zion is the starting point of the message of salvation.

173. Westermann, *Isaiah 40–66*, p. 296.

174. McKenzie, *Second Isaiah*, p. lxix.

175. Von Rad, *Old Testament Theology*, II, p. 280.

176. Jenni, 'Eschatology', p. 131, argues for the postexilic origin of the passages.

priestly worship is, however, common among the other restoration prophets such as Haggai and Zechariah. Keeping the Sabbath (56.4) is one of three qualifications for foreigners to become Yahwists (56.3, 6). By choosing things which please God, they are qualified to be Yahweh-worshippers.

The restoration is also the fulfillment of Israel's covenant tradition.[177] That Israel will lead the nations in the service of Yahweh (61.5; cf. 56.1-8) echoes the promise of God to make Israel a 'nation of priests'. In addition, the restoration of Israel as the spouse of Yahweh is an intimate covenant expression (cf. Hosea). Two blessings promised to Israel further manifest the covenant motif: the possession of the land refers to the Abrahamic covenant, and the inheritance of the holy mountain is linked with the Davidic covenant. The two covenant traditions are combined and applied to Israel as a whole. This may be an indication of the democratization of kingship, so that Israel as a nation will have a royal function, especially to the nations. Emphasis on the covenant is also found in one of the three criteria by which Yahwistic foreigners are regarded as people of God. Besides the two qualifications, one must hold fast the covenant. It is an indication that the consciousness of the covenant relation with Yahweh is a distinctive mark of Israel, particularly when some fellow Israelites desert this unique privilege.

However, there seems to be more distant and sometimes apocalyptic eschatological expectation. Although the impending restoration should include the long-awaited fulfillment of God's promises, there are more radical expectations. The creation of the new heaven and earth (66.22) implies the cosmic extent of God's work.

2.2.2 *Universalism*. The acceptance of the Gentiles into the Israelite community and worship demonstrates two unique features of the exilic Isaianic thought. One is the astonishing universalism of the prophet. The concept is already well developed by Second Isaiah and the influence is certainly from the tradition (56.1-8; 61.5).[178] The participation

177. W.A.M. Beuken, 'The Main Theme of Trito-Isaiah, "The Servants of YHWH"', *JSOT* 47 (1990), pp. 67-87, understands that the postexilic expression of 'servants' continues the 'servant of Yahweh' of Second Isaiah. He also seems to identify the 'servants' with the restored people of God. If these two preconditions are correct, the restoration is also the fulfillment of the exilic Isaianic promise.

178. Newsome, *The Hebrew Prophets*, p. 172.

of foreigners and eunuchs in worship is a further development of Second Isaiah who introduced Cyrus as Yahweh's anointed (45.1). Some will even serve as priests and Levites (66.18-21, 22-23), although the priesthood will primarily remain the privilege of Israel. It is not quite clear which period is represented in this remarkably broad attitude toward the Gentiles. Considering the narrow attitude toward the Gentiles in Ezra–Nehemiah, and later the broad view in the book of Chronicles, the passages do not come from the time when the purity of blood is a 'rigorous test for admission to the Israelite community'.[179] This is consistent with the Israelites' attitude toward the Gentiles: from exclusive in Ezra–Nehemiah to inclusive in Chronicles.

On the other hand, the great emphasis on Cyrus in Second Isaiah may have contributed to the universalism of the postexilic Judeans. Yet the most serious weakness of this view is to make the trend inconsistent: from inclusive, then exclusive and inclusive again in Chronicles. For this reason the passages may have their origin in a period after Ezra–Nehemiah. The writer envisages that in the fullness of Israel, there will be no difference between Israelites and Gentiles.

Universalism is expressed in a way slightly different from the exilic tradition. Earlier, there are two features in the universalistic expectation: foreigners will be sharers of God's salvation (e.g. 44.1-5); and Yahweh will raise a foreign king, Cyrus, and his Persian empire to liberate Israel. In the postexilic tradition, the first element continues or even expands. It is not only foreigners, but also eunuchs who will be allowed to have full participation in the temple worship. It also attains a religious emphasis, for the participants are religiously devoted individuals. However, the second element is almost entirely missing. There is no prominent foreign figure in the postexilic expectation. There is no individual mentioned who will carry the Servant's mission except the prophet in 61.1-3. In contrast, Beuken argues that in the postexilic tradition, the 'servants' are the direct heirs of the exilic Servant.[180] These servants, according to him, as a collective entity, are true Israel. He further argues that the idea of the 'servants' is the major theme of Third Isaiah.[181] However, Beuken's argument is based on one crucial tentative presumption that Second Isaiah himself initiated the move

179. McKenzie, *Second Isaiah*, p. lxviii.
180. Beuken, 'The Main Theme', pp. 67-87.
181. This 'main theme' is missing only in 56.9–62.12 which explicitly deals with *aposiopesis*, Beuken, 'The Main Theme', pp. 69-79.

from the 'Servant' to the 'servants' in 54.17.[182] His thesis also assumes that the Servant in Second Isaiah refers to Israel.

It can then be concluded that the postexilic universalism is expressed within the community. This might reflect the internal preoccupation of the society. Universalism on a grand scale is missing, although its details develop within the limited extent, that is within the community.

2.2.3 *Prophets*. There is a sudden emergence of the prophetic emphasis. First of all, there is a prophetic voice, claiming God's commissioning with the endowment of God's spirit (61.1-3). In comparison with the vaguely prophetic Servant of the exilic tradition, this is a bold appearance of the prophetic figure. Although used in the present tense, this claim, together with 59.21, evidences the significance of the prophetic phenomenon in the restored eschatological society. The disappearance of the royal figure and reappearance of a prophet-like figure is already observed during the exilic period (especially 42.1-4).

The new age is characterized by the presence of the prophetic spirit and the words among his people as long as Israel exists (59.21). This has already begun in the prophetic voice of 61.1-3. The perpetuation of the prophetic spirit is promised among Israel. As a result, the teaching will also be perpetuated throughout generations.

Thus the prophetic רוח of Yahweh has a definite role to play in the coming age of salvation. The new age is ushered in through the preaching of the prophet who is 'anointed' by the spirit of Yahweh. It is also the spirit of God among the prophets which will perpetuate the teaching in the word in the coming age.

3. Concluding Observations

3.1 *The* רוח *in its Traditions*
The Babylonian and early Persian periods mark 'the most rapid development' in the meaning of the רוח of Yahweh. This becomes most evident when one compares it with the late pre-exilic period, or the Deuteronomistic time during which 'the least possible (or even negative) development of the concept is evident'.[183] Traditional ideas with a direct reference to Yahweh's powerful theophany and to the warrior

---

182. Beuken, 'The Main Theme', p. 68.
183. Schoemaker, 'Use of "Ruach" ', p. 23.

motif of God have experienced a tremendous development during the
exilic or postexilic time when his powerful presence is desperately
desired and sought. Even the frequent appearance of the spirit of God
itself is an indication that the concept is no longer consciously avoided,
and begins to acquire a much more religious significance than before.

The frequent emphasis on the spirit of Yahweh in the exilic and
postexilic period is explained by Lindblom,

> [It is due to] the double tendency in the conception of God—immanence
> of God expressed by the expectations that Yahweh dwells in Zion, in the
> midst of His people; on the other hand, distancing God from the human
> realm, the need for an intermediary between God and man and the spirit
> serves the purpose.[184]

Several of the spirit traditions are present in the postexilic Isaianic
tradition. The most obvious emphasis, in comparison with the exilic
tradition, is on the prophetic phenomenon generally and the prophetic
spirit specifically. There is the almost complete absence of the ecstatic
form of revelation during the postexilic time, although the claim of the
spirit of Yahweh reappears as the source of revelation. Without any
reference to vision or dream, the prophet bluntly claims that the רוח of
Yahweh is upon him through the 'anointing' of God (61.1).

As argued above (pp. 120-25), this new prophet's task includes an
implicit allusion to the leadership spirit. Therefore he is more than a
prophet. Besides being a preacher, messenger and healer, he is a spiritual ruler too. In spite of the affinity to the first Servant Song (42.1-4),
the straightforward self-declaration makes it clear that his call is to the
prophetic task. There is no room for the personal suffering which the
Servant expects. He is a powerful messenger of God who is going to
usher in the new age through the רוח of God.[185] The allusion to the
leadership/charismatic feature is probably not because of an intentional
merging of the two traditions, but because of the pastoral motif. The
prophet addresses a community which does not have a political leader.
If the tradition of the leadership spirit is ever present here, the reference
is presumably no longer to physical or military might but only to

184. Lindblom, *Prophecy in Ancient Israel*, p. 413.
185. For the background to the prophet as a messenger in comparison with the
secular messenger formula, see James F. Ross, 'The Prophet as Yahweh's Messenger', in Bernhard W. Anderson and Walter Harrelson (eds.), *Israel's Prophetic
Heritage: Essays in Honor of James Muilenburg* (New York: Harper & Row,
1962), pp. 98-107, particularly p. 107 for Isa. 61.1.

spiritual power. The role of the spirit in 61.1-2, however, is almost identical with that of the first Servant Song.

A more explicit reference to the spirit of God upon the leaders appears in 63.7-14. Although the spirit of God is given to the 'shepherds of his flock' (v. 11), it is obvious that Moses is referred to as the national hero upon whom Yahweh 'put his holy spirit' (v. 11). In spite of the textual uncertainties, the past hero is remembered to have had God's spirit which enabled him to liberate his people. The spirit strengthens, equips and dwells in him. However, the text gives a strong impression that the real hero is the spirit of God. The spirit upon the leaders somehow lost its grand features during the postexilic era. The national leader is only remembered vaguely. It is expected that the second exodus will come to its completion through the leading of the same spirit. But the presence of any human agent is not implied for the expected consummation.

The spirit also continues to represent God himself, but not in his fullness. Often, this representation carries the notion of God's power and also his caring. This representation appears to reflect a theological emphasis prevalent during the postexilic era, namely, the transcendence of Yahweh. As a result, some expressions which refer to God himself, his visible organs like פנים are substituted by less direct expressions, and one of them is רוח. Westermann argues that the 'deepest break in the history of its meaning' is that the idea becomes a 'static concept' to such an extent that all God's activity becomes 'an activity through', or even an activity of, the spirit.[186] When compared with the much older 'Song of the Sea' (Exod. 15.1-21),[187] which forms the 'paradigm for Israel's future salvation',[188] the static tendency becomes evident. The direct reference to God or Yahweh in Exodus is all replaced by 'his

186. Claus Westermann, *Elements of Old Testament Theology* (trans. Douglas W. Stott; Atlanta: John Knox Press, 1982), p. 76.
187. David N. Freedman, 'Early Israelite Poetry and Historical Considerations', in *idem, Pottery, Poetry and Prophecy: Collected Essays on Hebrew Poetry* (Winona Lake, IN: Eisenbrauns, 1980), pp. 167-78 (168). Frank Moore Cross, Jr, 'The Song of the Sea and Canaanite Myth', in *idem, Canaanite Myth and Hebrew Epic* (Cambridge, MA: Harvard University Press, 1973), pp. 112-44 (121), places the song in a premonarchic time, possibly in the late twelfth or early eleventh century BCE.
188. Millard C. Lind, *Yahweh Is a Warrior* (Kirchener, Ontario: Herald Press, 1980), p. 49.

[holy] spirit' in Isa. 63.10-14. Its full development is seen in the New Testament.

Whether the spirit of God is understood as having a separate personality is a divided matter. Traditionally the main role of the spirit is to function as the means or medium of God's operation upon individuals and nations. At the same time, the רוח of God is often viewed as an impersonal force or power, or even influence of God like the word of God.[189] In spite of the verb 'grieve' and the attribute of holiness, there is no explicit evidence of a belief in the separate personality of the spirit. Yet the later development of the personality of the spirit and the employment of the verb may be an indication of an early tendency toward such a personalization.[190]

It is also the spirit of God who completes the Exodus liberation (63.14). Unlike the 'glorious arm' of God which is specifically perceived as a tool, the spirit of God is almost the substitution of God himself. In v. 14, 'the spirit of God gave them rest' is in parallel with 'Thus you [God] led your people'.

The spirit of God is also used as an impersonal tool of God's judgment. Its specific function is indicated by its construct state with 'judgment' and 'burning' (4.5). In a sense, its use is similar to how the 'wind' is used to execute God's judgment. It is the wind that will carry the idols off (57.13).

Completely missing in the postexilic Isaianic tradition is the spirit of God as a life-giving force. It is a significant contrast with the exilic tradition where the creative work of the spirit of God appears with strong emphasis. It may mean that with the return from exile, the nation is viewed as having regained its life (e.g. Ezek. 37.9, 10). However, the same spirit is to bring prosperity in the physical and spiritual realms (32.15-20; 44.1-5). With the great hardship that the postexilic community endures, the reason for the absence of this usage is a question. The strong pastoral motif of the postexilic message further makes the absence strange.

---

189. Eichrodt, *Theology of the Old Testament*, II, pp. 46-68, contends that the spirit and the word are the two major media of God.

190. Mowinckel, ' "Spirit" and the "Word" ', p. 204 n. 18, seems to make a premature conclusion by saying that 'Trito-Isaiah...always shows tendency to personify the spirit and make it a hypostasis'.

3.2 *Characteristics*

3.2.1 *Continuing Refinement*. The decrease in references to the violent effect of the spirit is also unmistakable. Even the prophet's declaration of the spirit of Yahweh upon him has no violent effects. This makes a contrast to the early notion of the idea where the judges are given physical might and military strength (e.g. Judg. 6.34; 13.25) and where the prophetic spirit is violent and ecstatic (e.g. 1 Sam. 10.6). Yet the violent action of the spirit still remains particularly in terms of judgment. The reference to a violent move is expressed by various means. The 'rushing wind' imagery is seen in 59.19 and the powerful verb 'take away' is used in 57.2 for the judgment on the idols. In the context of judgment, the decisiveness and power of the spirit is the main emphasis. The powerful presence of God by the spirit is also referred to in the exodus and wilderness journey.

3.2.2 *Assumption of Qualifying Concept*. In the past, the spirit of God, when accompanied by a qualifying word, basically indicates its function rather than its nature. The lying spirit and sleeping spirit are good examples. Of course, the evil spirit from Yahweh (1 Sam. 16.14) is a descriptive qualification, although its result indicates that the qualifying word in fact suggests the function of the spirit.

In this period, for the first time, the holiness of Yahweh is extended to his spirit (63.10, 11). Although some attributes of God are applied to the spirit of Yahweh, particularly his righteousness and justice (e.g. 4.2-6), his holiness has never been applied to his spirit. However, the distancing tendency of God from human beings opens a way for the spirit of Yahweh, which is the expression of his real presence, to be described as holy (63.10, 12; cf. Ps. 51.13). The separateness and sacredness are the main emphases of the holiness of God, or 'his holy spirit'. This reinforces the remoteness of God.

However, the old functional qualification continues to appear. The spirit of judgment and the spirit of burning (4.4) are closely connected with Yahweh's cleansing work among his remnant. Thus the function is not much different from the 'sleeping spirit' (Isa. 19.14).

3.2.3 *Eschatological Connection*. The vital role of the רוח of Yahweh in the coming age becomes more prominent in the tradition especially since the exilic period and onward. The function of the spirit of Yahweh in the new age is diverse: Ezekiel's witness to the renewal of the moral life of the people; the חור of God as a power by which nature would be transformed (Isa. 32.15); the spirit guiding the people in the exodus (Isa. 63.11-14); the spirit abiding in the midst of the new community (Hag. 2.5); enabling Zerubbabel to overcome all difficulties in the building of the new temple (Zech. 4.6); the general outpouring of the prophetic spirit in the new age (Joel 3.1-3). And the coming of the new age is brought about by the same spirit of God (61.1; cf. 32.15).[191] The effect of the spirit, however, shows a substantial difference between the exilic and the postexilic descriptions. Agricultural prosperity (32.15-20) and almost mythical description of the transformation of the natural world are the characteristics in the exilic expectation (44.4). In the postexilic description, however, the effect is more spiritualized. In spite of the emphasis on the material prosperity, the spirit is not referred to as the direct or indirect cause of blessing. The life-giving role of the spirit of God is limited only to human existence (57.16) and implicitly to the nation (63.14), but never to the increasing harvest or miraculous transformation of the natural world.

3.2.4 *Limited Democratization*. Democratization is a distinctive mark in the development of the concept during the exilic and postexilic period. The writer clearly understands that in the time of old, the spirit of God was given exclusively to a limited number of leaders (here, Moses and other leaders, 63.11). There is also an indication that the prophetic spirit is given to a selected individual (61.1). Yet the coming age is envisaged as a time when every descendant of the prophet is given the prophetic spirit of Yahweh (59.21). The perpetuity of the prophetic spirit is not merely the internalized will of God.[192] That the prophets are still around and that they have a vital role in the society rule out the spiritualized interpretation of prophecy. The intimate closeness between God and his prophets and his people and, as a consequence, the clear understanding of his will is part of Israel's eschatological expectations in the early restoration period.

3.2.5 *Pastoral Contexts*. As the entire section of Third Isaiah shows, the idea of the spirit of Yahweh is used to meet the pastoral need of the suffering and frustrated community. For instance, there is no mention

191. That the eschatological role of the spirit of God is a later development is attested by the fact that those passages are exilic or postexilic in origin.
192. Gowan, *Eschatology*, p. 75.

of the link between the wisdom tradition and the spirit of God, which is one of the main motifs of the spirit of God in the preexilic Isaianic tradition (e.g. Isa. 11.1-5).[193] In the later period, it is also noted that the spirit of God and wisdom are almost identical.[194] Therefore, the silence in the post-exilic Isaianic tradition does not mean that there is a break of the tradition. The fact is that the writer simply does not have a pastoral need to make use of the tradition, since there is no political reality which functions as the counterpart to divine wisdom (e.g. 31.1-3).

3.2.6 *Loose Application of the Term.* This tendency began during the exilic period as is evident in the book of Ezekiel. The word is used rather widely to include heavenly creatures. Thus there seems to be a loose interchangeability between the spirit and angels or heavenly beings. In the Isaianic tradition, however, this tendency is not found during the exilic period. It is in the postexilic tradition that Moses, the old national hero, is simply assumed to have the spirit of God. The divine spirit is believed to have completed the exodus event. The latter is more than representation. As found elsewhere among the postexilic literature (Zech. 4.6), the actual meaning of the word seems to acquire more related meanings. Traditionally the meaning has been rather tightly and clearly defined, although the word represents numerous independent traditions. However, as the frequency of occurrences increases, the clear semantic boundaries grow fuzzy, and less clearly defined ideas are attached to the term. This phenomenon is fully developed among the rabbinic literature and in some Qumran writings.

193. For a discussion on the spirit of God in wisdom literature, see Benson, *Spirit of God.*
194. Rylaarsdam, *Revelation*, p. 103.

Chapter 4

THE SPIRIT OF GOD IN THE CANONICAL BOOK OF ISAIAH

The previous chapters have divided the book into three approximate historical units, namely, pre-exilic, exilic and postexilic, and have examined the divine 'spirit' passages in their own historical settings. This chapter, however, takes a more holistic approach by reading the passages in the literary and theological context of the entire book.

1. *Methodological Considerations*

After decades of critical analyses of the book of Isaiah, recent scholarship has turned its attention to the book as a whole.[1] Anderson aptly describes the current state:

> Today scholars are beginning to move from analysis to synthesis in the interpretation of the Book of Isaiah. The established practice of separating the book into several discrete parts, each of which is viewed in isolation from the whole, is giving way to exploratory efforts to understand the overall unity and the theological dynamic of the Isaiah tradition.[2]

This holistic approach is welcomed by both critical and conservative scholarship, but for different reasons. On one hand, the conservative camp has been persistent in maintaining the unity of the entire book based on single authorship.[3] On the other hand, for the critical scholar-

---

1. E.g. Watts, *Isaiah 1–33* and *Isaiah 34–66*, although recognizing the 'prehistorical' existence of independent sayings from various time periods, treats the entire book as a literary unit.
2. Bernhard W. Anderson, 'The Apocalyptic Rendering of the Isaiah Tradition', in Jacob Neusner, Ernest S. Frerichs, Peder Borgen and Richard Horsley (eds.), *The Social World of Formative Christianity and Judaism: Essays in Tribute to Howard Clark Kee* (Philadelphia: Fortress Press, 1988), pp. 17-38 (17).
3. Recent works by this group include commentaries by Motyer, *The Prophecy*

ship, enough attention has been directed to the analysis of the book, particularly through source and literary criticism. In this regard, the holistic reading can be seen as a swing of the critical scholarly pendulum from the fragmented analysis of the book.

Reading the book as a whole requires a consideration of methodology. As Anderson points out, various 'exploratory' approaches have been suggested, and new attempts are made every year. The approaches to achieving the unity of the book are, however, categorized into: (1) canonical unity; or (2) thematic and/or structural unity.

1.1 *Canonical Criticism*

This new methodology was highlighted by the publication of Childs's *Introduction*, and was later modified and defined.[4] In spite of many unsettled issues in this new attempt, it has dramatically affected the way in which the book of Isaiah is read. For Childs, Second Isaiah was deliberately removed from its historical context by omitting its own historical material. And by appending it to First Isaiah, the editor made the exilic literary work to be read within First Isaiah's eighth-century context.[5] For him, this is the new canonical context of the entire book. However, this argument was seriously disputed and, as a result, Childs acknowledged the presence of distinct historical material in Second Isaiah.[6] The ultimate goal of the 'canonical' editor is, according to

of Isaiah and Oswalt, *Isaiah Chapters 1–39*, as well as a monograph by Youngblood, *The Book of Isaiah*.

4.   For the initial response which followed the publication of *Introduction to the Old Testament as Scripture* (Philadelphia: Fortress Press, 1979), see the papers in *HBT* 2 (1980). One half of the entire volume is devoted to five evaluations and Childs's response: Bruce C. Birch, 'Tradition, Canon and Biblical Theology', pp. 113-25; Douglas A. Knight, 'Canon and the History of Tradition: A Critique of Brevard S. Childs' *Introduction to the Old Testament as Scripture*', pp. 127-49; James L. Mays, 'What Is Written: A Response to Brevard Childs' *Introduction to the Old Testament as Scripture*', pp. 151-63; David P. Polk, 'Brevard S. Childs' *Introduction to the Old Testament as Scripture*', pp. 165-71; James A. Sanders, 'Canonical Context and Canonical Criticism', pp. 173-87; Brevard S. Childs, 'A Response', pp. 199-211. Later, a volume dedicated to Childs was published, which contains numerous articles discussing this new discipline: Gene M. Tucker, David L. Petersen and Robert R. Wilson (eds.), *Canon, Theology, and Old Testament Interpretation: Essays in Honor of Brevard S. Childs* (Philadelphia: Fortress Press, 1988).

5.   Childs, *Introduction*, pp. 325-30.

6.   Childs, 'A Response', p. 205, a reply to Birch, 'Tradition', p. 121.

Childs, to reflect on the end of the process of the encounter between God and Israel through the text.[7] That is, the editorial freezing of the process is to bring forth normative messages as the word of God for future generations.

As seen above and as in other areas of research, the canonical approach has numerous points of disagreement among scholars. This is understandable, particularly when one considers its present formative nature. Several problems have emerged thus far.

The first question is whether canonical criticism should include the canonizing process or not. Childs's main interest is in the final form of the book as canon. Of course, he acknowledges different dynamics in the canonical process, yet it is the final form of the 'authoritative scripture for the Jewish community' which has come to serve as a normative expression of God's will to later generations.[8] In a strict sense, he divorces the 'development and growth of canonical literature from its historical provenances'.[9] For him, this belongs to the area of redaction criticism. Accordingly, the social dynamics of the believing community are not often discussed in the formation of the book. A similar view is held by Clements.[10] A canonical critic's task, according to Childs, is, first, to 'identify [him/herself] with the historical Jewish community in starting with the received form of the literature which comprised the Hebrew canon'; and with that sympathy, the reader needs, secondly, 'to discern the canonical function of the literature'.[11] This approach defines the discipline narrowly and makes a clear distinction between canon and redaction criticism. Brueggemann calls this a 'static' approach.[12] Contrary to the narrow definition of Childs's, a broader scope of the discipline is argued for by numerous scholars.[13] This is primarily

7. Childs, *Introduction*, p. 75.

8. Brevard S. Childs, 'The Canonical Shape of the Prophetic Literature', *Int* 32 (1978), pp. 46-68 (47).

9. Sanders, 'Canonical Context', p. 186.

10. R.E. Clements, 'The Unity of the Book of Isaiah', *Int* 36 (1982), pp. 117-29.

11. Childs, *Introduction*, p. 96.

12. Walter Brueggemann, 'Unity and Dynamic in the Isaiah Tradition', *JSOT* 29 (1984), pp. 89-107 (90). Also Birch, 'Tradition', p. 122.

13. For instance, James Barr, *Holy Scripture: Canon, Authority, Criticism* (Philadelphia: Westminster Press, 1983), chs. 3 and 5. Also Roy F. Melugin, 'Canon and Exegetical Method', in Tucker, Petersen and Wilson (eds.), *Canon, Theology, and Old Testament Interpretation*, pp. 48-61 (48). Also Paul D. Hanson, *Dynamic Transcendence* (Philadelphia: Fortress Press, 1978). Peter R. Ackroyd's

because there is a logical interweaving between the final editor's theological intention and the socio-religious context he was living in. Normative as he may have intended the text to be, the process was still another theological endeavor to respond to the historical issues and questions the community was struggling with. Where the delicate and fine line lies, if there is any, which divides between canonical and redactional criticism, is a matter of dispute.[14]

If and when one accepts, against Childs, that the canonical process is included in the discipline, the canon is viewed as 'a control point for our appropriation of the history of biblical interpretation'.[15] Given that, the essential question one has to ask is what force(s) made significant contributions toward that process. The crucial role of the community in the formation of the canon is one of consensus.[16] Mays, for instance, emphasizes that the history of 'canonization' is a community movement in which,

> the language of faith becomes tradition, tradition becomes scripture, and scripture becomes canon. The later official decisions of the church were only a recognition of what had happened in that history.[17]

'Isaiah I–XII: Presentation of a Prophet', in *Congress Volume: Göttingen, 1977* (VTSup, 29; Leiden: E.J. Brill, 1978), pp. 16-48, was published just one year before Childs's book. In the conclusion of his article, Ackroyd makes an insightful comment (pp. 47-48): 'Canon criticism, as a distinct area of discussion, involves a sensitive appraisal of both the final stages of the according of authority to the biblical writings, and the awareness of the different levels at which this has operated in the eventual determining of the texts which have come down to us, stamped with the hallmark of experiential testing in the life of the community to which they belonged.'

14. John Barton, *Reading the Old Testament: Method in Biblical Study* (Philadelphia: Westminster Press, 1984), p. 90.

15. Birch, 'Tradition', p. 122.

16. In a number of works, James A. Sanders elaborates the role of the community. For instance, the entirety of *Torah and Canon* (Philadelphia: Fortress Press, 1972); 'Adaptable for Life: The Nature and Function of Canon', in Frank Moore Cross, Werner E. Lemke and Patrick D. Miller, Jr (eds.), *Magnalia Dei, The Mighty Acts of God: Essays on the Bible and Archaeology in Memory of G. Ernest Wright* (Garden City, NY: Doubleday, 1976), pp. 531-60; 'Canonical Context', pp. 183-86. Childs, on the contrary, criticizes Sanders for the open-ended idea of canon which implies that textual canonization is still going on ('A Response', p. 202).

17. James L. Mays, 'Historical and Canonical: Recent Discussion about the Old Testament and Christian Faith', in Frank Moore Cross, Werner E. Lemke and Patrick D. Miller, Jr (eds.), *Magnalia Dei, The Mighty Acts of God: Essays on the*

Any significant historical event can contribute to the canonizing process.[18] In Brueggemann's words, the 'radically sustained critique of the dominant ideology of the…culture' and the message of judgment among the eighth-century prophets (e.g. Isa. chs. 1–39) are based on this social criticism.[19] Gerstenberger calls it the 'situational fixation of the Word of God', emphasizing the role of its own *Sitz im Leben*.[20] Whatever this factor may be called, certainly there are dynamics through which the community takes hermeneutical roles that 'attend to the historical reality of the community and to the diachronic reality of the text'.[21] Each historical context may have its distinctive hermeneutical process to actualize the old message in a new situation.[22] Therefore, the canonical meaning of a passage is the end product or the culmination of this on-going process. The next logical question to ask is whether one should attempt to single out all the different layers of meanings and various dynamics which created the layers. It is also a matter of debate if all the different layers of meanings are equally authoritative, that is, carrying an equal weight. The inquiry into the process and dynamics, in a strict sense, requires redactional rather than canonical criticism.

Related to the present discussion, one particular life situation has contributed to the formation of the normative scripture for the coming generations. The postexilic community stood in a unique theological dilemma between the conviction of the truthfulness of the prophecies and the unfulfilled, or partially fulfilled, reality of the prophetic message. The community has witnessed the fulfillment of pre-exilic predictions. Even in the pre-exilic time, the deliverance from the

Bible and Archaeology in Memory of G. Ernest Wright (Garden City, NY: Double-day, 1976), pp. 510-28 (514).

18. R.E. Clements, 'Patterns in the Prophetic Canon', in George W. Coats and Burke O. Long (eds.), *Canon and Authority: Essays in Old Testament Religion and Theology* (Philadelphia: Fortress Press, 1977), pp. 42-55 (51), points out that the fall of Jerusalem (587 BCE) provides a significant motivation to canonization.

19. Brueggemann, 'Unity and Dynamic', p. 92.

20. Erhard S. Gerstenberger, 'Canon Criticism and the Meaning of *Sitz im Leben*', in Tucker, Petersen and Wilson (eds.), *Canon, Theology, and Old Testament Interpretation*, pp. 20-31 (20). He goes as far as to include the reader-response involvement in his discussion of *Sitz im Leben*.

21. Brueggemann, 'Unity and Dynamic', p. 90.

22. This process is universally recognized, e.g. Childs, 'The Canonical Shape', p. 49, and Sanders, 'Adaptable for Life', pp. 531-60.

Syro-Ephraimite war and the Assyrian invasion could have become 'incidents of one and the same paradigm of divine intervention'.[23] This leads to the belief in the prophecies as the truthful word of God. In the community's conviction, history is 'caused by the word of God',[24] and the history in fact becomes part of his word to his people.[25] As a consequence, prophetic promises require their complete fulfillment; yet, the majority of the most splendid promises were never fully realized for generation after generation.[26] This real life situation caused the community not only to collect and preserve the materials, but also to arrange and edit them in such a way that the scripture gains a timeless and normative value as the word of God for the coming generations. The final stage of the canonical process is situational in that it closely corresponds to its own setting.

The second confusion has arisen from the word 'canon' or 'canonical'. The traditional use of the term would refer to the entire body of the sacred writing, although the exact make-up varies depending on religious traditions. Childs, as a Christian, contends that the entire Old and New Testaments form the context for the interpretation of any particular passage.[27] Barton also argues that the New Testament witness is the legitimate 'settling point'.[28] However, this certainly goes against the deliberate reading of the Old Testament on its own terms; the Jewish scripture is unjustly taken from the hands of the Old Testament people of God and put into the hands of Christians. Even this Christian view of the canonical context does not solve the problem, but leads to another question of 'which Old Testament canon?' LXX recognizes a different canonical environment, as Roman Catholics do, from that of

---

23. Roth, *Isaiah*, p. 4.

24. Claus Westermann, 'The Interpretation of the Old Testament: A Historical Introduction', in *idem* (ed.), *Essays on Old Testament Hermeneutics* (trans. James Luther Mays; Richmond, VA: John Knox Press, 1963), pp. 40-49 (47).

25. Westermann, 'Interpretation', p. 48.

26. A similar argument is presented by Bruce K. Waltke, 'A Canonical Process Approach to the Psalms', in John S. Feinberg and Paul D. Feinberg (eds.), *Tradition and Testament: Essays in Honor of Charles Lee Feinberg* (Chicago: Moody, 1981), pp. 3-18 (15), for royal Psalms some of which become messianic Psalms in the canonical context.

27. The publication of Brevard S. Childs, *Biblical Theology of the Old and New Testaments: Theological Reflection on the Christian Bible* (Minneapolis: Fortress Press, 1992) is indicative of this assumption of the 'canon'.

28. Barton, *Reading the Old Testament*, p. 83.

that of the MT, apparently followed by Protestants.

In this study, the 'canonical' context is not used to refer to the wider environment: it is the book in its entirety which defines the theological and literary context.[29] With this defined context, 'a passage will be lifted beyond the question of its historical point of origin and its wider literary connections are considered...'[30] And yet, canonical reading is more than literary criticism. In this study, it is assumed that this 'final and normative' fixation is again occasioned by, and thus reflects, a certain postexilic historical setting.

1.2 *Intertextuality: Thematic and/or Structural Unity*

There have been serious challenges to the canonical approach. To many, it is methodologically unacceptable to superimpose the canonical context, which is a late phenomenon, on the books which predate it. Clements voices his objection by stating that 'the reasons why the Book of Isaiah acquired its present shape' is not related to the canonization of the entire Old Testament. Therefore, for him, it is 'methodologically wrong to attempt to resolve these problems [i.e. of the book of Isaiah] by an all-embracing hermeneutical appeal to the perspective of the canon'.[31] Most recent works in the book of Isaiah endeavor to prove the coherence of the entire book as a theological whole.[32] These approaches basically search for the presence of superstructure and/or the continuity of several themes and ideas.

On the one hand, many 'clues' are suggested to prove the inter-textuality of the book across the traditio-historically divided parts of the book. Several scholars have scrutinized chs. 36–39 to see the seam by which the two parts (chs. 1–35 and 40–66) of the book are linked.[33]

---

29. Rolf Rendtorff, 'The Book of Isaiah: A Complex Unity: Synchronic and Diachronic Reading', in Eugene H. Lovering, Jr (ed.), *SBL 1991 Seminar Papers* (Atlanta: Scholars Press, 1991), pp. 8-20 (9), perceives that '...the term is mainly applied to the final shape of the respective book in which it eventually became part of the canon as a whole'.

30. R.E. Clements, 'Patterns in the Prophetic Canon: Healing the Blind and the Lame', in Tucker, Petersen and Wilson (eds.), *Canon, Theology, and Old Testament Interpretation*, pp. 189-200 (192).

31. Clements, 'Beyond Tradition-History', p. 97.

32. The emphasis on literary unity has been achieved by various approaches. E.g. Wiklander, *Prophecy as Literature*, against the critical view in general, concludes that chs. 2–4 demonstrate a literary coherence.

33. Peter R. Ackroyd, 'Isaiah 36–39: Structure and Function', in Delsman *et al.*

There is no doubt that, at the historical level, the section is to explain why Babylonians would destroy Judah and Yahweh's temple. Canonically, however, as the exilic incident is looked back upon, chs. 36–39 play a dual role: first, to provide a paradigm for God's promise of restoration; and secondly, to bridge the two main sections of the book by stating why God's promise of restoration will be fulfilled. Williamson, Vermeylen, Albertz and others have forcefully challenged Childs's contention that Second Isaiah stands independently of First Isaiah.[34] Still others contend that there is a recognizable and coherent structure in the book.[35] Tomasino, for example, argues that the beginning (1.2–2.4) and the ending sections (63.7–66.24) share not only similar themes in the same order, using a similar language but also structural similarity between 1.2-31 and 66.1-24 practically forming an inclusio for the entire book.[36] Sweeney detects a structure which unites

(eds.), *Von Kanaan bis Kerala*, pp. 3-21 (17-21). Also his earlier 'An Interpretation of the Babylonian Exile', *SJT* 27 (1974), pp. 328-52 (338); Klaas A.D. Smelik, 'Distortion of Old Testament Prophecy: The Purpose of Isaiah xxxvi and xxxvii', *OTS* 24 (1989), pp. 70-93; Seitz, *Zion's Final Destiny*; Clifford, 'The Unity', p. 2; Conrad, *Reading Isaiah*, esp. pp. 34-36, 110-20.

34. Williamson, 'First and Last in Isaiah', pp. 95-108; Vermeylen, 'L'unité du livre d'Isaïe', pp. 147-53; Rainer Albertz, 'Das Deuterojesaja-Buch als Fortschreibung der Jesaja-Prophetie', in Erhard Blum, C. Macholz and E.W. Stegemann (eds.), *Die hebräische Bibel und ihre zweifache Nachgeschichte: Festschrift für Rolf Rendtorff zum 65. Geburtstag* (Neukirchen–Vluyn: Neukirchener Verlag, 1990), pp. 241-56.

35. R. Rendtorff, 'Jesaja 6 im Rahmen der Komposition des Jesajabuches', in Jacques Vermeylen (ed.), *Le livre d'Isaïe: Les oracles et leurs relectures unité et complexité de l'ouvrage* (BETL, 81; Leuven: Leuven University Press, 1989), pp. 73-83, argues for many connections between ch. 6 and ch. 40; G. Fohrer, 'Jesaja 1 als Zusammenfassung der Verkündigung Jesajas', *ZAW* 74 (1962), pp. 251-69; C.A. Evans, 'On the Unity and Parallel Structures of Isaiah', *VT* 28 (1988), pp. 129-47; Edgar W. Conrad, 'The Royal Narratives and the Structure of the Book of Isaiah', *JSOT* 41 (1988), pp. 67-81; B.G. Webb, 'Zion in Transformation: A Literary Approach to Isaiah', in David J.A. Clines, Stephen E. Fowl and Stanley E. Porter (eds.), *The Bible in Three Dimensions: Essays in Celebration of Forty Years of Biblical Studies in the University of Sheffield* (JSOTSup, 87; Sheffield: JSOT Press, 1990), pp. 65-84 (67-81), argues that each of the six sections (chs. 1–12; 13–27; 28–35; 40.1–51.11; 52.12–55.13; chs. 56–66) ends with an eschatological singing, except the transitory chapters (36–39); and recently Anthony J. Tomasino, 'Isaiah 1.1–2.4 and 63–66, and the Composition of the Isaianic Corpus', *JSOT* 57 (1993), pp. 81-98.

36. Tomasino, 'Isaiah 1.1–2.4 and 63–66', pp. 83-93.

the book as a consciously developed coherent work, pointing out that chs. 2–66 are embraced by the theological agenda of 'exhortation to people to participate in YHWH's plan for new world order'. Chapters 2–35 are the 'announcement of YHWH's plan for the new world order centered in Zion'; chs. 36–39 a 'narrative explanation for delay in implementation of plan'; and chs. 40–66 are an 'exhortation to participate in YHWH's renewed covenant'.[37] O'Connell's entire work is devoted to the literary structure of the book.[38] Gileadi, following Brownlee, argues that the entire book is divided into two parallel parts: chs. 1–33 and 34–66.[39] However, in spite of the seemingly convincing arguments, the book neither contains any structure encompassing the entire book nor exhibits an exact structural correspondence even within several selected passages.

On the other hand, the search for thematic continuity appears to be more promising, for several themes appear in all three sections of the book. Rendtorff, among critical scholars, identifies several common themes, and Clements elaborates the ideas of blindness and deafness.[40] Webb argues for the sustained appearance of the remnant idea which will in turn fulfill the restoration of Zion.[41] Recently, Darr has traced the 'recurring female and child tropes and the themes to which they are integral'.[42] Clifford examines the presence (or the lack) of creation language in the three sections of the book;[43] but, as he openly admits,

37. Sweeney, *Isaiah 1–4*, pp. 96-99.

38. Robert H. O'Connell, *Concentricity and Continuity: The Literary Structure of Isaiah* (JSOTSup, 188; Sheffield: Sheffield Academic Press, 1994), especially pp. 235-39.

39. Avraham Gileadi, *The Literary Message of Isaiah* (New York: Hebraeus, 1994), pp. 33-43.

40. R. Rendtorff, 'Zur Komposition des Buches Jesaja', *VT* 34 (1984), pp. 295-320; Clements, 'Beyond Tradition-History', pp. 95-113. In a similar way, K.T. Aitken, 'Hearing and Seeing: Metamorphoses of a Motif in Isaiah 1–39', in Philip R. Davies and David J.A. Clines (eds.), *Among the Prophets: Language, Image and Structure in the Prophetic Writings* (JSOTSup, 144; Sheffield: JSOT Press, 1993), pp. 12-41, traces a transformation of the motif '[not] hear/see'/'[not] know/understand' within chs. 1–39.

41. Webb, 'Zion in Transformation', pp. 67-84.

42. Darr, *Isaiah's Vision*, p. 11. Also *idem*, 'Two Unifying Female Images in the Book of Isaiah', in Lewis M. Hopfe (ed.) *Uncovering Ancient Stones: Essays in Honour of H. Neil Richardson* (Winona Lake, IN: Eisenbrauns, 1994), pp. 17-30.

43. Clifford, 'The Unity', pp. 1-17.

the creation imagery does not appear evenly in all three sections of the book. Themes and ideas which do not recur far outnumber the corresponding ones, and it is also true that a concept may be used differently in various parts of the book, for example the idea of 'righteousness'.

All these considerations seem to indicate that the final editor had a limited authority to select the materials and arranged them within some theological guidelines. This editor might have composed some materials and modified the existing literary traditions, but obviously he did not act as if possessing the authority to force the existing material into a harmonious theological mold. Carr expresses it aptly, in his case, from the structural basis,

> Yet excessive confidence in the existence of a more complete unity in biblical texts—and our need to find it—can blind us to the unresolved, rich plurality built into texts like Isaiah.[44]

This study uses as its context the entire book as it stands today, and accordingly, canonical reading is reading the book as a theological whole. However, I am aware of the fact that the task of canonical reading is not primarily to investigate the intention of the final redactor, since that would make the discipline a 'branch of redaction criticism'.[45] Rather, it is 'concerned with the meanings each part of the text is constrained to have by its juxtaposition with all the others'.[46] At the same time, it is difficult to imagine that the new meaning was attained in a vacuum. However unknown it may be to us now, the real life situation of the community of faith and its attempt to counter the problem theologically became an inherent motif too. In this sense, the theological intentions of the final compilers should not be ignored. This makes it more difficult to exclude the redactional process, especially that of the last stage, from canonical criticism.

In this rereading of the passages with a deliberate theological intention, a combination of a modified form of canonical criticism and intertextual reading will be considered as a possible approach. Much of the investigation is made through a simple rereading of the book with literary structure and thematic links in mind. In addition, given passages will be examined within the overall theological context of the

---

44. David Carr, 'Reaching for Unity in Isaiah', *JSOT* 57 (1993), pp. 61-80 (80).
45. Barton, *Reading the Old Testament*, p. 90.
46. Barton, *Reading the Old Testament*, p. 90.

book of Isaiah. Accordingly, the theology of the book as a whole will be discussed first.

2. *Theology of the Book of Isaiah in its Entirety*

The basis of the canonical Isaianic theology is found in the first 39 chapters, just as the theologies of the exilic and postexilic Isaianic traditions have their roots in the pre-exilic tradition. This pre-exilic theology was often modified, developed and expanded in different historical stages until it assumed the canonical theological significance. There are a number of theological themes that the book of Isaiah in its entirety sets forth.

2.1 *Judgment/Salvation*

The theme of judgment and salvation is recognized as the main theological motif around which 'the final form is regularly redacted'.[47] The first two chapters display this theological pattern,[48] and the same phenomenon is observable in the first 35 chapters. Chapters 1–12 are mainly judgment messages against his people; chs. 13–23 and 27, judgment oracles against the nations; and chs. 24–25 and 28–35 contain promises of restoration. Yet, the pattern is not as obvious in Isaiah as in Ezekiel or in the Greek text of Jeremiah.[49]

The arrangement of the entire book is also analogous to the judgment/salvation pattern. In a simplistic form, the overall message of chs. 1–35 is judgment, that of chs. 40–55 is salvation, and chs. 56–66 is a combination of both, but with the ultimate message of salvation. The narrative in chs. 36-39 serves not only to supplement the judgment messages with the historical account of a divine deliverance, but also as a bridge between the judgment part of the book and that of salvation.[50] Others argue that 40.1-8 was not composed by an independent exilic

47. Clements, 'Patterns', pp. 43-44. Also Brueggemann, 'Unity and Dynamic', p. 90, among others. This oscillation is also observed by earlier writings for certain portions of the book, e.g. Ackroyd, 'Isaiah I–XII', pp. 16-48.

48. See below, pp. 179-80.

49. Eissfeldt, *The Old Testament*, p. 306.

50. Joseph Blenkinsopp, *Prophecy and Canon: A Contribution to the Study of Jewish Origins* (Notre Dame: University of Notre Dame Press, 1977), p. 104, argues that the Deuteronomic history exerts a strong influence in the redactional process of the prophets as seen in the borrowing of the historical supplement to the collection.

prophet and later joined to chs. 1–39, but intentionally composed for the reader to 'reenter the divine council where Isaiah was first commissioned'.[51]

The purpose of the oscillation, however, is not to smooth out the harsh pronouncement of judgment, but to make it clear that judgment is not the last word; rather, salvation is the ultimate destiny which God has prepared for his people. The overall plan of the book with the judgment–salvation–judgment/salvation scheme indicates this theological intention. The imagery of God puts Yahweh as Israel's kinsman-redeemer. Although the judgment is unavoidable, the salvation from Yahweh is certain.

God's judgment, although now reflected upon with hindsight, was not only inevitable, in spite of the invitation to repentance, but also essential in the prophetic tradition. Of course, judgment presupposes the presence of sin within Israel, and when the sin persisted because Israel was reluctant to repent, God's judgment came. This certainty is demonstrated clearly from the very beginning of Isaiah's ministry in ch. 6 which exerts a heavy influence on the theological shaping of the book.[52] In Isaiah's mind, and thus in the subsequent Isaianic traditions, judgment must take place before salvation is realized. Hence, it is not strange that judgment is viewed as God's purifying process for his people (e.g. 4.2-6),[53] because judgment prepares the people of God for the coming age of salvation.

51. Christopher R. Seitz, 'The Divine Council: Temporal Transition and New Prophecy in the Book of Isaiah', *JBL* 109 (1990), pp. 229-47 (243-44). Roy F. Melugin, 'The Servant, God's Call, and the Structure of Isaiah 40–48', in Eugene H. Lovering, Jr (ed.), *SBL 1991 Seminar Papers* (Atlanta: Scholars Press, 1991), pp. 21-30, basically agrees with Seitz.

52. Brevard S. Childs, *Old Testament Theology in a Canonical Context* (Philadelphia: Fortress Press, 1985), pp. 123-24, and von Rad, *Old Testament Theology*, II, p. 58. The unusual position of the call narrative in comparison to Ezek. 1 and Jer. 1 confirms the unique formation of the book. Christopher R. Seitz, 'Isaiah 1–66: Making Sense of the Whole', in *idem* (ed.), *Reading and Preaching the Book of Isaiah* (Philadelphia: Fortress Press, 1988), pp. 105-26 (121).

53. This passage is viewed as the conclusion of the promise of covenantal restoration by Wiklander, *Prophecy as Literature*, p. 141. However, it is unmistakable that the passage not only explains judgment as purification, but also complements the final promise of salvation. For this analysis, see Rolf Rendtorff, *The Old Testament: An Introduction* (trans. John Bowden; Philadelphia: Fortress Press, 1985), p. 191.

Salvation is as certain as judgment, which has become a historical as well as a theological reality from the canonical perspective. This affirmation is based on the very nature of Yahweh, but the full recognition of God's salvation is reserved until the eschatological fulfillment.

There are various expressions in the Isaianic tradition which contrast the state of judgment and salvation. Clements argues that the contrast between darkness and light, and deafness and hearing refers to the radical contrast of the coming restoration to the previous, and in some sense present, state of judgment.[54] The expression of the former and new things, from the viewpoint of the restored community, has to do with the contrast between the judgment and the full realization of God's salvation.

2.2 *Yahweh: The Supreme King*
The idea of the holiness of God is closely associated with the judgment/salvation pattern on a functional level.[55] However, the expression is used to describe the otherliness and loftiness of Yahweh: it is the divine quality *par excellence* and by this Yahweh is delineated as inviolable and unapproachably transcendent compared with human beings, idols or nations.[56] The concept was revealed to Isaiah in the very beginning of his prophetic vocation by the pronouncement of the superlative mode of God's holiness by the Seraphim (6.3). This concept dominates not only his oracles and ministry but also the theological formation of the entire book. The evenly distributed expression 'the Holy One

---

54. Clements, 'Patterns', pp. 189-200.

55. In chs. 1–39, there are 15 occurrences of the adjectival form and all those which refer to the present are used negatively in the context of judgment (1.4; 5.16, 19, 24; 6.3; 10.17; 30.11-12, 15; 31.1; 37.23), but all those which are applied to the future are used positively (10.20; 12.6; 17.7; 29.19, 23). On the other hand, in chs. 40–55, all the occurrences of the adjectival forms (40.25; 41.14, 16, 20; 43.3, 14, 15; 45.11; 47.4; 48.17; 49.7; 55.5) and noun forms (48.2; 52.1, 10) are used in the salvation context. In chs. 56–66, two occurrences of the adjectival form are positive (60.2, 14) while the two noun forms are distinct (63.10, negative; 63.11, positive). When the term or its derivatives refer to somebody/something other than God himself, the mood is mostly positive in the future references (4.3; 8.14; 11.9; 35.8; 56.7; 62.9, 12; 66.20), but in the present references, they are both positive (8.14; 57.13; 58.13; 63.15, 18) and negative (64.9-10; 65.11).

56. Joseph Jensen, *God's Word to Israel* (Wilmington, DE: Michael Glazier, rev. edn, 1982), p. 168.

of Israel' throughout the book is an unmistakable evidence of the importance of this concept.[57]

The holiness of God, in fact, is a forceful motif for both judgment and salvation. As seen in the prophet's encounter with Yahweh's holiness, this reality brings an immediate awareness of the sinfulness of the prophet and his people (6.5); neither can Yahweh's holiness tolerate sin nor can a sinner stand before it. Sin must be dealt with either by the destruction of the sinner (6.5) or through a divine provision of taking away of the sin (RSV, 6.6-7), that is, either through judgment or salvation. Therefore, God's special relationship with, and his abiding presence among, his people could make the situation even 'dangerous'.[58]

At the same time, the concept of holiness implies the sovereign and supreme power of God, particularly as Israel's benefactor. At the declaration of God's holiness, the foundations of the thresholds were shaken, and the house was filled with smoke (6.5). The shaking of the ground and smoke are basic elements of theophanic appearance, and they certainly emphasize his absolute power.

In the call account, crucial to the theology of the entire book, Isaiah calls Yahweh 'the king' (6.5). There is no doubt that he confesses Yahweh as the king of Israel. He is also often called 'Yahweh of hosts' (יהוה צבאות), which is an originally cultic term associated with the ark in Shiloh (1 Sam. 1.3, 11; 4.4; 15.2; 2 Sam. 5.10; 6.2, 18; 7.8, 26, 27).[59] With Isaiah's creativity,[60] the term is applied to God who, as Israel's ruler, spares a small remnant. In the 'borrowed' historical narrative (chs. 36–39), for instance, only minor variations are found: one of them

---

57. The term appears 12 times in First Isaiah (1.4; 5.19, 24; 10.20; 12.6; 17.7; 29.19; 30.11-12, 15; 31.1; 37.23), 11 times in Second Isaiah (41.14, 16, 20; 43.3, 14; 45.11; 47.4; 48.17; 49.7; 54.5; 55.5) and twice in Third Isaiah (60.9, 14). But the same expression occurs only six times in the rest of the Old Testament (2 Kgs 19.22; Jer. 50.29; 51.5; Ps. 71.22; 78.41; 89.19).

58. Jensen, *God's Word to Israel*, p. 169.

59. Friedrich Baumgärtel, 'Zu den Gottesnamen in den Büchern Jeremia und Ezechiel', in A. Kuschke (ed.), *Verbannung und Heimkehr: Beiträge zur Geschichte und Theologie Israels in 6. und 5. Jahrhundert v. Chr.: Wilhelm Rudolph zum 70. Geburtstage, dargebracht von Kollegen, Freunden und Schülern* (Tübingen: J.C.B. Mohr, 1961), pp. 1-24 (12); Otto Eissfeldt, 'Silo und Jerusalem', in George W. Anderson (ed.), *Volume du Congrès: Strasbourg, 1956* (VTSup, 4; Leiden: E.J. Brill, 1957), pp. 138-47; H.-J. Kraus, *Psalms 1–59: A Commentary* (trans. Hilton C. Oswald; Minneapolis: Augsburg, 1988), pp. 85-86.

60. Wildberger, *Isaiah 1–12*, p. 29.

is the expression 'the word of Yahweh of hosts' in 39.5 for the 'word of
Yahweh' in 2 Kgs 21.16. This typical idea of the book presents God as
the sovereign ruler over Israel, and this royal image is explicitly
revealed in the call narrative with the word מלך (6.5).

The emphasis upon Yahweh's sovereign kingship is seen in contrast
to the historical failure of human kings and the reduced role of the
traditional human agents. First, there is no significant emphasis upon
the prophet except in the two superscriptions, and the chapters are filled
with God's direct addresses.[61] Secondly, the earthly kings are described
to have failed in their traditional royal role which includes military
leadership, supreme judgeship and congruent priestly functions. The
king as the representative of the entire nation fails as he relies on foreign power rather than on Yahweh (Ahaz in chs. 7–9 and Hezekiah in
chs. 30–31).

Israelite kingship is already a diminished version of the known royal
ideology withholding from the king the priestly role.[62] At least one pre-
exilic royal oracle (ch. 11) demonstrates much evidence of de-royaliza-
tion by later hands. The champion–hero image of the king has faded
away and the wisdom aspect of the ideal king becomes the hallmark of
the future king.[63] In fact, the exilic and postexilic traditions picture the
expectation of divine rule without any human agent; Yahweh is the
king who rules directly over his people (43.15). However, the exilic
tradition replaces these traditional human agents with two unlikely
figures: Cyrus and the Servant. By this, Yahweh's supreme rulership—
which centers around his ability to judge and restore the people, the
temple and the nation—is accentuated. The silence of a human ruler
may indicate the democratization of the royal tradition.[64]

The concept of Yahweh's kingship over Israel is eventually expanded
to his rulership over the nations, their gods and idols, and the whole
universe (e.g. 40.15-20). The notion of Yahweh's universal kingship is

61. Seitz, 'Isaiah 1–66', p. 121. It is worth noting that the 'involved' nature of
Jeremiah and Ezekiel make a sharp contrast to the book of Isaiah.

62. For instance, 1 Sam. 13.5-14 and 2 Chron. 26.16-18. However, it is doubtful
if this 'reductional' process was practiced from the beginning of the monarchy.

63. Clements, *Isaiah 1–39*, p. 122, argues that this reflects a later theological
trend.

64. Here the uniqueness of the Isaianic tradition is evident as it is contrasted to
other postexilic literature, which maintains the expectation of a human messianic
figure (e.g. Hag. 2.23; Zech. 3.8; 4.6-7, 14).

apparent throughout the book, and this theological notion is achieved in various ways. First, the Isaianic tradition places Israel, the nations and the universe under his rulership (chs. 13–27), for the fate of the nations is determined by God. Assyria, and later Babylon, are viewed as God's 'hired' tool for judgment upon Israel (7.18-20; 39.5-7), but later still Yahweh will judge them for their arrogance. Secondly, Yahweh in his sovereignty raises Cyrus to be his servant, who is chosen to bring destruction to Babylon and to liberate God's people from bondage. Thirdly, in the eschatological consummation the nations will voluntarily subject themselves to Yahweh; foreigners will actively participate in Yahweh worship in Zion, and some will even serve as Levites and priests (66.21). Nations that have never heard of Yahweh will see God's glory and they will bring bountiful offerings to Yahweh, to his 'holy mountain Jerusalem' (66.20). Ultimately, however, nowhere in the earth can his throne be adequately set: heaven is his throne and the earth is his footstool (66.1a).

2.3 *Zion*

Related to the restoration of Yahweh's kingship is the returning of glory to Zion. In fact, Zion/Jerusalem is often suggested as the main theological element of the book. For instance, Dumbrell argues for the centrality of Zion based on the inclusio of the idea of Zion/ Jerusalem, because the rejected Jerusalem begins the book and the newly created Jerusalem concludes it (66.20-24).[65] Although this concept, among others, is considered to bind the entire book together,[66] Zion's significance is based on the rulership of Yahweh: this city will be called, 'City of Yahweh, Zion of the Holy One of Israel' (60.14b). In a sense, Zion serves as a partner of God in his plan, so one may call God the main character and Zion the second main character.[67] Israelite kingship is greatly diminished in the exilic and postexilic Isaianic traditions, and Zion occupies the center of God's rulership. Not much evidence is found for any link between Zion and any human figure, nor for a political role of the city. It is a substantial theological shift from the close

65. William J. Dumbrell, 'The Purpose of the Book of Isaiah', *TynBul* 36 (1985), pp. 111-28 (113); *idem, The Search for Order*, pp. 80-85. See also Webb, 'Zion in Transformation', pp. 65-84.

66. Rendtorff, 'Zür Komposition', p. 381, and Childs, *Introduction*, pp. 328-34. See also Schibler, 'Messianism and Messianic Prophecy', p. 94.

67. Seitz, 'Isaiah 1–66', p. 122.

connection between Davidic kingship and Zion theology. After losing its political element, the city became more of a religious center of the world, and Israel takes up a priestly role for the nations.

As Yahweh's kingship extends to the entire universe, Zion will also attain a universal role; being the seat of God's rulership, Zion will become the center of the world. The old Zion failed to reflect who Yahweh is—its king (1.21-25), but in the day of salvation, the nations and peoples will gather in Zion (2.2-3). There Yahweh will rule the nations (2.4a), from there the instruction will flow (2.3) and 'many may drink deeply with delight from her [Zion's] glorious bosom' (66.11b).

Consequently, the fortunes of Zion, once plundered because of its sin, will be restored as the wealth of the nations is given to her (66.12). This vindication and liberation will come from the hand of Yahweh, when he comes in fire and chariots like the whirlwind 'to pay back his anger' (66.15).

2.4 *Israel*

Also related to the rulership of Yahweh is Israel as the people of God. In his relation to the people, God bases his kingship over Israel on two grounds: the covenant metaphor via cultic associations (6.1-4) and God as the creator (40.12-31). The unique relationship between Yahweh and Israel is well observed from the very beginning of the book (e.g. language like 'rear children' 1.2; 'my people' 1.3; and numerous other metaphors). The creation motif becomes prominent starting from ch. 40, for Yahweh's rule over Israel (41.21-24; 43.15; 44.6-8; 52.7) and the nations (their pilgrimage to Zion, 45.14-15; 49.14-21, 22-23; 52.1-2) is based on his creator–creation relationship.

Israel is clearly depicted as the principal recipient of Yahweh's goodness and his special favor (e.g. 5.2; 63.7). In turn, Yahweh expected undivided loyalty and faithfulness from Israel, but they rebelled (1.2; 63.10), and did not even know God (1.3). Unwillingness to recognize God and his acts constitutes rebellion;[68] Yahweh becomes their enemy (1.24, 25; 63.10).

Furthermore, through his election, Yahweh has given Israel a mission to the nations. The canonical reading undoubtedly identifies the Servant with Israel, but it was deaf and blind (42.18, 19), instead of being 'a covenant to the people, a light to the nations' (42.6). The new Servant, the new Israel, will succeed in spite of difficulties (42.4), and he will

68. Watts, *Isaiah 34–66*, p. 3.

bring forth מִשְׁפָּט to the nations (42.1) and his teaching to the coastlands (42.4).

2.5 *Eschatology*

Eschatology is an unmistakable mark of the canonical intention of the book,[69] for eschatologization is an outcome of the long interpretive process of the Isaianic tradition. This move probably stems out of a concern for the unfulfilled prophecies, especially those of splendid restoration and exaltation of Zion,[70] while the fate of the nations, although closely linked with that of Israel, is secondary.

The eschatological plan perceived by the Isaianic tradition involves two main elements: judgment and salvation. As already seen above, the entire book is collected, edited, arranged and refined with a definite eschatological motif.[71] The entire plan of God for human history can be divided into four different steps (see the table below),[72] although sometimes events may not strictly follow the sequence, particularly in the second and third blocks,[73] or an event may have significance in more than one category.

	Israel	Nations
Judgment	I	II
Salvation	III	IV

Eschatological Plan (EP)

69. Gileadi, *The Literary Message*, p. 249, argues for an overall apocalyptic feature. Anderson, 'The Apocalyptic Rendering', p. 18, rereads the book 'from the viewpoint of its final apocalyptic *relecture* or rendering'.

70. Carroll, *When Prophecy Failed*, especially pp. 130-56, for the Isaianic tradition.

71. This canonical motif is well observed by Childs, 'The Canonical Shape', p. 53.

72. This simplified chart was suggested by Leslie C. Allen in his lecture on Old Testament Theology (Fuller Theological Seminary, Pasadena, CA, in 1986), and his permission for adaptation is gratefully acknowledged.

73. The sequence of the first three elements corresponds to the editorial structure of First Isaiah, Jeremiah and Ezekiel: (1) oracles of judgment; (2) oracles against the nations; and (3) oracles of salvation or eschatological oracles, P.-M. Bogaert, 'L'organisation des grands receuils prophétiques', in Jacques Vermeylen (ed.), *Le livre d'Isaïe: Les oracles et leurs relectures unité et complexité de l'ouvrage* (BETL, 81; Leuven: Leuven University Press, 1989); Vermeylen, 'L'unité du livre d'Isaïe', pp. 147-53. Ackroyd, 'Isaiah I–XII', p. 20, rules out the existence of such a structure.

The eschatology of the book derives from its unique standpoint in the scheme of the eschatological plan (EP hereafter). The canonical reading interprets the 'former things' and the 'new things' differently from the traditional understanding.[74] The judgment which has been announced by the earlier prophecies is a past reality, or the 'former things'. Through a series of crises climaxed by the exilic experience, the community has witnessed the fulfillment of the first block of the EP. As Judah relied upon foreign power instead of Yahweh himself, the foreign powers were used by Yahweh to bring judgment upon Judah. Most of the judgment oracles against Israel belong to EP I, which is inevitable as a purging and purifying process (e.g. 4.2-6). The viewpoint of the book comes after the major fulfillment of the EP I and at the beginning of the EP II and the EP III.

Surprisingly frequent oracles of judgment upon the nations[75] (EP II), especially those who have oppressed Israel (Assyria, 10.5-19; 14.24-27; Babylon, 13.1-22; 14.3-23) and enemies like Edom (ch. 34), signal the salvation of Israel (EP III). When the Lord has finished all his work of judgment upon Mount Zion and Jerusalem, he will punish the arrogant boasting of the king of Assyria and his haughty pride (Isa. 10.12). Oracles against the nations also serve various purposes for both Israel and the nations.[76]

Often another nation or an individual is used by God's supreme sovereignty to bring judgment upon the nations. All the judgment oracles

74. E.g. Christopher R. North, 'The "Former Things" and the "New Things" in Deutero-Isaiah', in H.H. Rowley (ed.), *Studies in Old Testament Prophecy* (Edinburgh: T. & T. Clark, 1950), pp. 111-26, detects the old and new exodus motif. For relevant discussions, see Bernhard W. Anderson, 'Exodus Typology in Second Isaiah', in Bernhard W. Anderson and Walter Harrelson (eds.), *Israel's Prophetic Heritage: Essays in Honor of James Muilenburg* (New York: Harper & Row, 1962), pp. 177-95; *idem*, 'Exodus and Covenant in Second Isaiah and Prophetic Tradition', in Cross, Lemke and Miller (eds.), *Magnalia Dei*, pp. 339-60.

75. F.I. Andersen and A.D. Forbes, '"Prose Particle" Counts of the Hebrew Bible', in C.L. Meyers and M. O'Connor (eds.), *The Word of the Lord Shall Go Forth: Essays in Honor of David Noel Freedman in Celebration of his Sixtieth Birthday* (Winona Lake, IN: Eisenbrauns, 1983), pp. 165-83, argue that 15 to 20 per cent of the Latter Prophets is made up of oracles against the nations.

76. Paul R. Raabe, 'Why Prophetic Oracles against the Nations?', in Astrid B. Beck *et al.* (eds.), *Fortunate the Eyes That See: Essays in Honor of David Noel Freedman in Celebration of his Seventieth Birthday* (Grand Rapids: Eerdmans, 1995), pp. 236-57, especially pp. 241-42.

to the nations in chs. 13–23 belong to EP II. God is to judge the nations as an act of vindication for, and vengeance on behalf of, Israel (e.g. 34.8). To some extent, Israel has witnessed and realized its fulfillment: Syria and Samaria have fallen (as predicted in 7.7-9) and Assyria has disappeared as promised. Babylonia's fall is predicted and about to be fulfilled (chs. 13 and 41); yet, it is not fully consummated. The post-exilic community which contributed to the formation of the book could have experienced its struggle under ungodly foreign powers. Much of this block of the EP remains as an expectation for the future.

The third block of the EP, the salvation of Israel, logically follows the judgment of the nations (EP II) which have brought destruction to Israel. However, the realization of EP III is not necessarily contingent upon the historical fulfillment of EP II, the judgment of the nations. As proclaimed in chs. 40–55, the salvation of Israel is the sovereign work of Yahweh as the covenant God and creator, and his sovereignty in EP III is not much different from his utilization of the nations for EP II.

Historically, salvation has dawned with the appearance of Cyrus (45.1-3). The expected salvation has the exodus event as its paradigm (e.g. 40.3-5); yet this time it will be more glorious and grandiose. The community understands that the 'new things' have begun, but are not yet fully realized. This becomes a crucial theological and historical motivation that influences the canonical process of the book. The community is 'sandwiched' between the fulfilled and unfulfilled nature of the promise: the fulfillment of the 'former things' confirms that the word of the prophet is the truthful word of God, and yet, the community's existential struggle has motivated the canonization of the book. Chapters 56–66 find the cause of the delayed salvation to be the unreadiness of the people.

Israel needs to fulfill righteousness and justice, in moral as well as in religious areas, before Yahweh's salvation can be realized (56.1),[77] for the completion of EP I does not guarantee the purity of the community. In fact, the day of Yahweh, to the postexilic mind, is not necessarily past once and for all in 586 BCE; it can reoccur at any time (e.g. 4.2-6 and Joel). The appearance of the coming ruler (particularly 11.1-5), the fruitfulness of the land (32.15), and the 'pouring out' of the spirit of God (32.15) remain part of the unfulfilled portion of this EP. Even the restoration of Zion, although the temple has been rebuilt and the walls

---

77. Rendtorff, *The Old Testament*, p. 200.

around the city re-erected from the canonical standpoint, has not been fully realized. Many of these splendid promises are moved to a distant future and become part of the expectation of the new age. The fulfillment of this plan is the fulfillment of God's covenant with his people (60.21).

Much of the last EP, the salvation of the nations, still remains to be fulfilled in the future. This universalistic theology is not commonly seen within the pre-exilic prophetic tradition. This block (EP IV) presupposes the fulfillment of EP II, the judgment upon the nations (e.g. 'survivors of the nations', 45.20), especially for the enemies of Israel. The fulfillment of EP III is essential for the realization of EP IV. Although the Servant has a role in proclaiming Yahweh's משפט to the nations (especially 42.1-4), this universalism is mainly the historical demonstration of God's power in the judgment of the nations and the salvation of Israel. The return of Israel and the restoration of Zion are, therefore, understood as the demonstration of Yahweh's supremacy over the nations and their gods. The future Zion is the world center, since Yahweh sits there and rules over the universe. The wealth of the nations will be brought in, kings will pay their homage to Yahweh (60.11), and even the former oppressors of Israel will come and bow down before the people of God (60.14). The salvation for the nations is different from that of Israel (EP III), in that there is no element of vindication for the nations involved; rather, it is a time that Israel will be further vindicated as God's people. Aliens and foreigners will do all the manual work (61.5) and the people of God will become priests of Yahweh (61.6), which can be called a nationalistically motivated (Zion-centered) universalism. Therefore, the fulfillment of EP IV is not necessary as God is not obligated to save the nations. Only when they turn to God, they will be helped (45.22)—it is a sort of historical appendix.

Theocracy is the norm of the coming age and the messianic expectation should be understood within this assumption. The salvation of the nations (EP IV), like the judgment upon them (EP II), is the fullest expression of the salvation of Israel (EP III). This not only completes the eschatological plan of God, but also the canonical plan of the book: the rejected Jerusalem (ch. 1) becomes a new Jerusalem (66.20-24) in its 'obvious conclusion'.[78]

---

78. Dumbrell, 'The Purpose', p. 112, correctly points out the overall inclusio of the book. However, it is questionable whether 'Yahweh's interest in and devotion to the city of Jerusalem' function as the 'overmastering theme'.

3. *Passages*

Due to the large number of passages to be considered, it is impossible to devote adequate attention to all the questions in a limited space. This is a simple theological re-reading of the book, and so the following investigations will not repeat the basic exegetical material, especially in its historical context, which has been dealt with in the previous chapters. Rather, an attempt will be made to highlight the significance of the passages and the concept in question within the literary and theological reading as a canonical book. Notes represent the new context in which the passages are re-read. The reading will follow a logical arrangement of material as seen in the subtitles of each section.

3.1 *Chapter 1: Introduction to the Book*[79]

Chapter 1 is often recognized as an editorial introduction to the entire book.[80] The chapter sets not only the tone for the entire book, but also the pattern of judgment–salvation. First of all, the superscription, as in other prophetic books (e.g. Hosea and Amos), is a literary attempt to reflect the theological message of the book.[81] It presupposes, at the same time, that the work of the prophet had been completed and his sayings have been committed to writing.[82] This indicates that the careful theological shaping of the book has been completed. The chapter starts with messages predominantly of judgment (vv. 2-8) with a slight but significant implication of the promise of salvation (v. 9). The succeeding indictments (vv. 10-17) are followed by, this time, an invitation with promise of subsequent salvation (vv. 18-19) and an 'or else' type

---

79. John Barton, *Isaiah 1–39* (OTG; Sheffield: JSOT Press, 1995), pp. 14-15, contends that the most generally agreed division of chs. 1–39 is: ch. 1; chs. 2–12; chs. 13–23; chs. 24–27; chs. 28–31; chs. 32–33; chs. 34–35; and chs. 36–39. However, one can see that the division of chs. 28–39 varies among scholars and commentators.

80. Among others, Dumbrell, 'The Purpose', p. 114; S. Niditch, 'The Composition of Isaiah 1', *Bib* 61 (1980), pp. 509-29.

81. Gene Tucker, 'Prophetic Superscriptions and the Growth of a Canon', in George W. Coats and Burke O. Long (eds.), *Canon and Authority: Essays in Old Testament Religion and Theology* (Philadelphia: Fortress Press, 1977), pp. 71-87 (68).

82. Wildberger, *Isaiah 1–12*, p. 3.

of judgment saying (v. 20). The third, short, single accusation (vv. 21-23) is succeeded by a longer promise of salvation (vv. 24-27) and also an alternative choice of judgment (vv. 28-31). This deliberate editorial oscillation between judgment and salvation is many times not difficult to detect. In fact, for Childs, an abrupt shift from judgment to salvation as well as from poetry to prose, without much of an attempt to smooth things out, is a clear mark of the undertaking of canonization.[83]

3.2 *Chapters 2–12: Yahweh, God of Israel*

This section may be divided into two parts: chs. 2–4 and chs. 5–12. The former sets the tone of the message surrounding the Syro-Ephraimite war in the following chapters. The oscillation between judgment and salvation continues as demonstrated by Wiklander in chs. 2–4 (2.2b-5; 2.8b-10d; 2.22; 3.16–4.6), and the present accusation is molded in a lawsuit pattern or judgment (2.6-8; 2.11-21; 3.1-15).[84]

For the latter part, ch. 5 sets the tone for the section. It begins with the powerful Song of the Vineyard, signaling the negative outcome of the prophetic judgment. But the literary combination of the Isaiah memoir and other oracles affirms a deliberate editorial process. The position of the call narrative in ch. 6 is deliberate in order to prepare for the rejection of Ahaz in ch. 7. On the other hand, ch. 12 sums up the whole section and serves as a transitional literary link to the next section. The overall message is basically judgment upon Judah (EP I), but with a suggestion of a move toward salvation to Israel (EP III) via EP II (judgment upon nations). A rough chiastic structure of the section, except the introductory ch. 5 and the concluding, transitional chapter (ch. 12), is discernible:

```
  A [ch. 5          Song of the Vineyard (EP I)]
    B ch. 6              Prophetic Call and the Dead King (EP I)
      C 7.1–8.10           Signs and Enemy's Threat (EP I, II & III)
        D 8.11-22             Holiness of the Lord
          E 8.23–9.7             Royal Savior (EP III)
        D' 9.8–10.4a          Anger of Yahweh
      C' 10.4b-34          Destruction of Enemy (EP II)
    B' ch. 11           New King and Restoration (EP III)
  A' [ch. 12        Song of the Redeemed (EP III)]
```

83. Childs, *Introduction*, p. 319.
84. Wiklander, *Prophecy as Literature*, pp. 140-41.

Obviously the idea of the coming savior not only runs through the section, but also occupies the core position. Yet the outline exhibits a clear development from EP I to EP III and the idea of the coming savior is further elaborated in the climactic chapter (11).

Isaiah 4.4. Isaiah 4.2-6 forms the concluding section of the first portion, which is certainly looking forward to the day when the judgment of God will serve as a purifying process.[85] The passage also makes a neat inclusio of chs. 2–4 with the promise of restoration. This explicit theological link between EP I and EP III constitutes a significant contrast to the presentation of the wilderness experience of the first exodus (e.g. Isa. 63.7-14).

In its eschatological framework, it is highly plausible that the 'branch' here refers to the coming messianic figure.[86] It is even more so within its larger literary context, particularly with the Immanuel oracles and 11.1-5. The spirits of judgment and burning (v. 4) are viewed as God's agents to purify the remnant so that it will be holy before Yahweh. If the realization of Zion's glory is the goal toward which the history has moved, then to purge it of its guilt is crucial for the eschatological hope. Here, God's spirit achieves the purging role without any human agent being involved. The spirit's immediate function falls in EP I (judgment for Israel), but to achieve EP III (salvation for Israel). The spirit here is so impersonal that one can almost say 'a spirit of judgment' or 'burning' as if there were many other functional spirits in Yahweh's court (cf. 1 Kgs 22.19).

Isaiah 11.1. There are several literary features that are evident. *The passage* is carefully placed in its present position, although the poetic arrangement makes an obvious contrast to the prose nature of the previous passage. The tree imagery from the immediately preceding judgment oracle (10.33-34) is neatly picked up, but it creates a reversal. The alteration from judgment to salvation is the main element of this reversal. Also a contrast is noted between 'lofty trees', 'tall trees' (10.33), 'forest thickets' (10.34) and 'a shoot...from the stump' (11.1). Certainly a comparison is made between the judgment upon the nations

---

85. The passage 'counteracts' the judgment oracles in ch. 3 with an 'image of bliss' (DeVries, *Yesterday, Today and Tomorrow*, p. 308).

86. Childs, 'The Canonical Shape', p. 52.

and the salvation for Judah. The development from the prevailing judgment at the beginning of the section, namely chs. 5 and 6, to the promise of restoration in chs. 11 and 12 is unmistakable. The present arrangement indicates that the passage serves as the beginning of the climax for chs. 5–12. Yet the same arrangement implies that restoration comes only after judgment.

The passage in its broader canonical context, especially together with the two Immanuel passages in chs. 7 and 9, offers a new meaning. As seen above, the 'shoot' in 4.2 is likely to be understood by the community at the time of canonization as referring to a messianic ruler. This is all the more true with the Immanuel passages. All these glorious announcements in their own historical settings become predictions and promises for the coming age—an eschatologizing feature. The stereotypical liturgical announcement, at least in the case of 11.1-5, is reinterpreted by the postexilic community as describing the coming ruler in a distant future.[87]

All of the qualifications for the coming ruler are attributed to the spirit of God which will rest upon him. The language used in the passage exhibits a heavy wisdom influence which is a postexilic development. The traditional link between wisdom and might in royal ideology undergoes a de-royalizing process, and Harrelson rightly detects this trend.[88] This 'absolute power' is solely for God's service,[89] and his political and military roles decrease as the moral and spiritual nature of his rule is emphasized. In chs. 1–39, the Hebrew term מלך is only once used to refer to the coming ruler (32.1),[90] whereas the same word is used of Yahweh several times (6.1; 7.1 [3 times], 6, 17, 20; 8.4, 7, 21; 10.12). For the coming ruler, numerous non-royal terms are used: 'child' (9.6) with a royal role and a Davidic reference (9.7); 'shoot' and

87. However, this reappropriation may also reflect the reduced expectation of a royal messianic figure during the postexilic era as evidenced by the near silence of such a figure in chs. 56–66. There are hints that some of the royal features are transferred to the 'servants'.

88. Harrelson, 'Nonroyal Motifs', p. 154.

89. Walther Eichrodt, 'Prophet and Covenant: Observations on the Exegesis of Isaiah', in John I. Durham and J.R. Porter (eds.), *Proclamation and Presence: Old Testament Essays in Honour of Gwynne Henton Davies* (Macon, GA: Mercer University Press, new corrected edn, 1983), pp. 167-88 (183).

90. In 28.6, even though the future ruler is undoubtedly referred to, the term is avoided. It is also true in Isa. 11 as pointed by Eichrodt, ' Prophet and Covenant', p. 154.

'branch' (11.1) also with a Davidic indication (11.1); and 'Immanuel' with no apparent royal function. The tautological synonymous parallelism between מלך and שׂרים[91] is also evident in the following series of parallel structures which do not make two separate points but a single one (11.2).[92] As a result, the role of the king is substantially reduced to that of a faithful regent of God, and the fear of Yahweh becomes the conclusive merit of the coming ruler (11.3). Consequently, God's divine rulership and its effect become more evident, and through the enablement of the spirit of God, the ruler is led to depend faithfully on Yahweh.

As the passage gains its eschatological significance, so does the רוח of God upon the expected ruler. Accordingly the effect involves not only the realization of righteousness and justice, but even mysterious and universal paradisiacal features. The latter includes harmony between human beings and animals, and among animals, that is, a perfect שׁלום in the earth which only God's spirit can bring about. Here, there is an irony in that as the significance of the king is reduced, the effect of his rule is drastically widened. What is realized here is the rulership of Yahweh and its full effect. This canonical modification of the king's rule is achieved by appending the mythical description of an ideal paradise in vv. 6-9.

Traditionally, the Davidic covenant and Zion theology are intimately intermingled. However, the exilic and postexilic, as well as the canonical perspectives, tend to depoliticize Zion and separate it from the Davidic tradition. Zion is instead depicted as the seat of Yahweh's kingship and the world's religious center where Yahweh's Torah will be learned (2.3). The appended mythical passage, in this sense, replaces the expected restoration of Zion as a result of the established Davidic kingship.

Here, the spirit of God assumes various functions, not only resulting in the ideal qualifications of but also singling out the individual as

91. This reading is supported by LXX followed by Syriac, Targum and Vulgate. Also see *BHS*.

92. Douglas K. Stuart, 'The Prophetic Ideal of Government in the Restored Era', in Avraham Gileadi (ed.), *Israel's Apostasy and Restoration: Essays in Honor of Ronald K. Harrison* (Grand Rapids: Baker Book House, 1988), pp. 283-92 (288), shows that parallelism between 'shelter' and 'refuge' (32.2), 'eyes' and 'ears' (v. 3), 'mind' and 'tongue' (v. 4), and 'fool' and 'scoundrel' (v. 5) follows the same pattern.

God's appointed one. The canonical expectation of the messiah has two distinct traditions behind it: the charismatic tradition often found in Judges (Judg. 3.10; 6.34; 11.29; 13.25; 14.16, 19; 15.13, 14; 19.9, 20, 23) and the first two kings (1 Sam. 10.6, 10; 11.6; 16.13, 14; 19.9), and the Davidic covenant (2 Sam. 7.12).

3.3 *Chapters 13–23: Yahweh, God of the Nations*

These chapters basically contain messages of judgment upon the nations (EP II), the scope of which will be expanded to the final universal judgment in the next section. This will usher in Israel's salvation,[93] and, in some cases, the salvation of Yahweh is extended to the nations or their remnant (e.g. 16.1-5; 23.17-18; cf. Hag. 2.6-9). This will result in relief and joy to the entire world (e.g. 14.4-8). The representative role of Babylon is a reflection of an exilic perspective.[94]

The only passage where God's spirit is mentioned is 19.14. In the middle of an oracle against Egypt, the failure of Egypt is attributed to the 'foolish' counselors and royal wise men (vv. 11-13). Verse 14, however, attests that it is Yahweh who 'mingled...a spirit of confusion' within Egypt. Probably the expression can be understood within the context of the divine court scene, where in that literary setting, spirits are often found as courtiers, especially in 2 Kgs 22.19-23, though whether the present passage has a personal element as in 2 Kings 22 is not clear. In the light of 19.3 where the רוח refers to human courage for battle, the impersonality of the spirit can be well argued. In all four occurrences in the Old Testament, the verb מסך is associated with either 'wine' (Prov. 9.2, 5; Isa. 5.22) in the literary usage or 'tears' (Ps. 102.10) in a figurative way. This also supports the impersonal view of the spirit. The passage shows a similarity with 29.10 where Yahweh 'pours out the spirit of deep sleep'. This impersonal power becomes an agent of God's judgment upon Egypt.

3.4 *Chapters 24–27: Yahweh, God of the Universe*

The crucial role of this section in providing the eschatological feature to the theology of the canonical book is recognized widely. This section primarily falls into EP II with some part of it in EP I, and it serves as an expansion of chs. 13–23 and an introduction to chs. 28–33. Here,

---

93. Childs, *Introduction*, p. 332.
94. For a more detailed discussion, see Raabe, 'Why Prophetic Oracles?', p. 238.

God is depicted as 'the cosmic Judge, Ruler of time, [and] gracious Redeemer'.[95] Interestingly, there is no occurrence of God's רוח in any manner. Only once, the human spirit is described as having the faculty to seek Yahweh (26.9). This may reflect a rather later development, as seen in Ps. 61.13(11) and in the Qumran literature such as 1QM in particular.

3.5 *Chapters 28–33: Not to Trust in Any Nation*[96]
The oscillation between judgment and salvation is evident throughout this section. Five out of the six woe sayings in chs. 28–33 are balanced with assurances (woe in 28.1 and assurance in 28.23-29; woe in 29.1 and assurance in 29.13-14; woe in 30.1 and assurance in 30.19-33; woe in 31.1 and assurance in 31.4–32.20; woe in 33.1 and 33.17-24). The leaders in the restored nation (EP III) are described as having the spirit of משפט, in contrast to the drunken leaders of Israel (cf. Eph. 5.18).

In the eschatological development, it is natural to warn the nation not to trust in the nations since God's eschatological plan against the nations was unfolded in the previous section (EP II). Here, Yahweh is presented as the ultimate defender of Zion, although immediate judgment upon Jerusalem is unavoidable.[97] To this, some apocalyptic typology is added in chs. 32 and 33 (e.g. 33.9, 12).[98]

Throughout the section, there are numerous occurrences of רוח, in addition to those that are discussed below: a familiar spirit out of the ground (29.4); and the spirit of deep sleep from the Lord which closed eyes (29.10). The former 'spirit' is not related to God at all, while the latter is a spirit sent by God.

Isaiah 28.6. The section is opened up with an oracle of judgment upon drunken Ephraimites (vv. 1-4, EP I). The next passage (vv. 5-6), in contrast to the drunken and unfaithful leaders of Israel, addresses the Jerusalemites, balancing the previous passage with an oracle of salvation

95. J.N. Oswalt, 'Canonical Criticism: A Review from a Conservative Viewpoint', *JETS* 30 (1987), pp. 317-25 (323).

96. This block division is not universally accepted among scholars. For the present division, see the commentaries of Duhm, *Das Buch Jesaja*, p. 13; Gray, *Isaiah I–XXVII*, p. li; Clements, *Isaiah 1–39*, pp. 2-3. And for the division that ends with ch. 32, see the commentaries of Fohrer, *Das Buch Jesaja*, I, p. 43; Kaiser, *Isaiah 1–12*, p. 234, and Scott, 'Isaiah Chapters 1–39', p. 152.

97. Dumbrell, 'The Purpose', p. 122.

98. Clements, 'Patterns', p. 194.

Until the Spirit Comes

(EP III). Landy understands vv. 1-8 in the context of a covenant with death:[99] 'a metaphorical Jew' who experienced a divine deliverance from death to life would experience God's restoration with the proper administration of מֹשֵׁפֹ and proper protection of the city. Although the future ruler is mentioned, the emphasis lies on Yahweh who means everything to the remnant (28.5), and with the avoidance of the usual term מֶלֶךְ, the de-royalizing trend continues. This ruler will fulfill, however, the expectation of the ideal ruler (11.1-5): the administration of מֹשֵׁפֹ. As Yahweh himself is the glory and beauty of the restored community (cf. 4.2-3), his spirit will enable the 'one who sits in judgment' to administer justice (EP III).

Verse 30.1. This third woe oracle displays—as the other oracles in the series as well as in the entire book—the oscillation between judgment and salvation. Following the second woe oracle (29.15-16), the destruction of Lebanon and the salvation of God is announced (17-24), and this passage is parallel to the second woe oracle (29.15-16) in form and to the fourth (31.1-3) in meaning. As in 31.1-5, reliance on the Egyptian help is attacked, for the entire plan is carried out 'in darkness' to hide from Yahweh (29.15). This strong condemnation, in a sense, prepares the hearers for the judgment stipulations pronounced thereafter.

The actual conflict between the prophet and the political leaders becomes a metaphor for that between Yahweh and his people. Consulting the prophet becomes a covenant norm since not consulting the prophet means not asking for 'my [God's] counsel'. A comparison is set well ahead in the preceding salvation oracle that even the deaf will hear the words of the scroll...[and the] eyes of the blind will see' (29.18). And the mighty redeemer of Abraham promises the presence of 'the holiness of the Holy One of Jacob' (29.23), until 'those who complain' will be able to accept his instruction (v. 24). With the added covenant implication, the role of a prophet is generally enhanced and attains eschatological significance (59.21; Joel 3.1-2).

Verse 31.3. This fourth woe oracle also follows the canonical pattern of the alternation between judgment and salvation. First, a judgment message is found (vv. 1-3); then a promise of salvation (vv. 4-5);[100] a plea

99. Landy, 'Tracing the Voice', pp. 140-62.
100. Michael L. Barré, 'Of Lions and Birds: A Note of Isaiah 31.4-5', in Philip R. Davies and David J.A. Clines (eds.), *Among the Prophets: Language, Image and*

to return (v. 6) and a promise (vv. 7-9). It is noted that two similar oracles in 30.1-5 and 31.3 are juxtaposed. Therefore, the message in this context is clear: refusal of a prophetic advice ('plan not by my spirit', 30.1) is 'their plans from the Lord' (29.15). That, in turn, is 'doing work in darkness and thinking "Who sees us?" and "Who will know?"' (29.15). By doing so these godless leaders, who are in fact relying upon the 'useless' people (vv. 5, 7), are destined to doom. Yet, to these people with false hope and security, a chance of hope is offered by God.

Here the confrontation between the 'wise men's' wisdom and the power of the Egyptian military, on the one hand, and Yahweh's wisdom and power, on the other, is perceived by the prophet as a confrontation between flesh and spirit. It is doubtful whether the 'spirit' here refers to life-giving and transforming energy. The prophet is not saying that the Egyptian horses and soldiers are as good as dead without life-giving spirit. Here the characteristic of God in his power, and possibly in his wisdom, is said to be רוח, but that of human beings and animals is בשר in their weakness and frailties. Human wisdom and military power are by no means to be compared to Yahweh's. The רוח is not understood to be a substance or an entity standing apart from Yahweh, but as the quality or aspect of God as opposed to human beings and animals.

Verse 32.15. In this eschatological passage, as in Isa. 44.3, Ezek. 39.29 and Zech. 12.10, the canonical oscillation between judgment and salvation is again clear: salvation (32.1-8); judgment (vv. 9-14); and salvation (vv. 15-20). The immediately preceding oracle (vv. 9-14) portrays total desolation and destruction until the land is outgrown by thorns and briars (v. 13) and becomes a wasteland and the delight of donkeys, a pasture for flocks (v. 14).

On this dark scene, a new age dawns by the 'pouring out' of the spirit from above (32.15), and a drastic reversal is brought in; it is the regeneration of the nation and its land. Security, peace, righteousness, justice and getting rid of enemies are all directly attributed to the coming of the רוח. The radical reversal is highlighted by taking the same language from vv. 9-14 and reapplying it in a positive sense. In the desolated

Structure in the Prophetic Writings (JSOTSup, 144; Sheffield: JSOT Press, 1993), pp. 55-59, observes a change within vv. 4-5 from the original negative to the canonical positive message.

land which was a delight of donkeys and pasture for flocks (v. 14b), his people will let their cattle and donkeys range freely (v. 20b).

Another reversal theme is seen in the use of רוח. In an earlier oracle the same term was used in the context of judgment (30.28, 'his רוח like a flood') as a destructive force like a rushing and forceful flood. Now the same רוח is to be 'poured out' from above. The familiar water imagery is used, which is irresistibly powerful, limitless and unconditional. Yet, it not only ushers in the age of salvation, but also remains as a characteristic of the coming age. That the רוח is likened to a stream of water implies its life-giving effect,[101] and the connection is well attested elsewhere (e.g. Ps. 104.29-30; Gen. 1.2). This life-giving spirit brings renewal and restoration in three different levels of life: (1) to the fate of the nation (from desolation, 32.9-14, to restoration); (2) to its land (from failed harvest, 32.9, to fruitfulness); and (3) to the people (from a thoughtless, complacent woman, 32.9, to righteous and just people). The repeated mention of שׁלום or 'rest' (vv. 17-18) delineates well the peaceful life of the people in the coming age. This motif is probably further developed in the exilic context as an ideal expression of restoration, for its scope is almost universal including land and animal.

Chapters 32 and 33 depict the full consequences of the new age. A just government is established (32.1-2); understanding prevails (v. 4); the former and the latter leadership are compared (vv. 5-8); Jerusalem is denounced (vv. 10-14); the new age is ushered in by the pouring out of the spirit (vv. 15-20); and a hymn is offered for the restored Zion (ch. 33). In the restoration of Zion, there are two essential elements expressed: the judgment of God upon the nations (EP II) and the salvation and glorification of Zion (EP III).

3.6 *Chapters 34–35: Yahweh, God of Judgment and Salvation*
The nature and origin of these two chapters have prompted much discussion without any consensus. Some have noted the apocalyptic element of the section,[102] but the position of the chapters and their

---

101. H. Niehr, 'ערה ʿārāh', *ThWAT*, VI, cols. 369-75 (369). However, John D.W. Watts, '"The Spirit" in the Prophets: Three Brief Studies', in Mark W. Wilson (ed.), *Spirit and Renewal: Essays in Honor of J. Rodman Williams* (JPTSup, 5; Sheffield: Sheffield Academic Press, 1994), pp. 84-91 (85), rejects the liquid imagery.

102. E.g. J. Vermeylen, *Du prophète Isaïe a l'apocalyptique: Isaïe i–xxxv,*

apparent message of restoration have generated an argument that the section actually belongs to Second Isaiah and serves here to link chs. 40–66 to the previous portion of the book.[103] R.E. Clements points out the connecting function of the section, and argues that these two chapters echo a major theme of chs. 1–33, 'opening of the eyes of the blind and recovery of hearing for the deaf' (Isa. 6.9-10).[104] H.G.M. Williamson finds that chs. 34 and 35 'stand much closer to the world of Trito-Isaiah', and concludes that 'the most natural identification...is with Deutero-Isaiah'.[105] In either case, a close connection of these chapters with chs. 40–66 is apparent. Throughout the chapters the universal scope of God's rulership is stressed with judgment and restoration, and particularly with Israel's restoration (EP III). The next section (chs. 36–39) serves as a historical proof of the universal claim of Yahweh's kingship found in chs. 34–35.

Isaiah 34.16. Obviously the chapter begins with a judgment oracle against the nations (EP II), which is represented by Edom (vv. 1-15). It is noted that the language employed here reflects the expression first applied to the destruction of Jerusalem (32.9-14). Then the passage reaffirms the certainty of the fulfillment of the prophecy in the 'scroll' (ספר). This motif is often found in the 'former things' and 'new things' in Second Isaiah and other postexilic literature (e.g. Ezra 1.1). In this historical recalling (e.g. Isa. 63.7-14), the role of the spirit is not that of the inspiration of the 'word' in the 'scroll'. On the other hand, in the canonical context, especially from the late postexilic standpoint, the passage could have alluded to that extended function of the spirit. The prophetic authority is closely linked to the spirit of God by the later writers (e.g. Neh. 9.30). However, it is God's 'mouth' that is directly related to the prophetic authority rather than the 'spirit' which executes what was uttered. Here, the spirit is explicitly involved in bringing what

miroir d'un demi-millénaire d'experience religieuse en Israel (Paris: J. Gabalda, 1977), pp. 439-41, contends that 34.1–35.7 is the 'little apocalypse of Isaiah' and illustrates, together with chs. 24–27, the apocalyptic trend of the Isaianic tradition. However, Kaiser, *Isaiah 13–39*, p. 353, argues for the independent nature of the section from chs. 24–27.

103. The argument has persisted from the nineteenth century on. For instance, Steck, *Bereitete Heimkehr*, and the treatment of the two chapters by McKenzie, *Second Isaiah*, pp. 3-12.

104. Clements, 'Patterns', p. 192.

105. Williamson, *A Book Called Isaiah*, p. 243.

is prophesied into realization, and more specifically, in bringing judgment to the nations. Probably this is the only passage where the spirit of God, within the present narrow definition, is used in the context of judgment.

The juxtaposition between the 'mouth' and the 'spirit' of God may reflect a later development where the 'spirit' more explicitly represents God as a whole or in part. It may be compared to the 'mouth' and 'hand' pair in 1 Kgs 8.24.

3.7 *Chapters 36–39: God's Deliverance in the Past*[106]

These chapters move mostly between EP II and EP III, but ch. 39 alludes back to EP I to justify the exile historically. Yet, in the literary function, it warns the reader and rationalizes the unfinished EP I argument in chs. 56–66. Hence, the bridging role of the section between the first 39 chapters (which reflect predominantly EP I and II) and chs. 40–55 (mostly EP III) is evident. This borrowed material from 2 Kings 18–20 does not contain any occurrence of רוח whatever the usage.

3.8 *Chapters 40–55: God's Immanent Deliverance*

The present section portrays a great and imminent hope for the restoration of Judah, and it is dominated by creation imagery. Johnston's chart, for instance, adequately illustrates this with five pairs of chiastic lines with 44.21–45.19 at the center. The entire portion is heavy with creation images.[107]

These chapters fully enter into EP III (salvation of Israel), and even EP IV (salvation of the nations) is alluded to with the introduction of Cyrus as the historical 'savior' and God's anointed (45.1). It is a great contrast to the first 39 chapters where judgment upon the nations (EP II) is the precondition of, and even the means for, the salvation of Israel (EP III). Historically, the fulfillment of the promise in full scale is set forth for the immediate future, hence becoming an eschatological hope.

Isaiah 40.13. The larger literary context of the passage is the rhetorical confrontation between Yahweh and the idols, but the specific scene is creation. This is part of Yahweh's argument of his claim for his people

---

106. The unique function of this section in the formation of the canonical book has been much argued by scholars, e.g. Ackroyd, 'Isaiah 36–39', pp. 17-21; the entire book of Seitz, *Zion's Final Destiny*.

107. Johnston, 'A Prophetic Vision, p. 37.

who are in exile and a demonstration of his supremacy in power and wisdom against the idols.

It is obvious that the specific context in which the spirit is found is that of creation, although the overall context is that of salvation. The spirit is viewed as the creating agent of God with the motifs first of wisdom and secondly of power. This reflects well the Priestly tradition of creation in Gen. 1.2. The spirit is not involved in specific 'life-giving' details of creation. If the connecting role of v. 13 is considered, the spirit refers to the wisdom of Yahweh to plan and the power of Yahweh to bring about his creation plan. No idol can match his wisdom and power. No one can ever judge (weigh, measure) what he has planned in his mind and surpass his wisdom and his infinite power to make real what he has intended. In contrast to the first half of the book, the creation faith is first referred to as the basis for God's claim to restore his people (EP III). The role of his spirit in creation becomes an example of proving Yahweh's supremacy over the idols in his wisdom and power.

Isaiah 42.1. Since the Servant is identified with Israel in the canonical context[108] as an ideal prophet–king (judge) figure, there is another passage to be considered in this aspect. Isaiah 40.6-7 is regarded by many as the only biographical description of the prophetic call of Second Isaiah.[109] Petersen, however, reads 40.6 as in 1QIsaᵃ, 'A voice says, "Cry"; and she said, "What shall I cry?"'[110] against the traditional rendering of '…and I say…' From this interpretation, one can argue that the speaker here is the prophetess or herald of Zion. With the fact that the Davidic election has been democratized to the promise of glory to the people (that is, Israel becomes the royal figure), it can be argued that Zion becomes a prophet–king. Second Isaiah sees Israel not only as

108. Originally intended to be unidentified, as argued by Barstad, 'Future of the "Servant Songs"', pp. 262-63, but the wider literary context appropriates the servant to be identified with Israel, as Isa. 41.8-10 and 42.5-9 would indicate. Youngblood, *The Book of Isaiah*, p. 157, notes that after Isa. 53 the servant is replaced by the 'servants', and this indicates that the role of an individual messianic figure has been transferred to the faithful people of God.

109. E.g. Westermann, *Isaiah 40–66*, pp. 40-41; Skinner, *Isaiah Chapters XL–LXVI*, p. 4.

110. David L. Petersen, *Late Israelite Prophecy: Studies in Deutero-Prophetic Literature and in Chronicles* (SBLMS, 23; Missoula, MT: Scholars Press, 1977), p. 20. Also Volz, *Jesaia*, pp. 1, 6.

the herald or prophet, but also as the recipient of the glory of a former institution, kingship (Isa. 40).[111]

This is an indirect contrast to how unfaithful and unsuccessful the old servant Jacob/Israel has been in accomplishing its mission. It takes the transforming and life-giving spirit of Yahweh for the old servant to become the Servant in whom Yahweh delights.

One significant feature of רוח is the democratization of the idea from individual heroes to the people of Israel (as in Isa. 32.15). Whether the Servant was historically intended to be Cyrus, the prophet himself, Israel, a future deliverer, or a messiah, it seems evident that the final editor wants the Servant to be understood as Israel. The previous context is Yahweh's verdict against the gods of the nations: the idols without breath (רוח) have been declared as 'nothing' (41.29). Here the Servant, or Israel, is endowed with the רוח (42.1) and is Yahweh's Servant (41.9).[112] The first two trials (41.1-20 and 41.21–42.4) closely correspond to each other. The summons to trial (41.1 and 41.21-22b) is followed by legal questioning, then the gods' inability to respond (41.2-7 and 41.22c-29), and finally an address to Israel (41.8-20 and 42.1-4) concludes the scenes.[113] Also the double 'behold' (41.29 and 42.1) is another clue that the present position of the passage is the result of a careful and deliberate effort of the editor. Therefore, it is reasonable to treat the passage with the editor's intention in mind.

The thoughtful literary arrangement has been noted by a number of scholars,[114] and specifically the parallel arrangement between 41.1-20 and 41.21–42.17 has been recognized. Isaiah 41.1-20 forms one block and 41.21–42.17 makes up the corresponding block. The correspondence, contrast and the development of the argument are evident as can be seen below:

41.1-7 (A)   Yahweh's Supremacy over the Nations and their Idols
  41.8-16 (B)   Yahweh's Servant
    41.17-20 (C)   Yahweh's Transforming Power
    42.14-17 (C')   Yahweh's Transforming Power
  42.1-9 (B')   Yahweh's Servant
41.21-29 (A')   Yahweh's Supremacy over the Nations and their Idols

---

111. Petersen, *Late Israelite Prophecy*, p. 31.
112. The LXX rendering of v. 1, 'Jacob my servant' and 'Israel my chosen'.
113. Clifford, 'Function of Idol Passages', p. 453. Also Beuken, '*Mišpaṭ*', p. 13.
114. Seitz, 'The Composition of Isaiah 40–55', pp. 207-28.

This literary sequence implies that Yahweh's supremacy, although already revealed, will be fully realized through the servant, and as a result, Yahweh's transforming power will be realized. Hence, the servant takes the central role in God's plan in this passage. Yet, there are numerous and significant contrasting points between the two blocks. In A and A', the argument of Yahweh's rulership over history is based on different issues: the former by executing what was announced by 'stirring up' Cyrus, and the latter through the ability of Yahweh to predict the future. In the same way, B and B' demonstrate a contrast in two ways: the mission and the means to bring forth their missions. The former servant which is Israel has the mission of judgment upon the nations (EP II), whereas the latter has that of bringing forth Yahweh's justice (מֹשׁפֵּט, 42.3) to the nations (EP IV). Likewise, the first servant is to accomplish his mission by becoming a 'sharp threshing sledge' for he will thresh, crush (41.15) and winnow (v. 16) the nations, but the second one is to do his task through proclaiming that which entails suffering. In the same manner, God's transforming power will be exhibited in an opposite way, by turning the desert into a garden (41.18), presumably for Israel in the first block (EP III which is the other side of EP II in the eschatological view), but by turning the garden into a desert (42.15) in the second block.[115]

The explicit reference to God's spirit is found in the first Servant Song (42.1), although interestingly enough, the same Hebrew term is found twice in this broad context. In 41.16, which is the corresponding section of the present song, רוּחַ refers to an impersonal instrument of God's judgment. The other occurrence is in 42.5 which clearly indicates it as human breath given by God.

The effect of the 'resting' of God's spirit upon this servant displays an interesting development of the concept of the spirit of God (42.2-4). Unlike the ancient tradition of God's רוּחַ upon the selected leaders, the spirit of God is not going to grant physical might to destroy enemies. Instead, it will enable him to overcome hardship and finally accomplish his mission. The effect is much more refined and spiritualized and results in submission, obedience, reliance and faithfulness as alluded to in 11.1-5. However, the present passage implies a more personal attachment to God of the Servant. God's personal promise to the Servant

---

115. The exact interpretation of the passage is difficult. Westermann, *Isaiah 40–66*, pp. 105-107, argues that v. 16 is the clue, and the allusion is to the return of the exile. Also he notes the correspondence between 41.18-20 and 42.15-17.

Until the Spirit Comes

follows immediately (and canonically) with an impressive description of who Yahweh is (42.5). He is to 'take hold of [his] hand' and make him 'a covenant for the people and a light for the Gentiles' (v. 6). The scope of his work goes beyond the horizon of Israel to the nations (EP IV). The positive attitude toward Cyrus may be a reaction to the negativity toward Babylon (e.g. ch. 13). His mission is more religious than political: to spread the Torah and establish justice, making the rulership of Yahweh known to the whole world. The universalism that is already indicated in the song itself (42.3) is reinforced in this promise. Also, the idea of suffering here aligns well with the early Jewish thought (cf. Job). The more spiritualized understanding is evident in the spirit of God as well as in its effect.

Isaiah 44.3. Isaiah 42.18–44.23 forms a larger context for this verse, which begins with an accusation of the blind and deaf servant (42.18-25). Following the judgment/salvation pattern, the coming divine intervention is announced, especially in contrast to the idols' impotence (43.1–44.8, 9-20). Then Yahweh's power is demonstrated (44.21-22) and a call to celebrate God's intervention concludes the section (44.23). This overall structure is not much different from chs. 41 and 42 as discussed above, and the verse is found in the second portion.

In 43.22-28 Jacob/Israel is identified as the rejected unfaithful servant and accused of sins of the fathers, prophets (v. 27) and princes (v. 28). Unfaithfulness had spread in religious, social and political spheres of the nation. The judgment of God against this unfaithful servant was the giving up of him to utter destruction and reviling (v. 28). Here again, the canonical pattern and sequence of judgment–salvation becomes evident. Judgment is essential for the cleansing of guilt (43.25) before salvation can be brought in.

A complete reversal is signaled by וְעַתָּה, 'but now', and a new servant is called. However, the new servant is not different from the old, unlike in 42.1: it is the same Jacob/Israel and is called 'my servant' and 'my chosen' (43.1), with the almost stereotypical expression found in 42.1 as well as in 41.8. The typical 'fear not' salvation oracle brings the judgment pronounced in 43.22-28 to an end. The reversal, this time, is created by repeating the same language found in the preceding salvation oracle (43.19-20) before the judgment message. The 'water on the thirsty land' and 'streams on the dry ground' are the reflection of 43.19-20, 'I am making a way in the desert and streams in the wasteland' (v. 19b) and 'I provide water in the desert and streams in the wasteland...' (v. 20).

Isaiah 44.3 has an excellent parallel construction. It is found not only between v. 3a and v. 3b, but also between v. 3aα and 3aβ, and v. 3bα and v. 3bβ. What the 'water/stream' does to the thirsty land and dry ground is compared with what the 'spirit/blessing' does to the 'children' and 'descendants'. The water imagery is more explicit here than in 32.15. The verb 'pouring out' (יצק) reminds one of forceful, limitless and unconditional endowment, and becomes the characteristic of the future age of salvation (see, e.g., Joel 3.1). The outpouring of 'my רוח' and/or 'water' on the thirsty land signifies God's coming (40.3-5) to transform Israel. This argument is supported by the similar imagery of transformation in 41.18-19.

The creation motif is articulated in 44.2 by the use of verbs like 'make' (עשׂה) and 'form' (יצר). As the water/stream brings revival and life to a dry and thirsty land, the spirit which is expressed as 'my blessing' will re-create the old unfaithful servant into a lofty figure. It is certainly the life-giving power of God which accomplishes the regeneration as a stream regenerates the desert (e.g. 32.15; Ezek. 37). The spirit of God is the source of the perpetual blessing of increase and prosperity.

One significant contribution of the passage to the theology of רוח is found in its universal (EP IV) and religious outcome. In v. 4, the increase of the people of Yahweh in number seems to suggest the Gentile proselytes,[116] and they will in turn actively testify about the God of Israel. This effect is aligned with the ministry of the Servant in 42.1-4 who will bring teachings to 'the coast-lands' and establish justice on the earth (42.4), for this Servant Israel has no active role except for being a witness to God's mighty act (42.8). The whole point is that the glorious manifestation of God's goodness and power upon the restored Israel will attract many nations causing them to say 'I am Yahweh's' and to inscribe on their hands 'Yahweh's'. They are simply convicted by the mighty work of Yahweh and return to him, and Israel has a minimum role of letting the 'spirit' and 'blessing' pour out upon his children (44.3). In a strict sense, Israel is not a mediator, but a witness of the fact that Yahweh is 'the first and the last' (44.6), and there is no one like him who can announce 'from of old the things to come' (v. 7).

---

116. See Chapter 2 for more discussion.

God is called Yahweh, the king of Israel, his redeemer and Yahweh of hosts.

Unlike the first Servant Song (42.1-4) and 32.15-20, there is no ethical element expressed by 'righteousness' and 'justice'. The emphasis here is heavily on the powerful kingship of Yahweh, and this idea is augmented by his explicit identification as the king of and redeemer of Israel. 'Yahweh of hosts' also has a strong notion of power, for the spirit of God brings vitality to the nation and, as a consequence, demonstrates the powerful kingship of Yahweh over Israel and the nations.

3.9 *Chapters 56–66: Human Responsibility in Restoration*
This section appears as a theological explanation for the delayed salvation. This and the preceding section (chs. 40–55) are analogous to Exodus 6 and 19, with God's monergistic work for the initial deliverance and yet human responsibility as a condition for the full realization of the promised restoration. It still looks forward to the full restoration not explicitly as a nation, but more as the people or servant of Yahweh. Hence, the section is not characteristic of EP II, but EP III which implies EP IV. However, the salvation of the nations (EP IV) is primarily based on nationalistically motivated universalism. This section leaves room for further judgment if human responsibility is not met, for the historical completion of EP I (judgment upon Israel) is not considered consummated once and for all.[117]

The entire section can be divided into three segments: chs. 56–59, 60–62 and 63–66. The initial verses (56.1-8) open the first segment with oracles of salvation for Israel (EP III) and for foreigners (EP IV). Then the typical oscillation between judgment and salvation dominates chs. 56–59: judgment to Israel (EP I, 56.9–57.13); comfort for his people (EP III, 57.14-17); accusation and lament (presumably EP I, 59.1-15a); a salvation oracle with an unknown individual under Yahweh's enablement (EP III, 15b-20). This first portion is concluded with the assurance of the perpetual presence of God's spirit and word (59.21). This forms a kind of inclusio with 56.1-8 and emphasizes the notion of the future salvation in spite of the considerable impression of judgment.

The next three chapters (60–62) bear one single concept consistently:

---

117. This is a common application that postexilic Judahites frequently make. See the reapplication of the Day of Yahweh theme in Joel.

salvation of Israel (EP III) and the nations (EP IV). Isaiah 60.1-22 promises the splendid restoration of Zion (EP III) with many foreigners voluntarily serving the temple and the Judahites (EP IV, vv. 10-14). Then a Servant-like individual is introduced (61.1-3), having been equipped by God through the 'anointing' (EP III, 61.1-3). Restoration and other blessings are promised through the anointed preacher (EP III, vv. 4-11). Chapter 62 repeats the theme of the restored Zion (EP III, IV).

The last four chapters resume the oscillation between judgment and salvation. The tone is set in 63.1-6 where God's anger (EP II) and redemption (EP III) are blended together. In the form of lamentation (63.7-19) and plea for deliverance (64.11) the history of Israel is reviewed, and the writer alludes to the future hope (EP III). Isaiah 65.1-7 proclaims judgment upon Israel (EP I) and vv. 8-10 balance it with the promise of salvation in the remnant motif (EP III). Verses 13-16 take up another judgment theme (EP I) and vv. 13-16 have judgment and salvation together (EP I, III). It is only in vv. 17-25 that the eschatological paradisiacal blessings are pledged (EP III). Again, 66.1-4 goes back to the theme of judgment (EP I), while vv. 5-14a depict the blessing to Jerusalem (EP III). Verses 14b-16 remind of God's judgment one more time (EP I) before moving on to God's salvation of Jerusalem (EP III, vv. 17-18, 20-21) with the recognition of Yahweh's kingship by the nations (v. 19, EP III and implicitly EP IV). This will be achieved by God's servants.

Isaiah 59.21. The literary arrangement clearly demonstrates that the canonical intention for this verse is to serve as the conclusion of chs. 56–59. After a series of oscillations between judgment and salvation, the present verse reinforces the certainty of the promise of God.

Historically, this verse may have been uttered to a prophet or prophets to assure the continuity of the prophetic spirit. It is also possible that the verse reflects the scarcity of the prophetic presence and the longing for the restoration of the prophetic spirit. However, in the broader literary context the 'covenant with them' becomes that of God with his people.[118] The covenant which is a sign of his affirmation is the restoration of his word and spirit upon the prophetic descendants in the

---

118. In contrast, Watts, ' "The Spirit" ', p. 89, argues that the addressee is 'the same as in 42.1 and 45.1 (and 49.6), the emperor of Persia', who was, at this time, Artaxerxes I. Also *idem*, *Isaiah 34–66*, pp. 285, 287.

coming age. By this covenant God affirms his plan of intervention for his people and judgment upon Israel's foes in the age to come.

The perpetual presence of the prophetic spirit is an eschatological event. The piling up of expressions like 'your children...their descendants' and 'from this time on forever' emphasize the uninterrupted continuity of the prophetic presence for the coming age. The presence of the spirit and the word assumes that the promise will come true. The passage also implies a sense of democratization to a limited degree. The same expression of 'from you[r mouth], your children...their descendants' suggests a gradual expansion of the prophetic spirit to a wider group of people. Yet the scope is far from what Joel envisions in 3.1-2 where even female servants are promised the same spirit. The point here is the continuity of the prophetic spirit.

At any rate, the identity of several elements of the verse is not certain. The addressee is not revealed. It may be the people of God in general with 'them' referring to the nations; then the idea is much like that of the Joel passage. It may be an individual, like the Servant figure, who will become the 'covenant' for the rest of Israel. The introduction of a Servant-like individual in the previous passage (vv. 15b-20) seems, at least in the broader literary context, to imply an endowment to a selected group of people. In this sense, the verse remains in the old tradition in which selected leaders are endowed with the divine spirit.

Isaiah 61.1. This prophetic call-like self-proclamation is placed between the two glorious messages of Zion and its people (60.1-22 and 61.4-7). In fact, the ones who will 'rebuild the ancient ruins' in 61.4 can easily be identified with the 'aliens' who will build their walls in 60.10. Only the insertion of 61.1-3 says that the Judeans will rebuild the ruins and that draws the attention of hearers/readers to their obligation to God.

In its literary context, the speaker 'I' (61.1) is identified with the one who speaks to the people in 60.19-20. The subject matter changes from God to the speaker himself. Before any ship can bring silver and gold in honor of Yahweh in their nationalistically inspired universalism (60.9, EP III with an implication to EP IV), Yahweh's people must first realize and experience the salvation of their own God (EP III).

The speaker is 'anointed' with the spirit of God to preach restoration, transformation and liberation. Here the anointing is connected with the endowment of the spirit and this reflects the old tradition of David's

anointing (1 Sam. 16.13). This ancient rite here denotes God's valida-
tion and authorization of the recipient. This preacher figure is more of a
prophetic than a royal character, and his task is that of comfort, 'bringing good news' and 'proclaiming' liberty support the argument. The
overall literary or canonical context 'de-royalizes' the figure, and as a
consequence, the 'captives' and 'prisoners' are seen in a more spiritual
or socio-economic sense than literal.

An affinity between the figure in this passage and the Servant is
unmistakable (the spirit of God rests upon the Servant, 42.1 and 61.1).
An obvious difference between the two is their missions: the Servant
for the gentiles (EP III, and also IV by its effect) and this figure for
undesignated underprivileged people, but presumably Israel (EP III).
This Servant-like preacher claims the anointing of the spirit of God to
help any kind of human misery. The literary arrangement implies that
by the comforting ministry through the 'anointing of the spirit' the
physical restoration of Zion will be accomplished (v. 4). Only after
that, strangers and aliens will come and serve them (v. 5), while the
Judeans will be 'called the priests of Yahweh' and 'ministers of our
God' (v. 6). Then they will 'enjoy the wealth of the nations' (v. 7) and
the world will offer homage to the bride Zion (v. 10). The transformation of nature will climax the coming age through the ministry of the
'spirit-anointed'. This becomes a familiar notion at least in the Isaianic
tradition (e.g. 11.1-5 and 32.15-20). The literary arrangement demonstrates the presupposition that the appearance of the spirit-anointed
figure and his ministry are a prerequisite for the realization of the grand
promise of God in chs. 60–61.

R.E. Clements concedes that the pair of blindness and deafness is a
running theme of the book.[119] According to him, the theme of blindness
and deafness forms 'a central element in the original divine commis-
sion' given to the prophet.[120] This not only influences the development
of the book, but also provides a 'convenient literary form of expression'.[121] This theme in fact runs throughout the book with an initially
negative imagery (Isa. 29.9, 10) but later with a positive one (29.18;
30.20-21; 32.3; cf. 42.18-21; 43.8; 44.18). Whether blindness and deafness are understood literally or metaphorically, the reader of the book
will not fail to see that the ministry of this individual will have a far

119. Clements, 'Patterns', p. 192.
120. Clements, 'Patterns', p. 192.
121. Clements, 'Patterns', p. 193.

greater effect than is found in its historical context.

The 'anointing' by the spirit of God chooses, commissions, enables the prophetic figure and gives him his message as well as the authority to proclaim it. The coming of the preacher anointed with the spirit is a characteristic of the coming age. In fact, he is the announcer and intro-ducer of the time of salvation; the spirit of God causes him to usher in the long awaited day of God. As seen in 11.1-5 and 42.1-4, this character becomes part of the expectation for the coming age.

Isaiah 63.10, 11, 14. Isaiah 63.10-14 has three references to the (holy) spirit of God (vv. 10, 11 and 14). The oracle begins with the remem-brance of God's saving acts in the past (63.7). The one who offers this prayer understands that God's deliverance is based on the covenant relationship with his people, as the expression 'they are my people' indicates (v. 8).

In v. 10, the rejection of God's gracious offer results in grieving his holy spirit. One can argue that 'his holy spirit' (רוח קדשׁו) here func-tions very much like פנים in that it represents God's presence. However, unlike פנים, רוח is rather loosely attached to God. To counter the rebel-lion, 'he', not his spirit, takes an action. More specifically, the identity of רוח is closer to a theophanic angel, yet other than Yahweh's angel. The 'angel of his presence' is already used in v. 9 and also in a later development, and the same role is attributed either to an angelic repre-sentation as seen in Qumran (e.g. 1QM 13.16; 1QS 3.20; CD 5.18) or God himself (e.g. 1QH 7.6-7; 13.1; 16.6, 7, 9). This signals the later usage of the spirit as responsible for 'each and all of his [God's] acts', although restricted to God's action in history.[122] The spirit here illus-trates the theophanic presence of God among his people.

The noun 'holiness' (the literal translation is 'spirit of his holiness') here and in v. 14 has attracted many discussions. By the time of the canonical formation of the book, the term may have acquired a more technical meaning. It is also possible that the expression accentuates the holiness idea of Yahweh in dealing with his people and the nations. Whether it is an angelic representative or a theophanic symbolism, the spirit serves as his own presence which is well termed as the 'extension of his personality' by Johnson.[123] The concept of holiness certainly

122. Westermann, *Isaiah 40–66*, p. 389.

123. Johnson, *Vitality of the Individual*, pp. 2-3. Also *idem, The One and the Many*, pp. 6-7, 19-20, 36-37.

reinforces the emphasis on God's otherliness.

Similarly in v. 14 the spirit of Yahweh gives rest to the people. The spirit's abiding presence in the exodus event is acknowledged by another postexilic prophet (Hag. 2.5). This interpretation goes back to v. 10, where the change from the third person (v. 14a) to the second (v. 14b) seems to imply that the spirit here has a more direct reference to God himself. In v. 11 the abiding presence of God is closely associated with the motif of saving power; again the idea of holiness is significant. Unlike v. 10 and Ps. 51.13, the holiness here is more linked with his saving power than the conviction of sinfulness. It is the same spirit of God that works, but with a different emphasis.

4. *The* רוח *of God in the Traditions*

The survey of these passages can be summarized under the several roles that the spirit of God assumes. Since the book is read as a whole, this integration of similar expressions can be justified.

4.1 *The* רוח *of God upon Individuals*
Several passages fall under this category: 11.1; 42.1 and 61.1. Interestingly enough, all the passages are announcements which were canonically moved to the future and, hence, become part of the eschatological expectation. Their link with the spirit of God continues the old 'charismatic' tradition where extraordinary physical strength was a direct result of the spirit of God and this becomes a trademark of God's endorsement and endowment. Basically, they are the saviors of Israel (EP III) bringing God's judgment upon the enemies (EP II). The judges and the first two kings are typical of this tradition.

All these passages have different figures in their historical settings: a king for 11.1, a prophet-like person for 61.1 and the 'Servant' for 42.1. However, there has been a deliberate redactional and editorial hand so that their identity goes beyond the historical level. It has been argued that the description of the coming king in ch. 11 is redactionally deroyalized. The canonical appending of the mythical portion (vv. 6-9) reflects this trend. Moreover, the composite reading with other relevant passages like chs. 7 and 9 makes the 'king' an unrealistic superhuman who can only appear in the end time. As the expectation of the king grows, the effect of the spirit of God expands also. The other two passages are more ambiguous when it comes to identity: the 'preacher' in 61.1 will have a comforting and restorational ministry among the Israel (EP III), whereas the Servant will have a 'missionary' type of work. These two have little military and political reference. The effect of the spirit of God is so spiritualized that suffering becomes part of the result of the 'empowerment' (42.4, cf. 53.1-13), and this is a radical departure from the old tradition.[124]

Regardless of whom these eschatological figures refer to, the development of the messianic expectation may have drawn expressions from these promises. As it further evolved, the figures of these passages may have emerged as part of the messianic expectation as evidenced in the Qumran community: the king of ch. 11 as the Davidic messiah, and the 'preacher(s)' as the priestly messiah (CD 19.10-11). The traditional charismatic spirit is not to be democratized, for the early tradition does not allow both David and Saul to have the spirit of God at the same time (1 Sam. 16.14). The identity of this figure may have been intentionally vague with the same theological motif that has removed the historical reference from the second and third part of the book.[125] The future leader is portrayed as a hybrid figure based on the royal tradition with strong prophetic functions.

4.2 The Prophetic רוח

Two passages, 30.1 and 59.21 refer to the רוח among the prophets. Historically, as well as canonically, 30.1-3 is understood as a past event, and 59.21 as a promise for the future with little reference to the present state, as in 61.1. It is also observable that the former is used in a judgment context against Judah (EP I), and the latter for the restoration of his people (EP III). This may be an indication of the restored Israelite understanding that the golden prophetic era belongs to both past and future, but not to the present. The frequent references to the earlier prophets in the postexilic literature and the expectation of a future prophet (1 Macc. 4.46) demonstrate this fact.

From the early tradition, the prophetic spirit has played a more

124. S. Talmon, 'The Concept of *Māšîaḥ* and Messianism in Early Judaism', in J.H. Charlesworth (ed.), *The Messiah: Developments in Earliest Judaism and Christianity* (First Princeton Symposium on Judaism and Christianity; Minneapolis: Fortress Press, 1992), pp. 79-115 (93), argues that the concept of the Messiah is multilinear, moving from historical reality to idealization.

125. Childs, *Introduction*, p. 335. For his revised position, see 'A Response', p. 205.

significant role than merely a communicational function. The presence of the prophetic spirit upon an individual is a typical sign of God's endorsement and his favorable presence in the community (1 Sam. 10.6, 10). L. Neve contends that, during the Second Temple era, the prophets became 'Israel's charismatic leaders' after the Davidic kingship was set up.[126] In 30.1, it is the human king who refuses the involvement of Yahweh, who in turn withdraws his favorable protection from the nation. Therefore, the perpetuation of the prophetic spirit is indeed a positive covenant of God with his people. Although the democratization is not fully developed to the extent of Joel 3.1-2, the range of the recipients is wider than that of the national/community leaders as discussed above.

4.3 *The* רוח *upon the Nation*

Two passages, 32.15 and 44.3, occur with this most universal and democratic expectation. The effect and result of the presence of the spirit is universal, although one may see the universal scope within the national limit. Both use strong water imagery alluding to the spirit of God as a liquid-like impersonal force or the effect of God. The absence of any human figure reinforces the impersonal image of the spirit. Yet another significance of the water imagery lies in its abundance as expressed in the verbs of 32.15 (hiphil of ערה) and the powerful parallelism in 44.3.

In 32.15, the 'pouring out' of the spirit signals the beginning of the end time, resulting in the establishment of righteousness and justice, and also giving rest to God's people. Isaiah 63.14 also stresses the same point of giving rest, but only in retrospect. However, 44.3 adds two new dimensions to the ethical effect of the spirit. The nation will experience numerical increase and this will result in the spiritual conviction of the nations. Together with 42.1, the passage indicates two understandings: first, the salvation of the nations is the goal of the eschatological plan; and secondly, the spirit of God in the eschatological era will accomplish the plan, either through a human agent or by a direct anointing[127] upon God's people.

---

126. Neve, *The Spirit of God*, p. 55.

127. The verb יצק is used with the object of water or oil in the context of religious rites and sacrifices (e.g. Gen. 28.18; 35.14; Lev. 8.12; 1 Sam. 10.1; 2 Kgs 9.3).

4.4 *The* רוח *Referring to God or Associated with his Presence*

In 31.3, 34.16, 40.13 and 63.10-14, the spirit either represents God as the 'extension of his personality'[128] or almost replaces Elohim or Yahweh. With the exception of 34.16, the canonical viewpoint sets the passages in the past, hence without any eschatological notion.[129] Only 34.16 foresees the complete judgment upon Edom, although it uses the prophetic perfect.

Some passages (40.13; 63.10, 11, 14) show a slight hint to imply a separate being like an agent of God with some personal element. In 34.16, the spirit is more closely associated with God's 'physical' being as an anthropomorphism. As the 'mouth' partially represents God's being and work, so does the spirit.

Isaiah 31.3 refers more to the quality of God. A more precise rendering would be 'their horses are of flesh, not of spirit'. The lack of a personal association like a possessive pronoun or a construct state strengthens the argument. This divine quality will bring a powerful judgment upon the nation (EP 1).

As the words of the pre-exilic prophets are greatly treasured, many significant works of the past are often attributed to the presence of the spirit of God, especially with its power motif. The creation was carried out through the active participation of the spirit (40.13; cf. Gen. 1.2). The deliverance and provision in the exodus and the conquest are credited to it (63.10-14). The addition of the idea of holiness may be a reflection of a transcendental theology during the postexilic period.

128. Johnson, *Vitality of the Individual*, pp. 2-3.
129. Volz, *Jesaia*, pp. 270-71, calls this 'the power that operates in Israel's history'.

CONCLUSION

In the foregoing study of the רוח in the book of Isaiah, the evolution of
the diverse spirit traditions has been observed. Before summary points
are made, a comment on the combination of historical and synchronic
readings is in order. Adding another historical layer (canonical level) to
the traditional three chronological blocks allows observation of an
additional and consummating stage of the development. The legitimacy
and strength of a holistic reading is without question. However, a holistic and macroscopic reading should be based on a fragmentary and
microscopic investigation. Although this study was not able fully to
explore, and take advantage of, the difference between the two
methods, the present methodological combination may exploit the fruits
of both opposing approaches.

The various רוח traditions not only retain their unique traits, but also
undergo their own evolution. As the Isaianic traditions emerge in various historical and social stages and attain their eschatological significance, the רוח traditions also gain eschatological significance.

1. *The Evolution of the* רוח *Traditions*

The usage of the רוח tradition, from the very beginning of this study,
shows its diversity in meaning. This is probably due to the complex
origin of the רוח concept. The traditions achieve their own unique
development in the various Isaianic strata.

1.1 *The* רוח *in Leaders*
The רוח among the national leaders finds its ancient Near Eastern counterpart in the royal ideology that the king is either divine (Egypt), demi-
god (as in the Mesopotamian king list), or God-designated. The king or
a chosen leader is viewed to have divinely endowed superhuman quality and capability. Early Israelite רוח tradition among the leaders is
characterized by superhuman physical or military prowess as seen
among the judges and Saul.

Isaianic evidence of the role of the רוח in leadership exhibits a major leap from the crude notion of God's equipment. The pre-exilic texts clearly show moral and religious emphasis on the leadership quality through the endowment of the רוח. In the future ideal king (11.1-3a), the main task is the administration of righteousness and justice in the community. Although the 'might' is part of the royal endowment, the future king is portrayed in his spiritual piety ('Fear of Yahweh', 11.3a). For the one who will sit in judgment, Yahweh promises to be the spirit of justice (משפט, 28.6). This ideal quality in the expected future ideal leader is intended to make a sharp contrast to the leaders Israel had throughout its history.

This moral and spiritual emphasis continues in the description of the Servant (42.1-4). The רוח enables him not only to accomplish the prophet-like task ('to proclaim Yahweh's justice [משפט]'), but also to endure difficulties. The strength which comes from the רוח is no longer physical or military, but moral and spiritual.

The postexilic text (63.9-14) looks back to Moses, the Israelite leader *par excellence*. The relatively reduced role of the future leader is clearly alluded to in the description of Moses as God's vice regent.[1]

The רוח in the canonical layer seems to hint at the notion of democratization of the existing moral and spiritual emphasis. As the Servant is freely identified with Israel or Jacob (e.g. 44.1), the endowment of the רוח is also applied to the restored community of God.[2] However, this does not replace the expectation of an individual figure. Hence, the leadership רוח remains reserved exclusively for the coming ruler.

1.2 *The* רוח *and Prophetism*

The presence of the רוח among earlier prophets is characterized by ecstatic behavior (e.g. 1 Sam. 10.10; 19.20). In fact, the prophetic phenomenon becomes a standard demarcation of the spirit's coming upon individuals including non-prophetic figures (Num. 11.25; 1 Sam. 10.10; 19.23-24). Traditionally the prophetic רוח is less exclusive than the leadership רוח. It is evident in that a group of people, often called the 'sons of the prophet', experiences God's רוח together.

---

1. Recently Hugenberger, 'Servant of the Lord', pp. 119-40, highlighted the paradigmatic role of Moses for the future leader.

2. The promise of God's רוח to Jacob in Isa. 44.1-5 strengthens this reappropriation.

Pre-exilic Isaianic texts have almost no reference to the prophetic spirit with one possible exception (30.1). This may be part of a large tendency to avoid the link between the רוח and the prophetic activity among the 'classical prophets'. The ecstatic behavior is no longer associated with genuine prophetism.

The exilic period evidences a sudden surge of prophetic references. This has to do with a fresh appreciation of old prophetic utterances. Isaiah 34.16 looks back to how the prophetic words uttered from God's mouth have been fulfilled through the execution of God's spirit. The frequent pairing between 'word' and the 'spirit' replaces the link between the רוח and ecstatic behavior. The prophetic nature of the Servant's task (42.1-4) is another evidence of the resurgent prophetic interest.

The postexilic period further characterizes the coming age of restoration with God's promise for the prophetic word and רוח (59.21). The prophetic presence corresponds to that of Yahweh (cf. 31.1). The perpetuity and wide availability of the word and the רוח, therefore, ensures Yahweh's covenantal presence in the community. The prophetic figure moves from mere proclamation, and will actively liberate people (61.1-3).

The canonical layer enhances the prophetic prominence in the community. As the prophet (61.1) is viewed along with the Servant passages, his political involvement is further emphasized. Also in the wider literary context, the promise for the perpetual prophetic word and רוח (59.21) goes beyond the prophetic circle and is now applied to the restored community in general. Thus, this achieves the full democratizing effect of Joel 3.1-3.

1.3 *Creation/Life-Giving and the* רוח

There is no evidence of this tradition in the pre-exilic Isaianic tradition. The exilic Isaianic tradition fully utilizes the idea of creation/life-giving in describing the restored fortune of Israel. First of all, the רוח as an extension of God's being is described as having a direct involvement in creation (40.13; cf. Gen. 1.2). The effect of the creation/life-giving רוח ranges from agricultural bounty (32.15) and increasing population (44.3-4) to physical security and moral/spiritual effects possibly including the proselytization of the Gentiles (44.5)

In the canonical context, the world becomes a paradise as a direct effect of the רוח of God upon the eschatological ideal leader (11.6-9).

The description of the coming world is similar to what the creation/life-giving רוח of God would achieve (32.15-20; 44.3-4). One can assert that eschatological restoration is the ultimate goal of the Isaianic tradition.

From the beginning, the creation/life-giving רוח is poured out to the entire community. Hence, this is a democratized רוח of God throughout its appearance. It is also noted that in this work of the רוח, there is no human agent present. This is a direct work of Yahweh.

1.4 *Representing God or his Character*
This is an anthropomorphic use of the רוח. The רוח refers to God's presence, his faculty, character or simply God himself.

In the pre-exilic texts, Yahweh is compared with Egyptian soldiers and their horses by a contrast between רוח and נפש (31.3). This comparison highlights human or animal mortal frailty versus Yahweh's immortality and power. God's being is expressed by the רוח.

Anthropomorphism continues in the exilic Isaianic tradition. In the creation context, Yahweh's רוח is the planning and executing aspect of God's being with wisdom and executing power. In another anthropomorphism the רוח appears in parallel to God's 'mouth' (34.16). As the message of judgment against Israel's enemy was pronounced by the earlier prophet through the (God's) 'mouth', it was Yahweh's רוח that executed the judgment.

In the postexilic layer, often God himself is referred to by his רוח. It is God's רוח that completed the entire exodus process (63.14). In the previous verses, not only God, but also his רוח, his servant, namely Moses, and his angel are an active part of the wilderness experience. And yet, in the concluding statement, the writer attributes the רוח of God to be responsible for the successful exodus. In this case, the רוח represents God in his entirety. This tendency is analogous to the later writers who attribute all the prophetic utterances to the רוח of God (e.g. Neh 9.30).

Thus, the רוח expands its representation of Yahweh from earlier references to an aspect or even part of God's being to the later reference to the entirety of Yahweh.

1.5 *'Wind' and Others*
There are usages of the רוח detached from God himself. They continue to function as Yahweh's instrument or agent, but are too detached to refer to as the extension of God's being.

This usage has too extremes: personal and impersonal. The רוח with personal characteristics is well attested in 1 Kgs 22.19. It is assumed in the Introduction that this רוח later evolves into the idea of angels.

In the Isaianic texts, the closest reference is the 'spirit of deep sleep' (29.10), although its personality is not obvious. The work of the 'angel' (63.9), in this sense, is not much different from what the רוח would have been. The extreme case of the impersonal רוח is either identical with, or close to, the 'wind'. It often functions as Yahweh's impersonal force to bring judgment (e.g. 11.4; 30.28; 33.11; 59.19). The 'spirit of judgment' and the 'spirit of fire' (4.4) seem to assume the judgment role as does the 'wind' רוח. The original emphasis on physical power remains in this usage.

2. *Eschatology and the* רוח

Throughout the study, it is argued that eschatology is one of a few major motifs the book of Isaiah takes through its various developmental stages. It has also been shown that the רוח takes an active part in the making of the Isaianic eschatology.

2.1 *The* רוח *and the Eschatological Plan*
An observation of the distribution of the passages within the eschatological plan (EP) may be summarized as follow:

	Israel	Nations
Judgment	*EP I* 4.4; (30.1);* (31.3)	*EP II* 34.16
Salvation	*EP III* 11.1; 28.6; 32.15; (40.13); 44.3; 59.21; 61.1; (63.10,11,14)	*EP IV* 42.1

*From the canonical viewpoint, the passages in parenthesis belong to past fulfillment and the rest represent future expectation.

In the context of judgment upon Israel (EP I), two passages are used: 30.1 and 31.3. However, in both cases, the רוח of God is not directly involved in bringing judgment. For judgment against the nations (EP II), 34.16 explicitly refers to the divine spirit as an agent of destruction. Once the issue moves to the salvation side, nine of the 13 occurrences of the concept fall in the EP III category (salvation of Israel). The restoration will be brought out in at least three different ways that the spirit works: (1) through an individual 'servant' upon whom the spirit of God will rest (11.1; 61.1); (2) through the prophetic spirit (59.21); and (3) through God's sovereign 'pouring out' of his spirit upon the nation (32.15; 44.3). The completion of the eschatological plan will also be consummated through the salvation of the nations (EP IV). This will be realized through the work of the servant (presumably an Israelite). EP IV in 44.3 is a by-product of EP III.

As indicated in the note, two passages in EP I are of the past, but the one in EP II is an eschatological expectation. The expectation of EP III has four verses in the past and five in the future. The former group becomes the basis of the future restoration of the latter passages. EP IV is not realized yet.

2.2 The רוח in the Eschatological Components

The רוח takes an active role in the various elements of the Isaianic eschatological expectation.

2.2.1 Inauguration of the New Age.
The coming of the new age is attributed to the 'outpouring' of the spirit from above (32.15). The long-awaited day of restoration will be ushered in by the overwhelming presence of the רוח. This signals the turn of Israel's fortune. Similar prosperity is described also in 44.3 where the רוח of God is poured out like a river. The water-imagery in both passages enhances the life-giving work of the רוח. As God's רוח planned and executed the initial creation, the restoration as God's second creation will come about by the presence of Yahweh's רוח. As mentioned above, a similar result is expected through the רוח given to the future ideal ruler of God.

The רוח is also involved in the preparatory acts. The רוח completes Yahweh's judgment upon Edom (34.16; EP II) which either prepares, or coincides with, the coming salvation of Israel. The רוח also prepares God's people by cleansing them (4.4). Thus, judgment (EP I) attains the purpose of salvation (EP III).

2.2.2 The Restoration of Israel.
As observed in the above discussion, God's restoration of Israel (EP III) is the ultimate goal of Isaianic eschatology. 'In that day' (ביום ההוא) the members of the restored community will experience God's cleansing through the spirit of משפט and fire (4.4). The Isaianic tradition views the 'perfection of a faithful

remnant' as the key to the full restoration of the community.[3] The immediate effect of the eschatological inauguration is characterized by God's full favor toward his people. As the spirit is lavishly poured out upon the members of the restored community, they will experience Yahweh's reversed fortunes for Israel:[4] agricultural abundance, physical and emotional security, and moral restoration (32.15-20, EP III). God's blessing with his רוח also causes the numerical growth of God's people (44.3) and this causes the Gentiles to turn to Yahweh. The spirit is closely involved in the restoration of Israel.

The absence of any human agent reinforces God's direct involvement in restoration through his רוח. For this, God's people are elevated to be the direct recipients of God's רוח, just as national leaders (32.15; 44.3). In fact, as Israel assumes the Servantship, the so-called 'missionary' call is added to the task of the restored nation (42.1-4).

2.2.3 *The Future Leader.* Expectation of the 'messianic' figure is an element of Isaianic eschatology. This figure is expressed in various forms in the various Isaianic layers. In the pre-exilic time, he appears within the framework of the present world. He will be either a Davidic king (11.1-3) or a judge (28.6). In both cases, the enablement comes through Yahweh's רוח. The leader will be reduced to a faithful regent of Yahweh, and God's direct rulership is asserted. The more Yahweh's kingship is realized, the less royal, and probably more prophetic, the leader's task is portrayed to become. Accordingly, the political and military role decreases and the moral and religious role increases. This trend continues in the Servant figure in the exilic period. His task is more prophetic than royal. While the leadership 'empowerment' is reduced to his ability to endure hardships and suffering, the scope of his leadership expands to the nations and coastlands (42.4).

As the marvelous work of Moses is totally attributed to the presence of Yahweh's רוח, so the future leader will accomplish his task only through God's רוח. This postexilic perception is well summed up in Yahweh's admonition to Zerubbabel through Zechariah (4.6-7). Super-leaders in the past as well as in the future are, hence, commonly perceived to achieve the God-given task לא בחיל ולא בכח כי אם־ברוחי ('not by might, nor by power, but by my spirit').

3. Webb, 'Zion in Transformation', p. 81.
4. DeVries, *Yesterday, Today and Tomorrow*, p. 310.

212 Until the Spirit Comes

2.2.4 *Prophecy*. The age of restoration is perceived as the time when the prophetic spirit is restored. The presence of the prophets or prophetic activity is long considered as the presence of Yahweh and his רוח. For this reason, the prophetic ecstasy is often used to indicate the coming of God's רוח (e.g. Num. 11.25; 1 Sam. 10.10; cf. Isa. 30.1).

With the historical reality that there is no visible political royal figure, the expectation of the prophets and prophetic activity takes on an added significance in the eschatological expectation. It is no wonder that the leader figure almost assumes the prophetic role (42.1-4), while the future prophet assumes some royal functions as well (61.3).

The expectation of the prophetic רוח in the future is based on the role of God's רוח in fulfilling the prophetic word in the past (34.16). The postexilic period witnesses the full eschatological significance of the prophetic רוח. First, the prophetic figure boldly claims not only God's commissioning and authority through the רוח, but also his task which is beyond the traditional prophetic activities: proclamation (61.1-3). He will actually liberate those who are under bondage (cf. 61.3).

In addition, the perpetual endowment of the prophetic word and רוח is promised to the prophetic circle, and later canonically to the nation. In this sense, the end time is the restoration of the prophetic golden age, as the Isaianic tradition often looks back to the great prophet Isaiah. This expectation, in its broad canonical context, fulfills together with Joel 3.1-2 the ideal democratization of the prophetic gift uttered by Moses (Num. 11.25).

2.2.5 *The Consummation of Restoration*. In an implicit reference, the same רוח is expected to consummate the restoration of the national fate. As the postexilic community looks back to the wilderness period, the community confesses that the רוח led the nation to rest, that is, the fulfillment of the exodus promise. The passage is more than a reflection of the past acts of God. It becomes a paradigm for the coming age. With the ideal figure endowed with God's רוח, the entire journey of restoration will be completed by the work of the רוח.

The various רוח traditions maintain their distinct characteristics through the complicated evolution of the book of Isaiah. This points to the presence of multiple traditions from the very beginning of the evolution. The ancient Near Eastern evidence of the ideas related to Hebrew רוח as well as early Israelite רוח texts have already substantiated this argument. Almost mutually exclusive lines of evolution among the various רוח traditions reinforce the thesis.

They also attain new significance and emphases throughout the development stages. Refinement may sum up the general development. The old idea of ecstasy or physical prowess is totally refined to refer to prophets' words or inner changes. The concept of רוח also attains moral and religious significance. Probably the most significant, however, is the role of the רוח in the Isaianic eschatological expectation. In every major element of eschatological expectation, the רוח plays a significant role.

Among the various רוח traditions, the leadership רוח and the prophetic רוח at times appear to show a tendency to overlap. From the early period, the coming of the רוח upon the leaders is accompanied by prophetic behavior. However, the seeming overlap in some cases may take place due to the hybrid personality of the individual to whom the רוח is given. The Servant (42.1-3) and the prophet (61.1) are two examples. The later reflection reckoning David with the prophets with the prophetic רוח is illustrious (2 Sam. 23.2). Otherwise, the exclusiveness of the various traditions is consistently maintained.

At the same time, the various exclusive traditions are functionally brought together in their eschatological usage. The role which the רוח of God plays in the Isaianic eschatological expectation is a strong indication of how subsequent periods will take and further develop the eschatological significance of the רוח. It is also true that, however different one tradition may be from the other, the spirit tradition always maintains its close proximity with God. The רוח sometimes even represents God's very self. The spirit as the extension of God's personality or being serves as the common and fundamental meaning of the רוח across the different traditions.

BIBLIOGRAPHY

Achtemeier, Elizabeth, *The Community and Message of Isaiah 56–66: A Theological Commentary* (TC; Minneapolis: Augsburg, 1982).

Ackroyd, Peter R., 'An Interpretation of the Babylonian Exile', *SJT* 27 (1974), pp. 328-52.

—*Exile and Restoration* (OTL; London: SCM Press, 1968).

—'Isaiah I–XII: Presentation of a Prophet', in *Congress Volume: Göttingen 1977* (VTSup, 29; Leiden: E.J. Brill, 1978), pp. 16-48.

—'Isaiah 36–39: Structure and Function', in W.C. Delsman *et al.* (eds.), *Von Kanaan bis Kerala* (Festschrift J.P.M. van der Plög; AOAT, 211; Neukirchen–Vluyn: Neukirchener Verlag, 1982), pp. 3-21.

—*Israel under Babylon and Persia* (Oxford: Oxford University Press, 1970).

Aitken, K.T., 'Hearing and Seeing: Metamorphoses of a Motif in Isaiah 1–39', in Philip R. Davies and David J.A. Clines (eds.), *Among the Prophets: Language, Image and Structure in the Prophetic Writings* (JSOTSup, 144; Sheffield: JSOT Press, 1993), pp. 12-41.

Albertz, Rainer, 'Das Deuterojesaja-Buch als Fortschreibung der Jesaja-Prophetie', in Erhard Blum, C. Macholz and E.W. Stegemann (eds.), *Die hebräische Bibel und ihre zweifache Nachgeschichte: Festschrift für Rolf Rendtorff zum 65. Geburtstag* (Neukirchen–Vluyn: Neukirchener Verlag, 1990), pp. 241-56.

Albright, William F., *Yahweh and the Gods of Canaan: A Historical Analysis of Two Contrasting Faiths* (University of London; Winona Lake, IN: Eisenbrauns, 1968).

Alexander, J.A., *The Prophecies of Isaiah* (Grand Rapids: Zondervan, 1953).

Allen, Leslie C., *The Books of Joel, Obadiah, Jonah and Micah* (NICOT; Grand Rapids: Eerdmans, 1976).

Alt, Albrecht, 'Das Königtum in den Reichen Israel und Juda', *VT* 1 (1951), pp. 2-22.

Anderson, Bernhard W., 'The Apocalyptic Rendering of the Isaiah Tradition', in Jacob Neusner, Ernest S. Frerichs, Peder Borgen and Richard Horsley (eds.), *The Social World of Formative Christianity and Judaism: Essays in Tribute to Howard Clark Kee* (Philadelphia: Fortress Press, 1988), pp. 17-38.

—'Exodus Typology in Second Isaiah', in Bernhard W. Anderson and Walter Harrelson (eds.), *Israel's Prophetic Heritage: Essays in Honor of James Muilenburg* (New York: Harper & Row, 1962), pp. 177-95.

Anderson, Bernhard W., and Walter Harrelson (eds.), *Israel's Prophetic Heritage: Essays in Honor of James Muilenburg* (New York: Harper & Row, 1962), pp. 177-95.

Anderson, Bernhard W., 'Exodus and Covenant in Second Isaiah and Prophetic Tradition', in Cross, Lemke and Miller (eds.), *Magnalia Dei*, pp. 339-60.

Andersen, F.I., and A.D. Forbes, ' "Prose Particle" Counts of the Hebrew Bible', in C.L. Meyers and M. O'Connor (eds.), *The Word of the Lord Shall Go Forth: Essays in Honor of David Noel Freedman in Celebration of his Sixtieth Birthday* (Winona Lake, IN: Eisenbrauns, 1983), pp. 165-83.

Barnes, W.E., 'Cyrus the "Servant of Jehovah" Isaiah xlii, 1-4(7)', *JTS* 32 (1931), pp. 32-39.

Barr, James, *Holy Scripture: Canon, Authority, Criticism* (Philadelphia: Westminster Press, 1983).

Barré, Michael L., 'Of Lions and Birds: A Note of Isaiah 31.4-5', in Philip R. Davies and David J.A. Clines (eds.), *Among the Prophets: Language, Image and Structure in the Prophetic Writings* (JSOTSup, 144; Sheffield: JSOT Press, 1993), pp. 55-59.

Barstad, Hans M., 'The Future of the "Servant Songs": Some Reflections on the Relationship of Biblical Scholarship to its Own Tradition', in Samuel E. Balentine and John Barton (eds.), *Language, Theology, and the Bible: Essays in Honour of James Barr* (Oxford: Clarendon Press, 1994), pp. 261-70.

Barth, Hermann, *Die Jesaja-Worte in der Josiazeit* (Neukirchen–Vluyn: Neukirchener Verlag, 1977).

Barton, John, *Isaiah 1–39* (OTG; Sheffield: JSOT Press, 1995).

—*Reading the Old Testament: Method in Biblical Study* (Philadelphia: Westminster Press, 1984).

Baumgärtel, Friedrich, 'Spirit in the OT', *TDNT*, VI, pp. 359-67.

—*Spirit of God* (London: A. & C. Black, 1960).

—'Zu den Gottesnamen in den Büchern Jeremia und Ezechiel', in A. Kuschke (ed.), *Verbannung und Heimkehr: Beiträge zur Geschichte und Theologie Israels in 6. und 5. Jahrhundert v. Chr.: Wilhelm Rudolph zum 70. Geburtstage, dargebracht von Kollegen, Freunden und Schülern* (Tübingen: J.C.B Mohr, 1961), pp. 1-24.

Becker, Joachim, *Messianic Expectation in the Old Testament* (trans. David E. Green; Philadelphia: Fortress Press, 1980).

Benson, Alphonsus, *The Spirit of God in the Didactic Books of the Old Testament* (Catholic University of America, Studies in Sacred Theology, Second Series, 29; Washington: Catholic University Press of America, 1949).

Beuken, W.A.M., 'The Main Theme of Trito-Isaiah, "The Servants of YHWH"', *JSOT* 47 (1990), pp. 67-87.

—'*Mišpaṭ*: The First Servant Song and its Context', *VT* 22 (1972), pp. 1-30.

Birch, Bruce C., 'Tradition, Canon and Biblical Theology', *HBT* 2 (1980), pp. 113-25.

Blank, S.H., 'Studies in Deutero-Isaiah', *HUCA* 15 (1940), pp. 1-46.

Blenkinsopp, Joseph, *A History of Prophecy in Israel* (Philadelphia: Westminster Press, 1983).

—*Prophecy and Canon: A Contribution to the Study of Jewish Origins* (Notre Dame: University of Notre Dame Press, 1977).

—'The "Servants of the Lord" in Third Isaiah: Profile of a Pietistic Group in the Persian Epoch', *Proceedings of the Irish Biblical Association* 7 (1983), pp. 1-23.

Block, Daniel I., 'The Prophet of the Spirit: The Use of *rwḥ* in the Book of Ezekiel', *JETS* 32 (1989), pp. 27-50.

Boer, P.A.H. de, 'The Counselor', in M. Noth and D. Winton Thomas (eds.), *Wisdom in Israel and in the Ancient Near East: Essays Presented to H.H. Rowley* (VTSup, 3; Leiden: E.J. Brill, 1955), pp. 42-71.

—'Second-Isaiah's Message', *OTS* 11 (1956), pp. 1-126.

Box, G.H., *The Book of Isaiah* (London: Pitman & Sons, 1908).

Breasted, James H., *Development of Religion and Thought in Ancient Egypt* (New York: Harper & Brothers, 1959).

Briggs, Charles A., 'The Use of *Ruach* in the Old Testament', *JBL* 19 (1900), pp. 132-45.

Bright, John, *A History of Israel* (Philadelphia: Westminster Press, 3rd edn, 1981).

Brownlee, William H., 'From Holy War to Holy Martyrdom', in H.B. Huffmon, F.A. Spina and A.R.W. Green (eds.), *The Quest for the Kingdom of God: Studies in Honor of George E. Mendenhall* (Winona Lake, IN: Eisenbrauns, 1983), pp. 281-92.

Brueggemann, Walter, 'Unity and Dynamic in the Isaiah Tradition', *JSOT* 29 (1984), pp. 89-107.

Budde, K., 'The So-called "Ebed-Jahwe Songs" and the Meaning of the Term "Servant of Yahweh" in Isaiah Chaps. 40–55', *AJT* 3 (1899), pp. 499-540.

Buttenwieser, Moses, *The Psalms, Chronologically Treated with a New Translation* (Chicago: University of Chicago Press, 1938).

Campbell, J.C., 'God's People and the Remnant', *SJT* 3 (1950), pp. 78-85.

Carr, David, 'Reaching for Unity in Isaiah', *JSOT* 57 (1993), pp. 61-80.

Carroll, R.P., 'Twilight of Prophecy or Dawn of Apocalyptic?', *JSOT* 14 (1979), pp. 3-35.

—*When Prophecy Failed: Cognitive Dissonance in the Prophetic Traditions of the Old Testament* (New York: Seabury, 1979).

Cazelles, Henri S., 'Les milieux de Deutéronome', in Heather A. McKay and David J.A. Clines (eds.), *Of Prophets' Visions and the Wisdom of Sages: Essays in Honour of R. Norman Whybray on his Seventieth Birthday* (JSOTSup, 162; Sheffield: JSOT Press, 1993), pp. 288-306.

—'Prolegomenes à une étude de l'esprit dans la Bible', in W.C. Delsman *et al.* (eds.), *Von Kanaan bis Kerala* (Festschrift J.P.M. van der Plög; AOAT, 211; Neukirchen–Vluyn: Neukirchener Verlag, 1982), pp. 75-90.

Černy, L., *The Day of Yahweh and Some Relevant Problems* (Prague: Filosoficka Fakulta Karlovy University, 1948).

Cheyne, T.K., *Introduction to the Book of Isaiah* (London: Black, 5th edn, 1895).

—*The Prophecies of Isaiah: A New Translation with Commentary and Appendices* (2 vols.; New York: Thomas Whittaker, 5th edn, 1892).

Childs, Brevard S., *Biblical Theology of the Old and New Testaments: Theological Reflection on the Christian Bible* (Minneapolis: Fortress Press, 1992).

—'The Canonical Shape of the Prophetic Literature', *Int* 32 (1978), pp. 46-68.

—*Introduction to the Old Testament as Scripture* (Philadelphia: Fortress Press, 1979).

—*Isaiah and the Assyrian Crisis* (SBT, Second Series, 3; Naperville: Allenson, 1965).

—*Memory and Tradition in Israel* (Naperville, IL: Allenson, 1962).

—*Myth and Reality in the Old Testament* (SBT, 27; Naperville: Allenson, 1960).

—*Old Testament Theology in a Canonical Context* (Philadelphia: Fortress Press, 1985).

—'A Response', *HBT* 2 (1980), pp. 199-211.

Chisholm, Robert B., Jr, 'Wordplay in the Eighth-Century Prophets', *BSac* 144 (1987), pp. 44-52.

Clements, R.E., 'Beyond Tradition-History: Deutero-Isaianic Development of First Isaiah's Themes', *JSOT* 31 (1985), pp. 95-113.

—*Isaiah 1–39* (NCBC; London: Marshall, Morgan & Scott, 1980).

—'Patterns in the Prophetic Canon: Healing the Blind and the Lame', in Gene M. Tucker, David L. Petersen and Robert R. Wilson (eds.), *Canon, Theology, and Old Testament Interpretation: Essays in Honor of Brevard S. Childs* (Philadelphia: Fortress Press, 1988), pp. 189-200.

—'Patterns in the Prophetic Canon', in George W. Coats and Burke O. Long (eds.), *Canon and Authority: Essays in Old Testament Religion and Theology* (Philadelphia: Fortress Press, 1977), pp. 42-55.

—'The Unity of the Book of Isaiah', *Int* 36 (1982), pp. 117-29.

Clifford, R.J., 'The Function of Idol Passages in Second Isaiah', *CBQ* 42 (1980), pp. 450-64.

—'The Unity of the Book of Isaiah and its Cosmogenic Language', *CBQ* 55 (1993), pp. 1-17.

—'The Use of *Hoy* in the Prophets', *CBQ* 28 (1966), pp. 458-64.

Cole, D.P., 'Archaeology and the Messiah Oracles of Isaiah 9 and 11', in M.D. Coogan *et al.* (eds.), *Scripture and Other Artifacts: Essays on the Bible and Archaeology in Honor of Philip J. King* (Louisville, KY: Westminster/John Knox Press, 1994), pp. 53-69.

Condamin, Albert, *Le livre d'Isaïe* (Paris: Librairie Victor le Coffre, 1905).

Conrad, Edgar W., 'The "Fear Not" Oracles in Second Isaiah', *VT* 34 (1984), pp. 129-52.

—*Reading Isaiah* (Minneapolis: Fortress Press, 1991).

—'The Royal Narratives and the Structure of the Book of Isaiah', *JSOT* 41 (1988), pp. 67-81.

Cook, S.A., 'The Prophets of Israel', in S.A. Cook *et al.* (eds.), *Cambridge Ancient History* (3 vols.; Cambridge: Cambridge University Press, 1970–), III, pp. 458-99.

Crenshaw, James L., *Old Testament Story and Faith: A Literary and Theological Introduction* (Peabody, MA: Hendrickson, 1992).

Cripps, R.C., 'The Holy Spirit in the Old Testament', *Theology* 24 (1932), pp. 272-80.

Crook, Margaret B., 'A Suggested Occasion for Isa 9.2-7 and 11.1-9', *JBL* 68 (1949), pp. 213-24.

Cross, Frank Moore, Jr, 'The Song of the Sea and Canaanite Myth', in *idem, Canaanite Myth and Hebrew Epic* (Cambridge, MA: Harvard University Press, 1973), pp. 112-44.

Dahood, Mitchell, 'Accusative ʿēṣāh, "Wood", in Isaiah 30,1b', *Bib* 50 (1969), pp. 57-58.

Dalglish, Edward R., *Psalm Fifty-One in the Light of Ancient Near Eastern Patternism* (Leiden: E.J. Brill, 1962).

Darr, Katheryn Pfisterer, *Isaiah's Vision and the Family of God* (Literary Currents in Biblical Interpretation; Louisville, KY: Westminster/John Knox Press, 1994).

—'Two Unifying Female Images in the Book of Isaiah', in Lewis M. Hopfe (ed.), *Uncovering Ancient Stones: Essays in Memory of H. Neil Richardson* (Winona Lake, IN: Eisenbrauns, 1994), pp. 17-30.

Davidson, A.B., *Hebrew Syntax* (Edinburgh: T. & T. Clark, 3rd edn, 1901).

Davies, Philip R., 'God of Cyrus, God of Israel: Some Religio-Historical Reflections on Isaiah 40–55', in Jon Davies, Graham Harvey and Wilfred G.E. Watson (eds.), *Words Remembered, Texts Renewed: Essays in Honour of John F.A. Sawyer* (JSOTSup, 195; Sheffield: JSOT Press, 1995), pp. 207-25.

Davis, Ellen F., 'A Strategy of Delayed Comprehension: Isaiah liv 15', *VT* 40 (1990), pp. 217-21.

Day, John, 'The Problem of "So, King of Egypt" in 2 Kings XVII 4', *VT* 42 (1992), pp. 289-301.

Delitzsch, Franz, *Bible Commentaries on the Prophecies of Isaiah* (trans. James Martin; 2 vols.; Grand Rapids: Eerdmans, 1954).

DeVries, Simon John, *Yesterday, Today and Tomorrow: Time and History in the Old Testament* (Grand Rapids: Eerdmans, 1975).

Dobbs-Allsopp, F.W., *Weep, O Daughter of Zion: A Study of the City-Lament Genre in the Hebrew Bible* (BibOr, 44; Rome: Pontificio Istituto Biblico, 1993).

Donner, H., *Israel unter den Völkern: Die Stellung der klassischen Propheten des 8. Jahr-hunderts v. Chr. zur Aussenpolitik der Könige von Israel und Juda* (VTSup, 2; Leiden: E.J. Brill, 1964).

Dreytza, Manfred, *Der theologische Gebrauch von RUAḤ im Alten Testament: Eine wort- und satzsemantische Studie* (Basel: Brunnen, 1992).

Driver, G.R., 'Hebrew Notes', *VT* 1 (1951), pp. 241-50.

—'Isaiah I–XXXIX: Textual and Linguistic Problems', *JSS* 13 (1968), pp. 36-57.

Duhm, Bernhard, *Das Buch Jesaja: Übersetzt und erklärt* (HKAT, 3; Göttingen: Vanden- hoeck & Ruprecht, 1902).

Dumbrell, William J., 'The Origin of the Book of Isaiah', *VT* 9 (1959), pp. 138-57.

—'The Purpose of the Book of Isaiah', *TynBul* 36 (1985), pp. 111-28.

—*The Search for Order: Biblical Eschatology in Focus* (Grand Rapids: Baker Book House, 1994).

Eaton, John H., *Festal Drama in Deutero-Isaiah* (London: SPCK, 1979).

—'The Isaiah Tradition', in R. Coggins, A. Phillips and M. Knibb (eds.), *Israel's Prophetic Tradition: Essays in Honour of Peter Ackroyd* (Cambridge: Cambridge University Press, 1982), pp. 58-76.

Eichrodt, Walther, *Der Heilige in Israel: Jesaja 1–12* (BAT, 17.1; Stuttgart: Calwer Verlag, 1960).

—'Prophet and Covenant: Observations on the Exegesis of Isaiah', in John I. Durham and J.R. Porter (eds.), *Proclamation and Presence: Old Testament Essays in Honour of Gwynne Henton Davies* (Macon, GA: Mercer University Press, new corrected edn, 1983), pp. 167-88.

—*Theology of the Old Testament* (OTL; trans. J.A. Baker; 2 vols.; Philadelphia: West- minster Press, 1967).

Eissfeldt, Otto, 'The Ebed-Jahwe in Isaiah xl-lv. in the Light of the Individual, the Ideal and the Real', *ExpTim* 44 (1932–33), pp. 261-68.

—*The Old Testament: An Introduction* (trans. Peter R. Ackroyd; New York: Harper & Row, 1965).

—'Silo und Jerusalem', in George W. Anderson (ed.), *Volume du Congrès: Strasbourg, 1956* (VTSup, 4; Leiden: E.J. Brill, 1957), pp. 138-47.

Elliger, Karl, *Deuterojesaja. I. Jesaja 40,1–45,7* (BKAT, 11.1; Neukirchen–Vluyn: Neukirchener Verlag, 1978).

—*Deuterojesaja im seinem Verhältnis zu Tritojesaja* (BWANT, 63; Stuttgart: W. Kohl- hammer, 1933).

—*Die Einheit des Tritojesaja* (Stuttgart: W. Kohlhammer, 1928).

—'Der Prophet Tritojesaja', *ZAW* 49 (1931), pp. 112-41.

Emerton, J.A., 'A Further Note on Isaiah xxx.5', *JTS* 33 (1982), p. 161.

—'A Textual Problem in Isaiah xxx.5', *JTS* 32 (1981), pp. 125-28.

Emmerson, Grace I., *Isaiah 56–66* (OTG; Sheffield: JSOT Press, 1992).

Engnell, I., 'The Ebed Yahweh Songs and the Suffering Messiah in "Deutero-Isaiah"', *BJRL* 31 (1948), pp. 54-93.

Evans, C.A., 'On the Unity and Parallel Structures of Isaiah', *VT* 28 (1988), pp. 129-47.

Everson, A. Joseph, 'Isaiah 61.1-6 (To Give Them a Garland Instead of Ashes)', *Int* 32 (1978), pp. 69-73.

Exum, J. Cheryl, '"Whom Will He Teach Knowledge?" A Literary Approach to Isaiah 28', in David J.A. Clines, David M. Gunn and Alan J. Hauser (eds.), *Art and Meaning:*

Rhetoric in Biblical Literature (JSOTSup, 19; Sheffield: JSOT Press, 1982), pp. 108-39.

Fensham, F. Charles, 'Father and Son as Terminology for Treaty and Covenant', in Hans Goedicke (ed.), *Near Eastern Studies in Honor of William Foxwell Albright* (Baltimore: The Johns Hopkins University Press, 1971), pp. 121-35.

Fichtner, J., 'Jahves Plan in der Botschaft des Jesaja', *ZAW* 63 (1951), pp. 16-33.

Fischer, J., *Das Buch Isaias* (2 vols.; Bonn: Peter Hanstein, 1937–39).

Fohrer, Georg, *Das Buch Jesaja* (Zürcher Bibelkommentar; 3 vols.; Zürich: Zwingli-Verlag, 1960–64).

—'Jesaja 1 als Zusammenfassung der Verkündigung Jesajas', *ZAW* 74 (1962), pp. 251-69.

Franke, Chris, *Isaiah 46, 47, and 48: A New Literary-Critical Reading* (Biblical and Judaic Studies from University of California, San Diego, 3; Winona Lake, IN: Eisenbrauns, 1994).

Frankfort, Henri, *Kingship and the Gods: A Study of Ancient Near Eastern Religion as the Integration of Society and Nature* (Chicago: University of Chicago Press, 1948).

Freeman, Daniel N., 'Is Justice Blind? (Isaiah 11.3f)', *Bib* 52 (1971), p. 536.

Freedman, David N., 'Early Israelite Poetry and Historical Considerations', in *idem, Pottery, Poetry and Prophecy: Collected Essays on Hebrew Poetry* (Winona Lake, IN: Eisenbrauns, 1980), pp. 167-78. (Originally in Frank Moore Cross [ed.], *Symposia Celebrating the Seventy-Fifth Anniversary of the Founding of the American Schools of Oriental Research [1900–1975]* [Cambridge, MA: American Schools of Oriental Research, 1979], pp. 85-99).

Frost, S.B., 'Eschatology and Myth', *VT* 2 (1952), pp. 70-80.

Gehman, Henry S., 'The Ruler of the Universe: The Theology of First Isaiah', *Int* 11 (1957), pp. 269-81.

Gerstenberger, Edhard S., 'Canon Criticism and the Meaning of *Sitz im Leben*', in Tucker, Petersen and Wilson (eds.), *Canon, Theology, and Old Testament Interpretation*, pp. 20-31.

—'The Woe-oracles of the Prophets', *JBL* 81 (1962), pp. 249-63.

Gileadi, Avraham, *The Literary Message of Isaiah* (New York: Hebraeus, 1994).

Gibson, J.C.L., *Canaanite Myths and Legends* (ed. G.R. Driver; Edinburgh: T. & T. Clark, 1956).

Gitay, Yehoshua, 'Deutero-Isaiah: Oral or Written?', *JBL* 99 (1980), pp. 185-97.

—*Isaiah and his Audience: The Structure and Meaning of Isaiah 1–12* (Studia Semitica Neerlandica; Assen: Van Gorcum, 1991).

—*Prophecy and Persuasion: A Study of Isaiah 40–48* (Forum Theologiae Linguisticae, 14; Bonn: Linguistica Biblica, 1981).

Goedicke, Hans, *The Report about the Dispute of a Man with his Ba: Papyrus Berlin 3024* (Baltimore: The Johns Hopkins University Press, 1970).

Goldingay, John, 'The Arrangement of Isaiah xli–xlv', *VT* 29 (1979), pp. 289-99.

Gordon, Cyrus H., *Ugaritic Textbook: Grammar, Texts in Transliteration, Cuneiform Selections, Glossary, Indices* (AnOr, 38; Rome: Pontifical Biblical Institute, 1965).

Gottwald, Norman K., *All the Kingdoms of the Earth: Israelite Prophecy and International Relations in the Ancient Near East* (New York: Harper & Row, 1964).

—*Studies in the Book of Lamentations* (London: SCM Press, 1954).

Gowan, Donald E., *Eschatology in the Old Testament* (Philadelphia: Fortress Press, 1986).

—'Isaiah 61.1-3, 10-11', *Int* 35 (1981), pp. 404-409.

Gray, George B., *A Critical and Exegetical Commentary on the Book of Isaiah I–XXVII* (ICC; Edinburgh: T. & T. Clark, 1912).

Gray, John, *The Legacy of Canaan* (VTSup, 5; Leiden: E.J. Brill, 1957).

Gressmann, Hugo, *Der Messias* (Göttingen: Vandenhoeck & Ruprecht, 1929).

—*Der Ursprung der israelitisch-judischen Eschatologie* (Göttingen: Vandenhoeck & Ruprecht, 1905).

Gunkel, H., *Schöpfung und Chaos in Urzeit und Endzeit* (Göttingen: Vandenhoeck & Ruprecht, 1895).

Hanson, Paul D., *The Dawn of Apocalyptic: The Historical and Sociological Roots of Jewish Apocalyptic Eschatology* (Philadelphia: Fortress Press, rev. edn, 1979).

—*Dynamic Transcendence* (Philadelphia: Fortress Press, 1978).

—*Isaiah 40–66* (Interpretation: A Bible Commentary for Teaching and Preaching; Louisville, KY: Westminster/John Knox Press, 1995).

Haran, Menahem, 'The Literary Structure and Chronological Framework of the Prophecies in Is. xl–xlvii', in *Congress Volume: Bonn 1962* (VTSup, 9; Leiden: E.J. Brill, 1963), pp. 127-55.

Harrelson, Walter, 'Isaiah 35 in Recent Research and Translation', in Samuel E. Balentine and John Barton (eds.), *Language, Theology, and the Bible: Essays in Honour of James Barr* (Oxford: Clarendon Press, 1994), pp. 247-60.

—'Nonroyal Motifs in the Royal Eschatology', in Bernhard W. Anderson and Walter Harrelson (eds.), *Israel's Prophetic Heritage: Essays in Honor of James Muilenburg* (New York: Harper & Row, 1962), pp. 147-65.

Hasel, Gerhard F., *The Remnant: The History and Theology of the Remnant Idea from Genesis to Isaiah* (Berrien Springs, MI: Andrews University Press, 3rd edn, 1980).

Hayes, John H. and Stuart A. Irvine, *Isaiah, the Eighth-Century Prophet: His Time and his Preaching* (Nashville: Abingdon Press, 1987).

Hehn, Johannes, 'Zum Problem des Geist im Alten Orient und im Alten Testament', *ZAW* 43 (1925), pp. 210-25.

Herbert, A.S., *The Book of the Prophet Isaiah: Chapters 40–66* (CBCOT; Cambridge: Cambridge University Press, 1975).

Hermisson, H.-J., 'Israel und der Gottesknecht bei Deuterojesaja', *ZTK* 70 (1982), pp. 1-24.

Hertzberg, H.W., 'Die Entwicklung des Begriffes *mšpṭ* im AT', *ZAW* 41 (1923), pp. 16-76.

Hildebrandt, Wilf, *An Old Testament Theology of the Spirit of God* (Peabody, MA: Hendrickson, 1995).

Hillers, Delbert R., *Micah* (Hermeneia; Philadelphia: Fortress Press, 1984).

—*Treaty-Curses and the Old Testament Prophets* (Rome: Pontifical Biblical Institute, 1964).

Hindson, Edward E., *Isaiah's Immanuel* (Grand Rapids: Baker Book House, 1978).

Holladay, William L., *Jeremiah. I. A Commentary on the Book of the Prophet Jeremiah Chapters 1–25* (Hemeneia; Philadelphia: Fortress Press, 1986).

Horton, Stanley M., *What the Bible Says about the Holy Spirit* (Springfield, MO: Gospel Publishing House, 1976).

Hugenberger, G.P., 'The Servant of the Lord in the "Servant Songs" of Isaiah: A Second Moses Figure', in Philip E. Satterthwaite, Richard S. Hess and Gordon J. Wenham (eds.), *The Lord's Anointed: Interpretation of Old Testament Messianic Texts* (Carlisle: Paternoster Press; Grand Rapids: Baker Book House, 1995), pp. 105-40.

Imschoot, Paul van, 'L'action de l'esprit de Jahvé dans l'Ancien Testament', *RSPT* 23 (1934), pp. 553-87.
—'L'esprit de Jahvé et l'alliance nouvelle dans l'Ancien Testament', *ETL* 13 (1936), pp. 201-20.
—'L'esprit de Jahvé, principe de vie morale dans l'Ancien Testament', *ETL* 16 (1939), pp. 457-67.
—'L'esprit de Jahvé, source de la piété dans l'Ancien Testament', *Bible et Vie Chretienne* 6 (1954), pp. 17-30.
—'L'esprit de Jahvé, source de vie dans l'Ancien Testament', *RB* 44 (1935), pp. 481-501.
—'Sagesse et esprit dans l'Ancien Testament', *RB* 47 (1938), pp. 23-49.
—*Theology of the Old Testament* (trans. Kathryn Sullivan and Fidelis Buck; Paris: Desclée de Brouwer, 1965).
Irwin, William H., *Isaiah 28–33: Translation with Philological Notes* (Rome: Pontifical Biblical Institute, 1973).
Janzen, Waldemar, *Mourning Cry and Woe Oracle* (BZAW, 125; Berlin: W. de Gruyter, 1972).
Jenni, E., 'Eschatology of the OT', *IDB*, II, pp. 126-33.
Jensen, Joseph, *God's Word to Israel* (Wilmington, DE: Michael Glazier, rev. edn, 1982).
—*The Use of* tôrâ *by Isaiah: His Debate with the Wisdom Tradition* (CBQMS, 3; Washington: Catholic Biblical Association, 1973).
—'Yahweh's Plan in Isaiah and in the Rest of the OT', *CBQ* 48 (1986), pp. 443-55.
Jeppesen, Knud, 'Mother Zion, Father Servant: A Reading of Isaiah 49–55', in Heather A. McKay and David J.A. Clines (eds.), *Of Prophets' Visions and the Wisdom of Sages: Essays in Honour of R. Norman Whybray on his Seventieth Birthday* (JSOTSup, 162; Sheffield: JSOT Press, 1993), pp. 109-25.
Jeremias, Jörg, '*Mišpaṭ* im ersten Gottesknechtslied (Jes. xlii. 1-4)', *VT* 22 (1972), pp. 31-42.
Johnson, Aubrey R., *The One and the Many in the Israelite Conception of God* (Cardiff: University of Wales Press, 1961).
—'The Psalms', in H.H. Rowley (ed.), *The Old Testament and Modern Study* (repr.; Oxford: Oxford University Press, 1961), pp. 162-209.
—*The Vitality of the Individual in the Thought of Ancient Israel* (Cardiff: University of Wales Press, 1964).
Johnston, Ann, 'A Prophetic Vision of an Alternative Community: A Reading of Isaiah 40–55', in Lewis M. Hopfe (ed.), *Uncovering Ancient Stones: Essays in Memory of H. Neil Richardson* (Winona Lake, IN: Eisenbrauns, 1994), pp. 31-40.
Johnston, L., 'The Spirit of God', *Scripture* 8 (1956), pp. 65-74.
Jones, Douglas R., 'The Cessation of Sacrifice after the Destruction of the Temple in 586 BC', *JTS* 14 (1963), pp. 12-31.
Jones, Holland, 'How I Would Use Messianic Prophecy in Advent', *CurTM* 9.6 (1982), pp. 349-59.
Kaiser, Otto, *Introduction to the Old Testament* (trans. John Sturdy; Minneapolis: Augsburg, 1975).
—*Isaiah 1–12* (OTL; trans. John Bowden; Philadelphia: Westminster Press, 1983).
—*Isaiah 13–36: A Commentary* (OTL; trans. R.A. Wilson; London: SCM Press, 1974).
Kapelrud, Arvid S., 'The Main Concern of Second Isaiah', *VT* 34 (1982), pp. 50-58.
—'The Spirit and the Word in the Prophets', *ASTI* 11 (1977–78), pp. 40-47.
Kendall, D.J., 'The Use of *Mišpaṭ* in Isaiah 59', *ZAW* 96 (1984), pp. 391-405.

Kissane, Edward, *The Book of Isaiah* (2 vols.; Dublin: Browne & Nolan, 1941–43).

Klausner, Joseph, *The Messianic Idea in Israel: From its Beginning to the Completion of the Mishnah* (trans. W.F. Stinespring; New York: Macmillan, 1955).

Klein, Ralph W., *Israel in Exile: A Theological Interpretation* (Philadelphia: Fortress Press, 1979).

Knight, Douglas A., 'Canon and the History of Tradition: A Critique of Brevard S. Childs' *Introduction to the Old Testament as Scripture*', *HBT* 2 (1980), pp. 127-49.

Knight, George A.F., *Isaiah 56–66* (ITC; Grand Rapids: Eerdmans, 1985).

Koch, Robert, *Der Geist Gottes im Alten Testament* (Bern: Peter Lang, 1991).

—'Der Gottesgeist und der Messias', *Bib* 27 (1946), pp. 241-68, 376-403.

—*Geist und Messias* (Freiburg: Herder, 1950).

—'La théologie de l'esprit de Yahvé dans le livre d'Isaïe', in J. Coppens, A. Descamps and E. Massaux (eds.), *Sacra Pagina: Miscellanea biblica: Congressus Internationalis Catholici de Re Biblica* (2 vols.; Gembloux: Duculot, 1959), I, pp. 419-33.

Kraus, Hans-Joachim, 'Die ausgebliebene Endtheophanie: Ein Studie zu Jesaja 56–66', *ZAW* 78 (1966), pp. 317-32.

—*Psalms 1–59: A Commentary* (trans. Hilton C. Oswald; Minneapolis: Augsburg, 1988).

Kruse, C.G., 'The Servant Songs: Interpretive Trends since C.R. North', *Studia Biblica et Theologica* 8 (1978), pp. 3-18.

Laato, Antti, 'The Composition of Isaiah 40–55', *JBL* 109 (1990), pp. 207-28.

—*The Servant of YHWH and Cyrus: A Reinterpretation of the Exilic Messianic Programme in Isaiah 40–55* (ConBOT, 35; Stockholm: Almqvist & Wiksell, 1992).

Lampe, G.W.H., 'Holy Spirit', *IDB*, II, pp. 623-37.

Landy, Francis, 'Tracing the Voice of the Other: Isaiah 28 and the Covenant with Death', in J. Cheryl Exum and David J.A. Clines (eds.), *The New Literary Criticism and the Hebrew Bible* (JSOTSup, 143; Sheffield: JSOT Press, 1993), pp. 140-62.

Lee, Stephen, 'Power not Novelty: The Connotations of ברא in the Hebrew Bible', in A. Graeme Auld (ed.), *Understanding Poets and Prophets: Essays in Honour of George Wishart Anderson* (JSOTSup, 152; Sheffield: JSOT Press, 1993), pp. 199-212.

Leupold, Herbert C., *Exposition of Isaiah* (2 vols.; Grand Rapids: Baker Book House, 1968).

Lind, Millard C., *Yahweh Is a Warrior* (Kirchener, Ontario: Herald Press, 1980).

Lindblom, J., 'Gibt es eine Eschatologie bei den alttestamentlichen Propheten?' *ST* 6 (1953), pp. 79-114.

—*Prophecy in Ancient Israel* (Philadelphia: Fortress Press, 1962).

—*The Servant Songs in Deutero-Isaiah: A New Attempt to Solve an Old Problem* (Lund: C.W.K. Gleerup, 1951).

—'Wisdom in the Old Testament Prophets', in M. Noth and D. Winton Thomas (eds.), *Wisdom in Israel and in the Ancient Near East: Essays Presented to H.H. Rowley* (VTSup, 3; Leiden: E.J. Brill, 1955), 192-204.

Love, J.P., 'The Call of Isaiah: An Exposition of Isaiah 6', *Int* 11 (1957), pp. 282-96.

Lys, Daniel, *La chair dans l'Ancien Testament 'basar'* (Paris: Editions Universitaires, 1967).

—*'Rûach', le souffle dans l'Ancien Testament* (Etudes d'histoire et de philosophie religieuses; Paris: Presses Universitaires de France, 1962).

Ma, Julie, 'A Comparison of Two Worldviews: Kankana-ey and Pentecostal', in Wonsuk Ma and Robert P. Menzies (eds.), *Pentecostalism in Context: Essays in Honor of*

William W. Menzies (JPTSup, 11; Sheffield: Sheffield Academic Press, 1997), pp. 265-90.

Malamat, Abraham, 'A New Prophetic Message from Aleppo and its Biblical Counterparts', in A. Graeme Auld (ed.), *Understanding Poets and Prophets: Essays in Honour of George Wishart Anderson* (JSOTSup, 152; Sheffield: JSOT Press, 1993), pp. 136-241.

Marcus, Ralph, 'The "Plain Meaning" of Isaiah 42.1-4', *HTR* 30 (1937), pp. 249-59.

Marshall, Robert J., 'The Structure of Isaiah 1-12', *BibRes* 7 (1962), pp. 19-32.

Marti, K., *Das Buch Jesaja* (KHAT, 10; Tübingen: J.C.B. Mohr, 1900).

Mathews, Claire R., *Defending Zion: Edom's Desolation and Jacob's Restoration (Isaiah 34-35) in Context* (BZAT, 236; Berlin: W. de Gruyter, 1995).

Mays, James L., 'Historical and Canonical: Recent Discussion about the Old Testament and Christian Faith', in Frank Moore Cross, Werner E. Lemke and Patrick D. Miller, Jr (eds.), *Magnalia Dei, The Mighty Acts of God: Essays on the Bible and Archaeology in Memory of G. Ernest Wright* (Garden City, NY: Doubleday, 1976), pp. 510-28.

—*Micah: A Commentary* (OTL; Philadelphia: Westminster Press, 1976).

—'What Is Written: A Response to Brevard Childs' *Introduction to the Old Testament as Scripture*', *HBT* 2 (1980), pp. 151-63.

McKane, William, *Prophets and Wise Men* (SBT, 44; London: SCM Press, 1965).

McKenzie, John L., *Second Isaiah* (AB, 20; Garden City, NY: Doubleday, 1968).

Melugin, Roy F., 'Canon and Exegetical Method', in Gene M. Tucker, David L. Petersen and Robert R. Wilson (eds.), *Canon, Theology, and Old Testament Interpretation: Essays in Honor of Brevard S. Childs* (Philadelphia: Fortress Press, 1988), pp. 48-61.

—'Deutero-Isaiah and Form Criticism', *VT* 21 (1971), pp. 326-37.

—*The Formation of Isaiah 40-55* (BZAW, 141; Berlin: W. de Gruyter, 1976).

—'The Servant, God's Call, and the Structure of Isaiah 40-48', in Eugene H. Lovering, Jr (ed.), *SBL 1991 Seminar Papers* (Atlanta: Scholars Press, 1991), pp. 21-30.

Mendenhall, George E., *The Tenth Generation: The Origins of the Biblical Tradition* (Baltimore: The Johns Hopkins University Press, 1973).

Mettinger, Tryggve N.D., *King and Messiah: The Civil and Sacral Legitimation of the Israelite Kings* (ConBOT, 8; Lund: C.W.K. Gleerup, 1976).

Miscall, Peter D., *Isaiah* (Sheffield: JSOT Press, 1993).

Montague, George T., *The Holy Spirit: Growth of a Biblical Tradition* (New York: Paulist Press, 1976; repr.; Peabody, MA: Hendrickson, 1994).

Morgenstern, Julian, 'Deutero-Isaiah's Terminology for "Universal God"', *JBL* 62 (1943), pp. 269-80.

—*The Message of Deutero-Isaiah in its Sequential Unfolding* (Cincinnati: Hebrew Union College Press, 1961).

Motyer, J. Alec, *The Prophecy of Isaiah: An Introduction and Commentary* (Downers Grove, IL: InterVarsity Press, 1993).

Mowinckel, Sigmund, 'Die Komposition des deuterojesajanischen Buches', *ZAW* 49 (1931), pp. 87-112, 242-60.

—*He That Cometh* (trans. G.W. Anderson; New York: Abingdon Press, 1954).

—'The "Spirit" and the "Word" in the Pre-Exilic Reforming Prophets', *JBL* 53 (1934), pp. 199-227; 56 (1937), pp. 261-65.

Muilenburg, James, 'The Book of Isaiah, Chapters 40-66', *IB*, V, pp. 382-773.

—'The Literary Character of Isaiah 34', *JBL* 59 (1940), pp. 339-65.

Naidoff, Bruce D., 'The Rhetoric of Encouragement in Isaiah 40.12-31: A Form-Critical Study', *ZAW* 93 (1981), pp. 62-76.

Neve, Lloyd, *The Spirit of God in the Old Testament* (Tokyo: Seibunsha, 1972).

Newsome, James, D., Jr, *The Hebrew Prophets* (Atlanta: John Knox Press, 1984).

Niditch, S., 'The Composition of Isaiah 1', *Bib* 61 (1980), pp. 509-29.

Niehr, H., 'ערה ʿārāh', *ThWAT*, VI, cols. 369-75.

Nielsen, Kirsten, *There Is Hope for a Tree: The Tree as Metaphor in Isaiah* (trans. Christine Crowley and Frederick Crowley; JSOTSup, 65; Sheffield: JSOT Press, 1989).

North, Christopher R., 'The "Former Things" and the "New Things" in Deutero-Isaiah', in H.H. Rowley (ed.), *Studies in Old Testament Prophecy* (Edinburgh: T. & T. Clark, 1950), pp. 111-26.

—*Isaiah 40–55* (Torch Bible Commentary; London: SCM Press, 2nd edn, 1964).

—'The Religious Aspects of Hebrew Kingship', *ZAW* 50 (1932), pp. 8-38.

—*The Second Isaiah* (Oxford: Clarendon Press, 1964).

—*The Suffering Servant in Deutero-Isaiah: An Historical and Critical Study* (Oxford: Oxford University Press, 1948).

Noth, Martin, 'Gott, König, Volk im Alten Testament', *ZTK* 47 (1950), pp. 159-91.

O'Connell, Robert H., *Concentricity and Continuity: The Literary Structure of Isaiah* (JSOTSup, 188; Sheffield: Sheffield Academic Press, 1994).

Odeberg, H., *Trito-Isaiah: A Literary and Linguistic Analysis* (Uppsala Universitets Arsskrift, Teologi, 1; Uppsala: Lundeqvist, 1931).

Odendaal, Dirk H., *The Eschatological Expectation of Isaiah 40–66 with Special Reference to Israel and the Nations* (Nutley, NJ: Presbyterian and Reformed Publishing, 1970).

Orlinsky, Harry M., 'The So-called "Servant of the Lord" and "Suffering Servant" in Second Isaiah', in *Studies on the Second Part of the Book of Isaiah* (VTSup, 14; Leiden: E.J. Brill, 1967).

Oswalt, John N., *The Book of Isaiah Chapters 1–39* (NICOT; Grand Rapids: Eerdmans, 1968).

—'Canonical Criticism: A Review from a Conservative Viewpoint', *JETS* 30 (1987), pp. 317-25.

Pauritsch, K., *Die neue Gemeinde: Gott sammelt Ausgestossene und Arme (Jesaja 56–66): Die Botschaft des Tritojesaia-Buches literar-, form-, gattungskritisch und redaktionsgeschichtlich untersucht* (AnBib, 47; Rome: Biblical Institute Press, 1971).

Pedersen, Josh, *Israel, its Life and Culture* (4 vols. in 2; London: Milford, 1926–40).

Perdue, Leo G., *Wisdom and Creation: The Theology of Wisdom Literature* (Nashville: Abingdon Press, 1994).

Petersen, David L., 'Isaiah 28, A Redaction Critical Study', in Paul J. Achtemeier (ed.), *SBL 1979 Seminar Papers* (2 vols.; Missoula, MT: Scholars Press, 1979), II, pp. 101-22.

—*Late Israelite Prophecy: Studies in Deutero-Prophetic Literature and in Chronicles* (SBLMS, 23; Missoula, MT: Scholars Press, 1977).

Pezhumkattil, Abraham, 'Anthropological Concept of Spirit in the Old Testament', *Bible Bhashyam* 18 (1992), pp. 5-17.

—'The Spirit as the Power of God in the Old Testament', *Bible Bhashyam* 19 (1993), pp. 283-99.

Plög, J.P.M. van der, 'Eschatology in the Old Testament', *OTS* 17 (1978), pp. 89-99.

—'Šapaṭ et Mišpaṭ', *OTS* 2 (1943), pp. 144-55.

Polk, David P. 'Brevard S. Childs' *Introduction to the Old Testament as Scripture*', *HBT* 2 (1980), pp. 165-71.

Polzin, Robert, *Samuel and the Deuteronomist: A Literary Study of the Deuteronomic History*. II. *1 Samuel* (San Francisco: Harper & Row, 1989).

Pope, Marvin, 'Isaiah 34 in Relation to Isaiah 35, 40–66', *JBL* 71 (1952), pp. 235-43.

Porteous, N.W., 'Royal Wisdom', in M. Noth and D. Winton Thomas (eds.), *Wisdom in Israel and in the Ancient Near East: Essays Presented to H.H. Rowley* (VTSup, 3; Leiden: E.J. Brill, 1955), pp. 247-61.

Raabe, Paul R., 'Why Prophetic Oracles against the Nations?', in Astrid B. Beck *et al.* (eds.), *Fortunate the Eyes That See: Essays in Honor of David Noel Freedman in Celebration of his Seventieth Birthday* (Grand Rapids: Eerdmans, 1995), pp. 236-57.

Rad, Gerhard von, *Old Testament Theology* (trans. D.M.G. Stalker; 2 vols.; New York: Harper & Row, 1962–65).

—'The Origin of the Concept of the Day of Yahweh', *JSS* 4 (1959), pp. 97-108.

—'The Theological Problem of the Old Testament Doctrine of Creation', in *idem, The Problem of the Hexateuch and Other Essays* (London: SCM Press, 1966), pp. 131-43.

Reider, J., 'Contributions to the Scriptural Text', *HUCA* 24 (1952–53), pp. 85-106.

Rendtorff, Rolf, 'The Book of Isaiah: A Complex Unity: Synchronic and Diachronic Reading', in Eugene H. Lovering, Jr (ed.), *SBL 1991 Seminar Papers* (Atlanta: Scholars Press, 1991), pp. 8-20.

—'Jesaja 6 im Rahmen der Komposition des Jesajabuches', in J. Vermeylen (ed.), *Le livre d'Isaïe: Les oracles et leurs relectures unité et complexité de l'ouvrage* (BETL, 81; Leuven: Leuven University Press, 1989), pp. 73-83.

—*The Old Testament: An Introduction* (trans. John Bowden; Philadelphia: Fortress Press, 1985).

—'Zur Komposition des Buches Jesaja', *VT* 34 (1984), pp. 295-320.

Ringgren, Helmer, *Israelite Religion* (trans. David E. Green; Philadelphia: Fortress Press, 1966).

—*The Messiah in the Old Testament* (SBT, 18; London: SCM Press, 1956).

Roberts, J.J.M., 'The Divine King and the Human Community in Israel's Vision of the Future', in H.B. Huffmon, F.A. Spina and A.R.W. Green (eds.), *The Quest for the Kingdom of God: Studies in Honor of George E. Mendenhall* (Winona Lake, IN: Eisenbrauns, 1983), pp. 127-36.

—'Isaiah in Old Testament Theology', *Int* 36 (1982), pp. 130-43.

Robinson, H. Wheeler, *Corporate Personality in Ancient Israel* (Philadelphia: Fortress Press, rev. edn, 1980).

—*The Cross in the Old Testament* (London: SCM Press, 1955).

Rofé, Alexander, 'Isaiah 59.19 and Trito-Isaiah's Vision of Redemption', in Jacques Vermeylen (ed.), *Le livre d'Isaïe: Les oracles et leurs relectures unité et complexité de l'ouvrage* (BETL, 81; Leuven: Leuven University Press, 1989), pp. 407-10.

Ross, James F., 'The Prophet as Yahweh's Messenger', in Bernhard W. Anderson and Walter Harrelson (eds.), *Israel's Prophetic Heritage: Essays in Honor of James Muilenburg* (New York: Harper & Row, 1962), pp. 98-107.

Roth, Wolfgang, *Isaiah* (Knox Preaching Guides; Atlanta: John Knox Press, 1988).

Rowley, H.H., *The Faith of Israel* (London: SCM Press, 1956).

—*Prophecy and Religion in Ancient China and Israel* (London: Athlone Press, 1956).

—*The Servant of the Lord and Other Essays on the Old Testament* (London: Lutterworth, 1952).

—'The Suffering Servant and the Davidic Messiah', *OTS* 8 (1950), pp. 100-36.

Rylaarsdam, John Coert, *Revelation in Jewish Wisdom Literature* (Chicago: University of Chicago Press, 1946).

Sanders, James A., 'Adaptable for Life: The Nature and Function of Canon', in Frank Moore Cross, Werner E. Lemke and Patrick D. Miller, Jr (eds.), *Magnalia Dei, The Mighty Acts of God: Essays on the Bible and Archaeology in Memory of G. Ernest Wright* (Garden City, NY: Doubleday, 1976), pp. 531-60.

—'Canonical Context and Canonical Criticism', *HBT* 2 (1980), pp. 173-87.

—*Torah and Canon* (Philadelphia: Fortress Press, 1972).

Sawyer, John F.A., *Isaiah* (DSB; 2 vols.; Philadelphia: Westminster Press, 1984).

Schibler, Daniel, 'Messianism and Messianic Prophecy in Isaiah 1–12 and 28–33', in Philip E. Satterthwaite, Richard S. Hess and Gordon J. Wenham (eds.), *The Lord's Anointed: Interpretation of Old Testament Messianic Texts* (Carlisle: Paternoster Press; Grand Rapids: Baker Book House, 1995), pp. 87-104.

Schmid, Hans Heinrich, 'Ekstatische und charismatische Geistwirkungen im Alten Testament', in C. Heitmann and H. Mühlen (eds.), *Erfahrung und Theologie des Heiligen Geistes* (Hamburg: Agentur des Rauhen; Munich: Kösel, 1974), pp. 83-100.

Schoemaker, William R., 'The Use of "Ruach" in the Old Testament and of "Pneuma" in the New Testament', *JBL* 23 (1904), pp. 13-67.

Schoors, Antoon, *I Am God your Saviour: A Form-Critical Study of the Main Genres in Is. XL–LV* (VTSup, 24; Leiden: E.J. Brill, 1973).

Schramm, Brooks, *The Opponents of Third Isaiah: Reconstructing the Cultic History of the Restoration* (JSOTSup, 193; Sheffield: Sheffield Academic Press, 1995).

Schniedewind, William M., *The Word of God in Transition: From Prophet to Exegete in the Second Temple Period* (JSOTSup, 197; Sheffield: Sheffield Academic Press, 1995).

Schweizer, Harold, 'Praedikationen und Leerstellen im 1. Gottesknechtslied (Jes 42.1-4)', *BZ* 26 (1982), pp. 251-58.

Scott, R.B.Y., 'Biblical Research and the Work of the Pastor: Recent Study in Isaiah 1–39', *Int* 11 (1957), pp. 259-68.

—'The Book of Isaiah Chapters 1–39', *IB*, V, pp. 149-381.

—'Solomon and the Beginning of Wisdom', in M. Noth and D. Winton Thomas (eds.), *Wisdom in Israel and in the Ancient Near East: Essays Presented to H.H. Rowley* (VTSup, 3; Leiden: E.J. Brill, 1955), pp. 262-79.

Scullion, John, *Isaiah 40–66* (OTM, 12; Wilmington, DE: Michael Glazier, 1982).

Seitz, Christopher R., 'The Divine Council: Temporal Transition and New Prophecy in the Book of Isaiah', *JBL* 109 (1990), pp. 229-47.

—*Isaiah 1–39* (Interpretation: A Bible Commentary for Teaching and Preaching; Louisville, KY: Westminster/John Knox Press, 1993).

—'Isaiah 1–66: Making Sense of the Whole', in *idem* (ed.), *Reading and Preaching the Book of Isaiah* (Philadelphia: Fortress Press, 1988), pp. 105-26.

—*Zion's Final Destiny: The Development of the Book of Isaiah: A Reassessment of Isaiah 36–39* (Minneapolis: Fortress Press, 1991).

Sekine, S., *Die tritojesajanische Sammlung (Jes 56–66) redaktionsgeschichtlich untersucht* (BZAW, 175; Berlin: W. de Gruyter, 1989).

Simon, U.E., *A Theology of Salvation: A Commentary on Isaiah 40–55* (London: SPCK, 1953).

Skinner, J., *The Book of the Prophet Isaiah, Chapters I–XXXIX* (Cambridge Bible for Schools and Colleges; Cambridge: Cambridge University Press, 1958).

—*The Book of the Prophet Isaiah Chapters XL–LXVI* (Cambridge Bible for Schools and Colleges; Cambridge: Cambridge University Press, rev. edn, 1917).

Sklba, Richard J., *Pre-Exilic Prophecy: Words of Warning, Dreams of Hopes, Spirituality of Pre-Exilic Prophets* (Collegeville, MN: Liturgical Press, 1990).

—'"Until the Spirit from on High is Poured out on Us" (Isa 32.15): Reflections on the Role of the Spirit in the Exile', *CBQ* 46 (1984), pp. 1-17.

Slotki, I.W., *Isaiah: Hebrew Text and English Translation with an Introduction and Commentary* (rev. A.J. Rosenberg; London: Soncino, rev. edn, 1983).

Smart, James D., *History and Theology in Second Isaiah: A Commentary on Isaiah 35, 40–66* (Philadelphia: Westminster Press, 1965).

Smelik, Klaas A.D., 'Distortion of Old Testament Prophecy: The Purpose of Isaiah xxxvi and xxxvii', *OTS* 24 (1989), pp. 70-93.

Smith, P.A., *Rhetoric and Redaction in Trito-Isaiah: The Structure, Growth and Authorship of Isaiah 56–66* (VTSup, 62; Leiden: E.J. Brill, 1995).

Snaith, Norman H., *The Distinctive Ideas of the Old Testament* (London: Epworth Press, 1944).

—'Isaiah 40–66: A Study of the Teaching of the Second Isaiah and its Consequences', in *Studies on the Second Part of the Book of Isaiah* (VTSup, 14; Leiden: E.J. Brill, 1967), pp. 137-264.

—*Notes on the Hebrew Text of Isaiah Chapters XXVIII–XXXII* (London: Epworth Press, 1945).

—'The Servant of the Lord in Deutero-Isaiah', in H.H. Rowley (ed.), *Studies in Old Testament Prophecy Presented to Professor Theodore H. Robinson by the Society for Old Testament Study on his Sixty-Fifth Birthday* (Edinburgh: T. & T. Clark, 1950), pp. 187-200.

—'The Spirit of God in Jewish Thought', in *The Doctrine of the Holy Spirit: Four Lectures* (London: Epworth Press, 1937), pp. 11-37.

Spykerboer, H.C., 'Isaiah 55.1-5: The Climax of Deutero-Isaiah, an Invitation to Come to the New Jerusalem', in Jacques Vermeylen (ed.), *Le livre d'Isaïe: Les oracles et leurs relectures unité et complexité de l'ouvrage* (BETL, 81; Leuven: Leuven University Press, 1989), pp. 357-59.

Stacey, David, *Isaiah 1–39* (Epworth Commentaries; London: Epworth Press, 1993).

Stadelmann, Luis I.J., *The Hebrew Conception of the World* (AnBib, 39; Rome: Biblical Institute Press, 1970).

Steck, O.H., *Bereitete Heimkehr: Jesaja 35 als redaktionelle Brücke zwischen dem ersten und dem zweiten Jesaja* (SBS, 121; Stuttgart: Katholisches Biblelwerk, 1985).

—'Jahwes Feinde in Jesaja 59', *BN* 36 (1987), pp. 51-56.

Stuart, Douglas K., 'The Prophetic Ideal of Government in the Restored Era', in Avraham Gileadi (ed.), *Isreal's Apostasy and Restoration: Essays in Honor of Ronald K. Harrison* (Grand Rapids: Baker Book House, 1988), pp. 283-92.

Stuhlmüller, C., *Creative Redemption in Deutero-Isaiah* (AnBib, 43; Rome: Pontifical Biblical Institute, 1970).

Sweeney, Marvin A., *Isaiah 1–4 and the Post-Exilic Understanding of the Isaianic Tradition* (BZAW, 171; Berlin: W. de Gruyter, 1988).

Talmon, S., 'The Concept of *Māšîaḥ* and Messianism in Early Judaism', in J.H. Charlesworth (ed.), *The Messiah: Developments in Earliest Judaism and Christianity* (First Princeton Symposium on Judaism and Christianity; Minneapolis: Fortress Press, 1992), pp. 79-115.

—*King, Cult and Calendar in Ancient Israel* (Jerusalem: Magnes Press, 1986).

Tanghe, Vincent Tanghe, 'Lilit in Edom (Jes 34,5-15.)', *ETL* 59 (1993), pp. 125-33.

Tengström, S., 'רוח *rûaḥ*', *ThWAT*, VII, cols. 385-418.

Thompson, Michael E.W., *Situation and Theology: Old Testament Interpretations of the Syro-Ephraimite War* (Sheffield: Almond Press, 1982).

Tomasino, Anthony J., 'Isaiah 1.1–2.4 and 63–66, and the Composition of the Isaianic Corpus', *JSOT* 57 (1993), pp. 81-98.

Torrey, Charles C., *The Second Isaiah: A New Interpretation* (New York: Charles Scribner's Sons, 1928).

Tucker, Gene M., 'Prophetic Superscriptions and the Growth of a Canon', in George W. Coats and Burke O. Long (eds.), *Canon and Authority: Essays in Old Testament Religion and Theology* (Philadelphia: Fortress Press, 1977), pp. 71-87.

Tucker, Gene M., David L. Petersen and Robert R. Wilson (eds.), *Canon, Theology, and Old Testament Interpretation: Essays in Honor of Brevard S. Childs* (Philadelphia: Fortress Press, 1988).

Tur-Sinai, N.H. 'A Contribution to the Understanding of Isaiah I–XII', *Scripta Hierosolymitana* 8 (1951), pp. 154-241.

Vermeylen, Jacques, *Du prophète Isaïe a l'apocalyptique: Isaïe i–xxxv, miroir d'un demi-millénaire d'experience religieuse en Israel* (Paris: J. Gabalda, 1977), pp. 144-55.

—'Le motif de la création dans le Deutéro-Isaïe', in F. Blanquart (ed.), *La création dans l'Orient ancien* (Paris: Cerf, 1987), pp. 183-240.

—'L'unité du livre d'Isaïe', in J. Vermeylen (ed.), *Le livre d'Isaïe: Les oracles et leurs relectures unité et complexité de l'ouvrage* (BETL, 81; Leuven: Leuven University Press, 1989), pp. 147-53.

Vermeylen, Jacques (ed.), *Le livre d'Isaïe: Les oracles et leurs relectures unité et complexité de l'ouvrage* (BETL, 81; Leuven: Leuven University Press, 1989).

Volz, Paul, *Der Geist Gottes und die verwandten Erscheinungen im Alten Testament und im anschliessenden Judentum* (Tübingen: J.C.B. Mohr [Paul Siebeck], 1910).

—*Jesaia: 2. Hälfte, Kap. 40–66* (KAT, 9; Leipzig: Deichertsche, 1932).

Vriezen, T.C., 'Essentials of the Theology of Isaiah', in Bernhard W. Anderson and W. Harrelson (eds.), *Israel's Prophetic Heritage: Essays in Honor of James Muilenburg* (New York: Harper & Brothers, 1962), pp. 128-46.

—*An Outline of Old Testament Theology* (Oxford: Basil Blackwell, 1958).

—'Prophecy and Eschatology', in George W. Anderson (ed.), *Congress Volume: Copenhagen, 1953* (VTSup, 1; Leiden: E.J. Brill, 1953), pp. 199-229.

Waltke, Bruce K., 'A Canonical Process Approach to the Psalms', in John S. Feinberg and Paul D. Feinberg (eds.), *Tradition and Testament: Essays in Honor of Charles Lee Feinberg* (Chicago: Moody, 1981), pp. 3-18.

Watts, John D.W., 'Images of Yahweh: God in the Prophets', in Robert L. Hubbard, Jr, Robert K. Johnston and Robert P. Meye (eds.), *Studies in Old Testament Theology: Historical and Contemporary Images of God and God's People* (Dallas: Word Books, 1992), pp. 135-47.

—*Isaiah* (Word Biblical Themes; Dallas: Word Books, 1989).

—*Isaiah 1–33* (WBC, 24; Waco, TX: Word Books, 1985).

—*Isaiah 34–66* (WBC, 25; Waco, TX: Word Books, 1987).

—'"The Spirit" in the Prophets: Three Brief Studies', in Mark W. Wilson (ed.), *Spirit and Renewal: Essays in Honor of J. Rodman Williams* (JPTSup, 5; Sheffield: Sheffield Academic Press, 1994), pp. 84-91.

Webb, B.G., 'Zion in Transformation: A Literary Approach to Isaiah', in David J.A. Clines, Stephen E. Fowl and Stanley E. Porter (eds.), *The Bible in Three Dimensions: Essays in Celebration of Forty Years of Biblical Studies in the University of Sheffield* (JSOTSup, 87; Sheffield: JSOT Press, 1990), pp. 65-84.

Wegner, P.D., *An Examination of Kingship and Messianic Expectation in Isaiah 1–35* (Lewiston, NY: Edwin Mellen Press, 1992).

Weinfeld, Moshe, ' "Justice and Righteousness"—וצדקה משפט—The Expression and its Meaning', in Henning Graf Reventlow and Yair Hoffman (eds.), *Justice and Righteousness: Biblical Themes and their Influence* (JSOTSup, 137; Sheffield: JSOT Press, 1992), pp. 228-46.

Weiser, Artur, *The Old Testament: Its Formation and Development* (trans. Dorothea M. Barton; New York: Association Press, 1961).

Westall, M.R., 'The Scope of the Term "Spirit of God" in the Old Testament', *Indian Journal of Theology* 26 (1977), pp. 29-43.

Westermann, Claus, *Basic Forms of Prophetic Speech* (trans. Hugh C. White; London: Lutterworth, 1967).

—*Elements of Old Testament Theology* (trans. Douglas W. Stott; Atlanta: John Knox Press, 1982).

—'Geist im Alten Testament', *EvT* 41 (1981), pp. 223-30.

—'The Interpretation of the Old Testament: A Historical Introduction', in *idem* (ed.), *Essays on Old Testament Hermeneutics* (trans. James Luther Mays; Richmond, VA: John Knox Press, 1963), pp. 40-49.

—*Isaiah 40–66: A Commentary* (OTL; trans. David M.G. Stalker; Philadelphia: Westminster Press, 1969).

Whedbee, W., *Isaiah and Wisdom* (Nashville: Abingdon Press, 1971).

Whybray, R.N., *The Heavenly Counsellor in Isaiah xl 13-14: A Study of the Sources of the Theology of Deutero-Isaiah* (SOTSMS, 1; Cambridge: Cambridge University Press, 1971).

—*Isaiah 40–66* (NCBC; London: Marshall, Morgan & Scott; Grand Rapids: Eerdmans, 1975).

Widengren, G., *Sakrales Königtum im Alten Testament und im Judentum* (Stuttgart: W. Kohlhammer, 1955).

Widyapranawa, S.H., *The Lord Is Savior: Faith in National Crisis: A Commentary on the Book of Isaiah 1–39* (ITC; Grand Rapids: Eerdmans, 1990).

Wiebe, John M., 'The Form of the "Announcement of a Royal Savior" and the Interpretation of Jeremiah 23.5-6', *Studia Biblica et Theologica* 15 (1987), pp. 1-22.

Wiklander, Bertil, *Prophecy as Literature: A Text-Linguistic and Rhetorical Approach to Isaiah 2–4* (ConBOT, 22; Lund: C.W.K. Gleerup, 1984).

Wildberger, Hans, *Isaiah 1–12: A Commentary* (trans. Thomas H. Trapp; Minneapolis: Fortress Press, 1991).

—*Jesaja 28–39* (BKAT, 10.3; Neukirchen–Vluyn: Neukirchener Verlag, 1982).

—'Jesajas Verständnis der Geschichte', in *Congress Volume: Bonn, 1962* (VTSup, 9; Leiden: E.J. Brill, 1962), pp. 83-117.

Williams, J.G., 'The Prophetic "Father": A Brief Explanation of the Term "Sons of the Prophets"', *JBL* 85 (1966), pp. 344-48.

Williamson, H.G.M., *The Book Called Isaiah: Deutero-Isaiah's Role in Composition and Redaction* (Oxford: Clarendon Press, 1994).

—'First and Last in Isaiah', in Heather A. McKay and David J.A. Clines (eds.), *Of Prophets' Visions and the Wisdom of Sages: Essays in Honour of R. Norman Whybray on his Seventieth Birthday* (JSOTSup, 162; Sheffield: JSOT Press, 1993), pp. 95-108.

Wilson, Andrew, *The Nations in Deutero-Isaiah: A Study on Composition and Structure* (Lewiston, NY: Edwin Mellen Press, 1986).

Wilson, Robert R., 'Prophecy and Ecstasy: A Reexamination', *JBL* 98 (1979), pp. 321-37.

—*Prophecy and Society in Ancient Israel* (Philadelphia: Fortress Press, 1980).

Wolff, Hans W., *Anthropology of the Old Testament* (trans. Margaret Kohl; Philadelphia: Fortress Press, 1974).

—*Micah: A Commentary* (trans. Gary Stansell; Minneapolis: Augsburg, 1990).

—'The Understanding of History in the O.T. Prophets', in Claus Westermann (ed.), *Essays on Old Testament Hermeneutics* (trans. James L. Mays; Richmond, VA: John Knox Press, 1963), pp. 336-55.

Wood, Irving F., *The Spirit of God in Biblical Literature* (London: Hodder & Stoughton, 1904).

Wood, Leon J., *The Holy Spirit in the Old Testament* (Contemporary Evangelical Perspectives Series; Grand Rapids: Zondervan, 1976).

Young, Edward J., *The Book of Isaiah* (NICOT; 3 vols.; Grand Rapids: Eerdmans, 1965–69).

Young, G. Douglas, *Concordance of Ugaritic* (AnOr, 36; Rome: Pontificio Istituto Biblico, 1956).

Youngblood, Ronald F., *The Book of Isaiah: An Introductory Commentary* (Grand Rapids: Baker Book House, 2nd edn, 1993).

Ziegler, J. *Das Buch Isaias* (Würzburg: Echter Verlag, 1948).

Zimmerli, Walther, 'The עֶבֶד יהוה in the OT', *TDNT*, V, pp. 656-77.

—'Das Gnädenjahr des Hernn', in Arnulf Kuschke and Ernst Kutsch (eds.), *Archäologie und Altes Testament: Festschrift für Kurt Galling z. 8. Jan. 1970* (Tübingen: J.C.B. Mohr, 1970), pp. 321-32.

—*Old Testament Theology in Outline* (trans. David E. Green; Edinburgh: T & T Clark, 1978).

INDEXES

INDEX OF REFERENCES

BIBLE

INDEX OF AUTHORS

JOURNAL FOR THE STUDY OF THE OLD TESTAMENT
SUPPLEMENT SERIES